Derek Jarman's Angelic Conversations

UCP Marjon

Derek Jarman's
Angelic Conversations

JIM ELLIS

University of Minnesota Press
Minneapolis
London

The University of Minnesota Press gratefully acknowledges the financial assistance provided for the publication of this book from the Department of English, University of Calgary.

The discussion of *Jubilee* in chapter 3 incorporates material originally published in "The Erotics of Citizenship: Derek Jarman's *Jubilee* and Isaac Julien's *Young Soul Rebels*," *Southern Quarterly* 39.4 (2001): 148–60. The section on *The Tempest* in chapter 3 is a revised version of "Conjuring *The Tempest*: Derek Jarman and the Spectacle of Redemption," *GLQ* 7.2 (2001): 265–84; copyright Duke University Press and reprinted with permission of the publisher. The sections on *The Angelic Conversation* in chapter 4 and on *Edward II* in chapter 7 contain material originally published in "Queer Period: Derek Jarman's Renaissance," in *Out Takes: Essays on Queer Theory and Film,* ed. Ellis Hanson (Durham, N.C.: Duke University Press, 1999), 288–315. The discussion of *War Requiem* in chapter 5 is a revised version of parts of "Strange Meeting: Wilfred Owen, Benjamin Britten, Derek Jarman, and the *War Requiem*," originally published in *The Work of Opera: Genre, Nationhood, and Sexual Difference,* ed. Richard Dellamora and Daniel Fischlin (New York: Columbia University Press, 1997), 277–96.

Quotations of poetry from *Blue* and from unpublished materials by Jarman held by the British Film Institute are included courtesy of the Estate of Derek Jarman; the author thanks Keith Collins.

Published by the University of Minnesota Press
111 Third Avenue South, Suite 290
Minneapolis, MN 55401-2520
http://www.upress.umn.edu

Library of Congress Cataloging-in-Publication Data
Ellis, Jim.
  Derek Jarman's angelic conversations / Jim Ellis.
    p.   cm.
  Includes bibliographical references and index.
  ISBN 978-0-8166-5312-6 (hc : alk. paper) — ISBN 978-0-8166-5313-3 (pb : alk. paper)
  1. Jarman, Derek, 1942-1994—Criticism and interpretation.   I. Title.
  PN1998.3.J3E44   2009
  791.4302'33092—dc22   2009027550

Printed in the United States of America on acid-free paper

The University of Minnesota is an equal-opportunity educator and employer.

20 19 18 17 16 15 14 13 12 11 10 09   10 9 8 7 6 5 4 3 2 1

Contents

Getting History Wrong

IN AN ENTRY OF *MODERN NATURE* dated April 4, 1989, Derek Jarman records a conversation with Mrs. Oiller, a ninety-four-year-old fellow inhabitant of Dungeness: "She tells me one sunny afternoon she saw two men fall out of a plane in a still blue sky, remain suspended in the azure while she held her breath, before they plummeted out of sight behind the holly bushes at Holmstone." On June 1 of the same year, the novelist Neil Bartlett visits Jarman at his cottage: "When I told him old Mrs. Oiller's story of the two men falling from a plane in a clear blue sky, he said that it was the first shot from *A Matter of Life and Death;* in Mrs. Oiller's story they had disappeared behind the Hoppen Pits, where the film was shot."[1] This is a characteristic Jarman anecdote for the way that it illustrates his belief in the power of cinema to re-make the world. Film, the episode suggests, can alter our experience of landscapes and other places, colonizing our memory and thereby transforming the real. On another level, the story is also characteristic of Jarman for the way that it (consciously or unconsciously) plays fast and loose with history: the location shooting for *A Matter of Life and Death* took place on the other side of the country, at Saunton Sands in North Devon, and the shot that Bartlett describes doesn't exist.[2]

"Getting its history wrong," wrote the French philosopher Ernest Renan, "is part of being a nation."[3] Eric Hobsbawm uses Renan as a starting point for a consideration of how the work of historians can alternately contribute to or challenge nationalist ideologies. Jarman was an artist who well understood the role history and mythology played in the psychic life of communities, whether these were mainstream or underground. His films hijacked some of the favorite stories of English nationalism, using them to create new mythologies that challenged the dominant version of the present. In other works he created new histories and alternative lineages for himself and the new communities in which he lived. The anecdote about *A Matter of Life and Death* is a small example of this tendency, serving partially to connect Jarman to a tradition of nonrealist, romantic, or expressionist filmmaking that exists in opposition to the dominant British schools of "heritage" films and social realism.[4] More particularly, it connects him to the filmmakers Emeric Pressburger and Michael Powell, filmmakers whom he greatly admired, and who, beyond the stylistic parallels, share with Jarman a deep love for traditional English landscapes and a concern about their disappearance. This investment in a version of pastoral was cause for accusations of political conservatism against all three, paradoxically existing alongside official suspicion and even condemnation of their films.[5] Jarman was aware of this irony, and occasionally highlighted it by claiming that he was a true conservative and patriot, as opposed to those Thatcherite politicians who were busily tearing down the welfare state previous generations had fought to establish. Although he clearly identified with oppositional and alternative communities, he was very much alive to the strategic value of claiming membership in the nation, and the crucial role that history could play in this claim.

Jarman's interest in historical subject matter was thus doubled-edged: both challenging official versions of history and claiming ownership of it. In films such as *The Tempest, The Angelic Conversation,* and *Edward II* he seized on canonical texts from what is perhaps the key site of British national glory, the English Renaissance, and used them to tell different stories about the nation. In films like *War Requiem, Wittgenstein,* and *Blue,* he constructed new traditions of gay or alternative artists and thinkers. Elsewhere he explored some of the dead ends of history, arcane and alternative knowledge systems, to offer different perspectives on the present. Beyond this strategic use of historical subject matter, however, Jarman strove in his work to invent new ways of seeing and of representing the relation between the past and the present, of exploring the ways in which history inhabits and informs the present.

In her overview of British cinema, Sarah Street writes that "In many senses, Jarman's films can be called *histories:* they revel in presenting history as a complex process which interweaves past and present."[6] Jarman's use of anachronistic props is the most obvious example of this mode of representation and one of the most commented on of his stylistic choices; what is less often explained is the complex historical vision that this signals. One model for thinking about this particular vision can be found in the work of the Renaissance painter Caravaggio, the subject of one of Jarman's most successful early films. Caravaggio painted his biblical subjects using his contemporaries as models, and deliberately mixed contemporary and period dress, which prompted the accusations that he had used a prostitute for the central figure in *Death of the Virgin*. Caravaggio's paintings require of the viewer a historical double vision, making two distinct temporalities occupy the same representational space. A similar claim might be made about many of Jarman's historical films, which often involve the juxtaposition of at least two historical periods.

For Jarman, the past, insofar as it can be said to exist, exists within the present, often imagined by Jarman in spatial terms. Even in his earliest films, Jarman is interested in how objects trail behind them their own histories, or, to put it another way, how objects import into the space of the present their own pasts. The represented space in the film is at times a collage or a palimpsest, combining or layering different temporalities that exist in productive relations with each other. History can function something like a building from the past, which brings into the present its original moment, as well as all of the transformations and accretions of the intervening years. We inhabit the myths and stories of the past much as we inhabit these buildings, and they can mold our consciousness much as a building shapes our movements and directs our activities. But we can also productively misuse the past just as we can deform the spatial regime of a piece of architecture, exploiting its program for our own purposes.

Collaging or juxtaposing historical styles was a hallmark of postmodernist art in the 1980s, but Jarman would have encountered it earlier as a student at the Slade School of Fine Art in the 1960s, during the heyday of British pop artists like Richard Hamilton and American modernists like Robert Rauschenberg. He glued objects onto his landscape paintings, and his early set designs for theater and ballet extended this interest in collage into three-dimensional spaces. His first work in film was as a set designer for a couple of films by Ken Russell (*The Devils* [1971], *Savage Messiah* [1972]). Russell was at that time reinventing the historical biopic, replacing the staid, unobtrusive style that marked earlier examples of the genre with showy camera work and startling fantasy sequences that insisted upon the contemporary relevance of his subjects.

In Jarman, Russell would find an apposite collaborator. Jarman's spectacular, nonnaturalist creation of the medieval city of Loudun in *The Devils* prefigures other architecturally striking sets that would follow in his own films, including the use of the derelict hospital in *War Requiem*, the prison-like set of *Edward II*, or the complete absence of sets in *Wittgenstein*. The Loudun set echoes to some degree his geometric designs for *Don Giovanni* at the London Coliseum in 1968, which Jarman says "reinterpreted the historical past in a contemporary manner."[7] *The Devils'* set is significant not only for its bold refusal of a surface historical accuracy (a hallmark of both Jarman's and Russell's films), but also for the way in which it works to define the different spatial regime of an oppositional community. This is not a matter simply of a different look, which would alert the audience to the opposition between the city of Loudun and the world of the court, but rather that the stark, clean, open set itself is an expression of what is at stake in that opposition between those two communities and their ideologies. Jarman's interest in history is linked to his interest in the spatial regimes of particular communities; the past offered him different examples of social organizations that allowed for different ways of being.

One of the aims of this book is to concentrate more fully and more closely on Jarman's engagements with the past. Although this was a career-long preoccupation, it did not always take the same form. Qualifying an earlier statement he made about his work "reclaiming the queer past," he later said, "I think I sort of made some of those things up. I'm not quite certain that I was really aware. Then it seemed the sensible thing to say. I don't think I ever actually had any plan."[8] Although he is overstating the case here, playing around with his own history, we should be alive to the fact that his work spans a very tumultuous period, during which thinking about sexual minorities and alternative communities changed rapidly and dramatically. Jarman's ongoing and shifting engagement with historical matter has to be seen as part of a larger project of responding to the challenges of his own time. By remaking the past, he was remaking the present, and allowing for the

Cathedral set by Derek Jarman for *The Devils* (Ken Russell, 1970). Photograph by Ray Dean.

invention of new possibilities for living. This invention extended to form, genre, and the cinematic apparatus itself: by changing the cinema, he could change the audience, and thereby the world.

Film allows for the creation of experimental worlds, and Jarman's films frequently explore how particular configurations of space open up possibilities for other kinds of social or sexual or political regimes. A number of people have observed that Jarman was first and foremost a painter. As a painter he understood that space and relationality are intimately and unavoidably connected, and that the arrangement of persons and objects in a painting is also a commentary on the relations between them. Social historians and cultural critics such as Fredric Jameson argue that one of the defining characteristics of the modern era is the separation between public and private space, and the particular mode of subjectivity—the bourgeois individual—this spatial regime guarantees. For homosexual men in Britain in the 1960s such as Jarman, the nature and definition of space was more than just an aesthetic or philosophical concern, but a very immediate and practical problem. Until 1967, homosexual relations between men were prohibited, even in private. Moreover, as Matt Houlbrook points out, "residential space was only defined as legally private if it were domestic space," and in the eyes of the law, "male persons living together [did] not constitute domestic life."⁹ In a very real sense, homosexuality, and by extension homosexuals, were thus specifically excluded from the private sphere, as well as, of course, from the public. Theorists of space argue that "space does not simply reflect social relations; it is constitutive of and is constituted by them."¹⁰ How, then, were homosexual subjects to locate themselves within this spatial regime? Further, what happens to these subjects when the law changes and the proscribed becomes licit? We can identify one of the projects of Jarman's career as addressing the questions that are ultimately rooted in this new cultural development: Where and how were these new subjects to find or invent themselves? How are to they accommodate themselves to this newly emergent world? What kinds of stories can be told or rewritten for them?

Historically speaking, we can identify two practical responses to this existential dilemma. One we can associate with the Campaign for Homosexual Equality, a political group originating in the 1950s with largely assimilationist goals: homosexuals should be granted the same rights as everyone. In relation to the law, we can identify their response as a demand for access to the private realm, and to a version of bourgeois subjectivity. The other response, which we will discuss in some detail in the next chapter, we can associate with the gay liberation movement. Rather than sue for access to the private, the liberationist response is to challenge societal definitions of space itself, and hence dominant modes of subjectivity. Central to the liberationist philosophy is a rejection of bourgeois individualism, and central to the activities of its adherents were affronts to dominant conceptions of spatial propriety.

Jarman's response, I will be arguing, follows the liberationist model. What we will see repeatedly in his work is an ongoing attempt to chart, comment on, and stimulate the emergence of new forms of sexual subjectivity. In keeping with the liberationist model, Jarman shows little or no interest in modes of subjectivity that are grounded in the private sphere of bourgeois individualism. We see this most immediately reflected in his films' utter lack of interest in characterization. There are virtually no examinations of individual psychology, not even when the film falls into the category of the biopic: neither *Caravaggio* nor *Wittgenstein* can be said to offer any real insight into the souls of their ostensible historical subjects. The films are to some degree interested in psychology, but this is better characterized as an interest in intersubjectivity or collective subjectivities, and the exploration of psychology is often tied in the film to examinations of or experiments with space, and the ways particular terrains are supportive of particular subjectivities. What we would characterize as private spaces rarely appear in his films, and the domestic, when we see it, is usually radically reconfigured.

What we have instead are what Michel Foucault would label heterotopias: real spaces that do not conform to a society's dominant spatial paradigm, that offer space for refuge, resistance, or retreat. Heteropias "are sorts of actually realized utopias in which the real emplacements, all the other real emplacements that can be found in culture are, at the same time, represented, contested, and reversed, sorts of places that are outside all places, although they are actually localizable."[11] One characteristic of heterotopias worth noting is their connection with heterochronias, or temporal dislocations, which is to say that different spatial regimes are often marked by different temporal regimes. Foremost among Foucault's examples of the heterotopia is the garden; other spaces include the theater, the cinema, prisons, cemeteries, and old-age homes. It is not surprising, but worth remarking, that Jarman's films are invariably set in some kind or other of heterotopia. In particular, the centrality of the garden in Jarman's imagination can hardly be overstated: in virtually every medium in which he worked, gardens figured to some degree, always as a space of refuge or opposition to the dominant culture. In terms of his artistic practice as a whole, we should also look beyond the representation of heterotopias to consider the heterotopic dimensions of each particular artistic medium in question. This is most crucial in the case of cinema. We have to think about both the projected, illusionary, three-dimensional space behind the screen and the spectatorial space in front of it, as well as the role of the screen itself in mediating those two spaces, and as a space in its own right. In all of these other spaces, Jarman explores the potential for new ways of being together.

Jarman's innovations go beyond the matter of what is represented to address the matter of representation itself. He was a lifelong experimenter with aesthetic forms, often reclaiming conservative genres for radical purposes. His autobiographical writings, for example, are a generically impure blend of personal, familial, and social history, along with aesthetic and political observations, often presented in the guise of another generic form, such as the saint's testament, the philosophical treatise, or the screenplay. I will be arguing that one of the things that Jarman is doing is inventing new forms of writing by rewriting old ones, with the aim of documenting new modes of being, modes of being that do not fit with genres that are premised on the exploration of privatized, interior psychologies. The films display a similar interest in formal innovation, for similar aims. These innovations frequently take the form of juxtaposition or disruption. His strategy of including anachronistic props to disrupt period realism exists on a continuum with other antirealist strategies, disruptions of familiar genres, and inclusion of different recording media to disrupt the smooth reception of the film by its audience. This last innovation, an attempt to reform the apparatus of reproduction, has to do with Jarman's interest in remaking the audience, partially through remaking the cinematic apparatus.

In thinking about the radical potential of cinema for responding to social change, we might turn to Walter Benjamin's theory of the cinema, as elaborated in the second version of his famous essay on the aura, "The Work of Art in the Age of Its Technological Reproducibility." Miriam Bratu Hansen has drawn attention to how this lesser-known version of the essay allows for a more optimistic view of the potential of the new technologies of modernism. In this version, Benjamin argues that cinema can act as both a compensatory and a revolutionary force in the modern era. Cinema, he argues, could help its audience to adjust to the new spatial regimes of modernity: "Our bars and city streets, our offices and furnished rooms, our railroad stations and our factories seemed to close relentlessly around us. Then came film and exploded this prison-world with the dynamite of the split second, so that now we can set off calmly on journeys of adventure among its far-flung debris. With the close-up, space expands; with slow motion, movement is extended."[12] Arguably, the new worlds opened up by the sexual and social revolutions of the 1960s posed as radical a challenge for some as did the advent of modernism, and it was to this challenge that Jarman was at least partially responding.

Drawing attention to the historical specificity of modes of perception ("The way in which human perception is organized—the medium in which it occurs—is conditioned not only by nature but by history"),[13]

Benjamin argues that cinema can retrain our perceptual apparatus to allow us to function critically in the age of technology, a process he calls "innervation": "The function of film is to train human beings in the apperceptions and reactions needed to deal with a vast apparatus whose role in their lives is expanding almost daily."[14] Noting the key role of play in Benjamin's theory, Hansen argues that for Benjamin, "The 'prismatic' work of film at once unveils and refracts the everyday, thus making it available for play—for a mimetic appropriation and re-configuring of its ruined fragments."[15] We will see in the next chapter that the Situationists had a similar investment in play, coming out of their own interest in surrealism, which will provide a useful way of understanding the work being performed by Jarman's very playful early films: inventing new ways of seeing to help its audience respond to new worlds of possibility.

Benjamin's theory of innervation is indebted to Sergei Eisenstein and the Soviet avant-garde's theory of montage, which was similarly premised on a belief in the revolutionary potential of cinema and its ability to remake its audience. Jarman, as we shall see, was himself pro-foundly influenced by the work of Eisenstein (who is the subject, or at least the starting point, of *Imagining October*). We can see links both to Eisenstein's use of montage as a way of producing knowledge in the audience and to Eisenstein's belief in the physical power of the cin-ema to shock or even assault the audience: the cine-fist. We will see Jarman playing with the possible physical effects of cinema early in the experimental films that often flash light into the camera, and late in the sound design of *Blue,* and mid-career in the disorienting, rapid-fire editing of films such as *The Last of England* or the music video for The Smiths, *The Queen Is Dead.* Just as Benjamin believed that cinema could ameliorate the disorientations of time and space caused by capi-talism, Jarman's work is marked by a belief in art's potential to aid the new subjectivities that appeared in his lifetime, in his own communities. Like the films of Kenneth Anger, Jack Smith, and Andy Warhol, his films participate in the creation of a new experience of intersubjectiv-ity for the gay or queer subject, an experience that is predicated to a large degree on the sexual revolution in the sixties, and more particu-larly for Jarman, the increasing visibility of homosexuality in the post-Stonewall, gay liberation era.

It is no exaggeration to state that Jarman is the most important Anglo-American gay director in the post-Stonewall era, although it is surprising that, to my knowledge, no one has ever made that claim for him. There are likely a number of reasons for this. First, it has never been easy to locate his work precisely within any artistic or filmic tradition, a task made more difficult by the fact that he produced work in so many different artistic forms: set design, painting, experimental and narrative film, memoir, gardens. He was a major inspiration for the New Romantic filmmakers of the early 1980s[16] and for activist video artists, and he was viewed as the Grand Old Man of the New Queer Cinema of the early 1990s, but it is not immediately obvious what actual influence his work has had.

Moreover, while he is often seen as a political artist, he was never firmly associated or easily aligned with any particular political movement (with the late exception of OutRage!), with one result being that his films were sometimes criticized more harshly by the gay media than they were by the mainstream. His radical politics were mixed, as I have said, with what seemed to be a conservative investment in certain aspects of Englishness, which led to further suspicion and confusion as to where on the political spectrum he should be located. Finally, while he was an artist who produced a great deal of autobiographical material and who was a well-known public figure, he was something of a conscious or unconscious fabulist, the facts of his life undergoing alteration in subsequent retellings. Autobiography serves for him as a source of material or a starting point for certain explorations, never really as the object of interest in itself, and so accuracy was beside the point. All of these factors make it difficult to pin Jarman and his work down, or to find the appropriate grounds on which to assess his accomplishment.

Criticism of his work has, quite naturally, tended to emphasize certain aspects of his work over others. Most frequently, his films are read from either a biographical or a political perspective. More than one critic, for example, has identified in his work an investment in homosexual passivity or masochism that they see as stemming from his own life.[17] His films have often been discussed by self-identified gay or queer critics (myself among them) who have wanted to see in them illustrations of theoretical or political programs. Certainly, the ascendancy of these and related interpretative approaches in the academic world gained him a wider audience than was granted most avant-garde directors, but the resulting criticism has tended to give short shrift to the formal aspects of the films.

Neither the biographical nor the political approach to Jarman's career is illegitimate or unjustified, and the work certainly encourages them. But Jarman's creative use of biography, and his complex relation to politics, make such approaches both limiting and potentially treacherous. It is my sense that the most interesting and, indeed, the most radical aspects of his work are not located in what we might call the surface politics of the narratives (which tend to attract the most comment), but rather in the ways in which politics and aesthetics are intertwined at a deeper level. The experiments with form, which often play with the ideological accretions of particular forms, are ultimately far more disruptive that the provocations offered by the content, as salutary as they might be. Thus a central aim of this book is to look more closely at the connections between Jarman's political interests and his artistic ones.

To complicate our understanding of the way the films work, this study will employ a series of complementary approaches. An important starting point will be fairly detailed descriptions and analyses of the works themselves, specifying as a carefully as possible what is happening in each, looking at them again in order to forestall overhasty conclusions. In examining the films, I will be paying close attention to such things as the overall structure of the work, the construction of spaces within it, the use of sound, choices about editing style, recording media, and the processing of the image, among other things. Related to these formal questions are considerations of Jarman's own ideas about the nature of the work of art, and the implications of his representations of artists, studios, and the act of painting. This will sometimes lead to considerations of conditions of production and exhibition, where Jarman challenged dominant notions about the boundaries of the work of art, and art's role in the world.

As already indicated, I will frequently be looking at Jarman's use of historical texts and historical figures. Some of this will involve investigations into forgotten knowledges and practices such as alchemy, the Renaissance masque, or the physic garden, in order to specify the particular use Jarman might be making of them. We will look at how he remakes popular forms, such as the home movie or the movie musical. Elsewhere we will consider Jarman's attraction to certain artists or writers of the past, the genealogies he constructs for his own thought and practice, and the oppositional traditions he creates. And, of course, we will look at the way that he seizes hold of certain moments of the past, rewriting them for the purposes of the present. What this book aims to do is to specify carefully how and why Jarman was invoking the past in a particular work. What precisely is at stake in how he resuscitates, resignifies, and mobilizes texts or artifacts of the past, making them serve in new contemporary contexts? How does each work answer to its own historical moment?

This leads to another central concern of the book: resituating Jarman's works more carefully in their own historical contexts. He was an artist who was very much interested in engaging with his world, which means that his works often sought to intervene in a particular cultural or political moment. Thus, while we can certainly see ongoing preoccupations throughout his career, Jarman was never invested in consistency for its own sake, and his thinking and aesthetic practice underwent significant changes over the course of his life. We will be interested, therefore, in examining Jarman's work in relation to contemporary aesthetic developments, such as 1960s pop art, 1970s punk music, and 1980s heritage cinema. Equally important, the works will be situated in their political contexts, both sexual and national.

We can see charted in Jarman's work most of the major developments in post-Stonewall gay history. *Sebastiane*, Jarman's first feature, can be clearly read within the context of the gay liberation movement. His films of the early 1980s reflect a growing wariness toward a gay mainstream, along with a sustained reflection on the ways in which his status as a gay artist shaped his career. The effects of the AIDS epidemic, and the conservative backlash toward the gay community that coincided with it, are registered very early in his films, arguably before his own diagnosis as HIV positive in 1986. The films and writings that followed reflect in a very open way the psychological experience of living with AIDS, as well as with being the most famous face of AIDS in Britain. This in turn led to Jarman's close identification with the rise of queer politics, a complex political development that emerged partly in response to government inactivity in the face of the AIDS crisis, and partly as a rejection of identity politics. Jarman's film *Edward II* was one of the films most frequently cited in discussions of the New Queer Cinema, although the films of his that followed cannot be so easily subsumed under this rubric.

In Jarman's films and writings we can thus chart a historical progress from homophile to homosexual to gay to queer. In his later writings especially, we can see him reflecting on the shifts in thinking that occurred in his own lifetime, and throughout his career we can see an interest in charting larger historical trajectories and traditions. His first film is clearly an homage to Pasolini, a director with whom he felt much sympathy, and other films would consciously put themselves in a tradition of gay filmmaking that for him included directors like Eisenstein, Cocteau, Genet, Anger, and Warhol. The lineage of gay artists he invents and invokes includes painters, poets, musicians, and philosophers. This interest in a gay tradition is associated with a constellation of related explorations, from the function of filmic history to what would become the more central and pressing question of a gay ethics, and of our responsibilities to each other.

The study that follows divides Jarman's career into several phases, discussing related works in each. These divisions will be useful for illustrating shifts in his thinking about art, sexuality, and politics, in response to various cultural and historical changes. Wherever possible, I discuss related works from different genres, attempting to discern how formal strategies employed in one might be working in parallel to those of another. Jarman's autobiographical writings will not be used as sources of explanation for the film, or for biographical insight, but rather read as parallel works of art that chart the emergence of new ways of being in the world. Although this book largely proceeds in chronological order, it is neither a biography nor a catalogue raisonné of Jarman's work, although I have tried to refer to and make sense of as much of his artistic output as possible.

Although the central focus is on his films, my aim is to isolate the major aesthetic concerns that characterize his work at different points in his career, and to look at how these are related to political (or other) aims. Thus one of the concerns of the first chapter is to explore two key contexts for Jarman's early development as an artist: the avant-garde artistic and political movements of the 1960s, including the Situationist International, and the Gay Liberation Front. One thing that unites these two disparate movements is a theoretical and political concern with social space. It is largely in this light that I look in the second chapter at Jarman's first filmmaking efforts. Jarman's early experimental super-8 films document the new spaces and social relations of the bohemian underground in which he moved. His first feature, *Sebastiane,* takes this exploration of space in a different direction, looking to the past for alternative worlds that might allow for different modes of relationality. This film thus starts off a career-long interest in the radical potential of historical subject matter, although the past that he would most often turn to is the English Renaissance.

Chapter 3 looks at an unlikely pair of films that themselves make an unusual set of connections: *Jubilee* and *The Tempest. Jubilee* is a punk apocalypse made in the Queen's Jubilee Year, 1977, while *The Tempest* is an adaptation of Shakespeare's most theatrical play. What is often forgotten about punk is that in its early stages it was unusually accommodating to women and gay men. This is the version of punk that interested Jarman and which in *Jubilee* he connects with one of the more disreputable figures of the English Renaissance, the alchemist and scholar John Dee. Jarman's version of *The Tempest* solidifies these connections, remaking Prospero as a version of Dr. Dee, and casting the punk star Toyah Willcox as Miranda. Here we see Jarman constructing an alternative past that encodes a different set of values for the nation, by constructing a punk version of Shakespeare.

Following the early successes of these first three features, Jarman's career went into an apparent stall as he struggled for seven years to get funding for *Caravaggio.* However frustrating they may have been, these years did produce a series of paintings, the first of Jarman's extraordinary experimental autobiographies *(Dancing Ledge),* and two other films: *Imagining October* and *The Angelic Conversation.* Chapter 4 looks at these along with the series of scripts written for *Caravaggio,* showing how the evolution of the script charts the evolution of Jarman's thinking about the emergence of a gay mainstream, and the effect his sexuality had on his career. The three films produced in the period explore from different perspectives the connections between art, sexuality, politics, and commerce. His study of the painter Caravaggio, and in particular his use of light and color to define space and to push the space of the painting outward into the world of the viewer, had a lasting effect on Jarman's style, just as his construction of layered temporal spaces influenced his thinking about the representation of the past.

After Jarman's diagnosis of his HIV-positive status, all of the following films would register in some way the effect of the disease on himself and on his sense of the nation. Chapter 5 looks at two early responses to the epidemic. *The Last of England* is a whirling, chaotic, experimental feature that savagely anatomizes the experience of living in a country that is willing to turn its back or even its forces on its own people. *War Requiem* has as its sound track Benjamin Britten's antiwar requiem mass, written in response to the Second World War, which itself incorporated the poetry of Wilfred Owen, written in response to the First. Jarman uses the film to construct a countertradition of three gay, antiwar artists, and in the process to construct a gay ethics.

Chapter 6 is the most consistently interdisciplinary of the book, considering three parallel works: Jarman's garden at Dungeness, his book about the making of the garden *(Modern Nature),* and the experimental film *The Garden.* It considers the ways in which these three works can be seen as exploring similar issues of space and time. All three works resist the comfort of narrative, while exploring the uses of the past. *Modern Nature,* for example, draws upon Renaissance books about gardening and herbal remedies to suggest an alternative mode of thinking about the relations between the body, the self, and the world. The construction of a garden becomes simultaneously an act of defiance toward received knowledge, an assertion of a continuity with alternative traditions of knowledge, and the creation of an open and welcoming work of art that is fully inhabited by the spectator.

Chapter 7 looks at the final books and films. Formally, we can see a development from what was learned in *Caravaggio,* as the films use increasingly minimal sets, stark lighting, and bold colors to make the images invade or envelope the space of the auditorium. *Edward II* is set in bare, dusty rooms with oppressive stone walls, while *Wittgenstein* dispenses with sets altogether, dressing its characters in primary colors that pop out against black backdrops. Most radically, *Blue* offers no image at all, opting instead for an unwavering blue screen accompanied by a sound track. *Edward II* is both a call to arms and a call to hope, and a meditation on how one is to live in the shadow of one's own death. *Wittgenstein,* a study of the philosopher, is an investigation of color and an acceptance of solitude. *Blue,* an homage to the French conceptual artist Yves Klein, is a powerful (at times overwhelming) meditation on death, disease, and art. Its blue screen recalls Klein's understanding of the void not as an absence, but rather as an infinity. The blue screen in the film is similarly an opening up of the infinite, while the sound track penetrates the audience, conjuring up images that are played out solely in the mind's eye. The film thus realizes in a potent way Jarman's long-standing ambition to break down the barrier between screen and spectator, art and world.

In order to deal with an artist as complex as Jarman, I will be drawing upon a wide range of texts, from Renaissance herbals to queer theory. It is only with such a diverse scope of reference that we can come to terms with such a career. Jarman's work offers an unprecedented and sustained investigation of the relations between sexuality, politics, and art, over the course of the turbulent history of sexual minorities in the latter half of the twentieth century. Equally important, Jarman's oeuvre is a rich and diverse body of artistic work that combines old forms and radical content, new media and canonical texts; his is a career dedicated to experiments both in artistic form and in ways of being in the world.

ONE

Artistic and Sexual Revolutions

ALTHOUGH JARMAN'S FAME came as a filmmaker, painting was his first and most enduring passion. His accounts of his public school days mention the art master's studio as a space of refuge and furious productivity, and he had his first solo exhibition in 1960, at the age of eighteen.[1] While pursuing a degree in English literature at King's College, University of London, he continued to paint landscapes, and won the award for "amateur" painting in the Student Union's annual exhibition in 1961 (David Hockney won the award that year for the art students). He subsequently studied painting and set design at the Slade School of Fine Art. His interest in set design was no doubt influenced by his tutor at Kings, the art historian and architectural critic Nikolaus Pevsner, who inspired in him a lifelong enthusiasm for the subject: "With Pevsner, architecture became a passion."[2] In *Dancing Ledge* he talks about having endless debates in the 1960s with the architecture students in his circle of friends, and mentions in particular a spirited argument he had one evening with the prominent architect Peter Cook, a member of the radical Archigram group. Upon graduation, he continued painting and won the Peter Stuyvesant Prize in the Young Contemporaries show at the Tate Gallery in 1967, an annual exhibition of considerable importance: the 1961 show is generally credited with heralding the arrival of pop art in Britain.

During the sixties Jarman circulated in a largely gay milieu that included some of the more important artists of this generation, including David Hockney and Patrick Procktor. His early successes as a set designer are partly attributable to being a member of this gay cultural underground. As he notes in *Dancing Ledge,* he started his career where others might hope to end theirs, designing for a ballet featuring Rudolf Nureyev at the Royal Court. His move into designing sets for films appears to have been entirely accidental. He happened to sit by a friend of Ken Russell's on a train ride back from Paris, and Russell showed up at his studio the next day to offer him the job of designing *The Devils*. This would be followed by work on Russell's next film, *Savage Messiah*.[3] Jarman's shift into experimental filmmaking is as serendipitous as his entry into studio filmmaking. While working on *The Devils*, an American friend staying with him gave him a super-8 camera, and he started experimenting with it.[4]

I recount this early history to establish a couple of things. First and foremost, it was as a painter and designer that Jarman initially came to filmmaking, and not through the world of experimental film. Jarman, more than one critic has observed, was a painter who made films; we might further add that he made these films not as a substitute for painting, but as a further avenue for exploring painterly or artistic questions. In order to understand his early films, particularly the super-8s, it is necessary to consider the particular worlds he inhabited in the 1960s, and the kinds of ideas and debates he was likely to have encountered there. He did, of course, have an enthusiastic interest in film that predates his own filmmaking career, but making films does not seem to have been an early ambition. It is the world of art (and to a lesser degree architecture) that provides the most formative aesthetic context.

The gay subculture that he moved in is, of course, the other major formative context, and the particularities of it demand some attention. There was a major cultural shift in gay politics in the late 1960s, following the student revolts in Paris in May 1968 and elsewhere. These uprisings have been seen as an important stimulus to various identity-based political movements, including women's liberation and gay liberation. Guy Debord and Gianfranco Sanguinetti of the Situationist International, a key group in the Paris uprisings, observed in 1972 of the aftereffects of these events:

> Ways of life improve. The meaning of words participates in this. Everywhere *the respect for alienation has been lost*. Young people, workers, coloured people, homosexuals, women and children, take it into their heads to want everything that was *forbidden* them; at the same time as they refuse the major part of the miserable results that the old organization of class society permitted them to obtain and to bear. They want no

more leaders, no more family, no more State. They criticize
architecture and they learn to speak to each other. And in
rising up against a hundred particular alienations, they in fact
challenge alienated labour.[5]

In gay history, the Stonewall riots of June 1969 in New York are generally seen as a turning point that heralded the emergence of an unapologetic gay activism and a new era of gay life. Although these events had
more symbolic importance in the United States than they did in
Britain, they certainly had an effect. Inspired by similar organizations
in New York and San Francisco, the Gay Liberation Front was founded
in London in the early 1970s. The appearance of this new activism
roughly coincides with Jarman's move to the Docklands in 1969 and
into filmmaking.

One thing that unites these two disparate worlds of the 1960s—the
aesthetic avant-garde and the new gay activism—is a concern with
the politics of space. Groups of artists, critics, and architects like the
Independent Group, Team 10, and the Situationist International challenged the modernist, high-rationalist ideal of the city, focusing instead
on how space is experienced at the level of the human. The actions of
the Gay Liberation Front put this theory into practice, both by claiming
public space for minority subjects and by challenging the established
outlines of public and private space.

These two contexts—aesthetic and political—offer productive ways
of understanding what is at stake in Jarman's early super-8 films and
his first feature, *Sebastiane*. Before addressing these films and the work
they are accomplishing, we will look in some detail at the cultural developments of the 1960s, and in particular the artistic and political
avant-gardes.

Situationism and Other Avant-gardes

I quoted the Situationist International (SI) on the aftereffects of Paris '68
because I will be using its ideas to highlight certain aspects of Jarman's
early career. This is not because I believe that Jarman was secretly a Situationist; I have seen no evidence to suggest that he had even heard of
the SI prior to the May 1968 uprisings, although, as I will demonstrate,

both they and their ideas circulated in Britain for some time before then. After the events of 1968, which included protests in London, it is unlikely that Jarman would not have heard of them, and we can see some fairly obvious evidence in the Situationist graffiti sprayed on the walls in Jarman's film *Sloane Square* (1974–76), and a late echo in the narration of *The Last of England* (1987). The clearest reflection of Situationist aesthetics is, however, the punk-inspired film *Jubilee* (1978). Although Greil Marcus may overstate the connections between the Situationists and the punk movement, the influence was certainly and clearly there.[6] More important than stylistic echoes, which could just as easily be a reflection of ideas that were simply in the air, are a set of aesthetic, cultural, and political theories most associated with the SI that surface with some frequency in Jarman's early work, and which help to clarify the point of what are generally seen as punk elements in his mature work.

The Situationist International was founded in 1957, out of the remnants of two earlier avant-garde groups, the Lettrist International and the International Movement for an Imaginist Bauhaus (itself founded out of CoBrA, an even earlier avent-garde group), which in turn had their roots in various forms of Dadaism and surrealism.[7] The SI's one British cofounder was Ralph Rumney, the only known member of the London Psychogeographical Association and a frequenter of the Institute of Contemporary Arts (ICA), which became an important center in London for the avant-garde. The SI consisted of artists, architects, and theorists who shared a Marxist analysis of alienation in modern society and a belief in the revolutionary potential of art in everyday life, especially through the liberation of the unconscious. The Situationists are known for their critique of what founder Guy Debord calls the society of the spectacle, a domination of reality by the commodity form. They fought the spectacle with the constructed situation, which they defined as "A moment of life concretely and deliberately constructed by the collective organization of a unitary ambiance and a game of events."[8] Connected to this critique of the spectacle is an interest in urban life and urban architecture, and in particular a critique of the functionalist ideas associated with modernist architecture and its key figure, Le Corbusier. There are some close associations between their early thinking on space and that of the French philosopher Henri Lefebvre, with whom they had some significant contact.[9]

Among the most important of the Situationists' aesthetic strategies or concepts are the *dérive*, psychogeography, and *détournement*, the first two of which were Lettrist practices. Psychogeography involved "the systematic observation of the effects produced by different urban ambiances upon the emotions."[10] Ralph Rumney's early psychogeography of Venice, for example, included photographs of and commentary on a progress through the streets of Venice ("The Leaning Tower of Venice"); parts of it were published in 1957 in London in *ARK: The Journal of the Royal College of Art.*[11] A key method for charting psychogeography was the *dérive* or drift. A group of two or more persons take a path based on an arbitrary principle through an urban environment and "let themselves be drawn by the attractions of the terrain and the encounters they find there. The element of chance is less determinant than one might think: from the *dérive* point of view cities have a psychogeographical relief, with constant currents, fixed points and vortexes."[12] The *dérive* has as its goal the discovery of a certain knowledge about the authentic life of the city and the everyday, knowledge that can be used to challenge modern urban alienation: "the *dérive* is a political use of space, constructing new social relations through its 'ludic-constructive behavior.'"[13] This specifically political and oppositional stance, felt Debord, distinguished the *dérive* from the stroll, and the activities of the *flâneur.*

Perhaps the most famous Situationist aesthetic strategy was *détournement*, which is short for "*détournement* of pre-existing aesthetic elements. The integration of present or past artistic production into a superior construction of a milieu."[14] As Jappe observes, this strategy was "a way of transcending the bourgeois cult of originality and the private ownership of thought."[15] Or, in Debord's words: "The literary and artistic heritage of humanity should be used for partisan propaganda purposes." *Détournement* could take the form of writing new thought bubbles for comics, quotation (or misquotation) without attribution, collaging elements together to form a new meaning, or, in the case of Debord's own films, the use of found footage or photographs.[16] The Situationists distinguished their use of mass-culture artifacts from that of the pop artists of the 1960s: "It was not enough for the intellectual simply to admit to enjoying American mass culture, nor to decoratively rearrange it, pop art style, into artistic products for distribution on the conventional art market. This merely elaborated on the spectacle."[17] Jappe points to a particular devaluing/revaluing dialectic in *détournement* that always makes productive use of what it is recycling, and that distinguishes it from other, largely ironic, uses of pop-culture artifacts (which, we will see, also distinguishes Jarman from filmmakers like Andy Warhol or Jack Smith). Anthony Vidler argues that this dialectic involves "a double identification: with the original and with its transformed state, which are both retained in the resulting milieu that conserves all possible past and future implications of the détourned work."[18] The essentially productive element of *détournement* is useful when thinking about Jarman's reuse of conservative forms—home movies, cottage gardens, landscape painting—for radical purposes. The point is not to mock but to hijack.

We can see some of the same ideas about urban space, modernist architecture, and commodity culture surfacing in Britain in the 1950s. Simon Sadler argues that "situationist sensibilities were most akin to those of the young British artists and theorists gathered around the Independent Group (IG), which met from 1952 to 1955 as a forum for avant-garde discussion at London's Institute for Contemporary Arts (ICA), and which affected ICA policy for a decade or more to come."[19] The Independent Group, a rather loose association, included Nigel Henderson, best known for his photographs of working-class life in Bethnal Green; Eduardo Paolozzi and Richard Hamilton, who would become central figures for British pop art (Hamilton's seminal collage "Just What Is It That Makes Today's Homes So Different, So Appealing?" is reproduced in Jarman's *Dancing Ledge*); Alison and Peter Smithson, architects who rejected modernist rationalism and focused instead on the social patterns of life, particularly as embodied in their emphasis on the street;[20] and Lawrence Alloway, a critic and curator who is credited with coining the term "pop art," which he originally used to refer to artifacts of popular culture.[21] The Independent Group was responsible for a few groundbreaking exhibitions, the most influential of which was *This Is Tomorrow* (1956), which comprised a series of ten collaborative environments constructed by various configurations of artists and architects. Alloway collaborated with Ralph Rumney in 1959 on a more Situationist-inspired exhibition at the ICA titled "Place" that stressed audience engagement and play; this would be followed by a similar exhibition in 1960–61 titled "Situation."[22]

The Independent Group shared with the Situationists an interest in the patterns of everyday life, a belief in the importance of play and contingency, a strong distrust of modernist urban planning, and an enthusiasm for popular culture; it was generally less critical in its embrace of American consumer culture than was the SI. The actual connections between the groups should not be overstated, although the Situationist International used the ICA as its London mailing address, and the last day of the 1960 Situationist conference in London was held at the ICA (the meeting appears not to have gone smoothly).[23] The SI and the IG should instead be seen as related parts of a larger artistic and intellectual movement, surveyed in 1964 in two special issues of the *Times Literary Supplement* devoted to the Anglo-American and the European avant-garde.[24] The first featured the work of IG members Eduardo Paolozzi and Richard Hamilton, as well as Allen Ginsberg and William S. Burroughs, two of the most important literary figures for Jarman, and the concrete poet Dom Sylvester Houédard, one of Jarman's early mentors. The second issue included statements by past and present SI members Michèle Bernstein and Jörgen Nash, and the Lettrist figure Isidore Isou. This gathering of avant-garde figures, published while Jarman was a student in London, gives a snapshot of an important matrix of thought for radicals and would-be radicals in the mid-1960s.

The Independent Group did not last past the 1950s (it disbanded after *This Is Tomorrow*), but its members would become prominent figures in the following decade. Art critic and IG member Lawrence Alloway observes that "English Pop Art emerged unmistakably at the 'Young Contemporaries' exhibition of 1961."[25] This was the generation that immediately preceded Jarman, and which included David Hockney, Peter Blake, Richard Smith, and R. B. Kitaj. Barry Curtis argues that British pop artists were more ambivalent about commodity culture than their American counterparts, and quotes Michael Bracewell's observation that the movement "was simultaneously futuristic and nostalgic, 'a sense of Englishness which had one foot in the future and one in the past, one half of the brain engaged with the banality of daily life in rainy old England, the other pioneering within extreme states of mind to bring back reports from the edges of consciousness.'"[26] Jarman was, if anything, more suspicious of American popular culture than the painters who preceded him, which moves his thinking closer to that of the Situationists. In a collaged design for a production of *Orphée*, for example, he used a détourned image of the Brooklyn Bridge for the gates of hell, which, he said, "delineated my attitude to 'American' Popism, nicely. The Elysian fields, on the other hand, are strewn with the fragments of the classical world we were casually discarding."[27] American culture he referred to occasionally as "The Billboard Promised Land," an unwitting but apt translation of Debord's "Society of the Spectacle."

It is Jarman's attitudes toward architecture and urban space, however, that bring him closest to the Situationists. His tutorials with Nikolaus Pevsner would have exposed him to contemporary debates among architectural theorists, both British and European, as would, presumably, his conversations with friends studying architecture. Pevsner was no doubt responsible for Jarman's interest (and expertise) in historical styles of architecture, but Jarman shared with the Independent Group and the Situationists an interest in the psychogeography of the city and a concern for the destruction of traditional neighborhoods in the name of urban planning, evident in his overview of the sixties: "Down came the tiled Lyons Corner Houses, the grocers' shop which weighed your orders, and packed them in blue bags; and the row houses, with their little back yards. In their place, curtain walling, Carnaby Street, supermarkets and finally, American hamburger joints—aptly known as The Great American Disaster."[28] It could be argued that his first mature artworks are not paintings or films at all, but rather the construction of two different spaces: the city of Loudun for Russell's *The Devils* and the series of studio spaces he occupied in Docklands warehouses. The super-8s films function, at least initially, as extensions of this studio space; the feature films reflect an interest seen in *The Devils* in the relation between created spaces and alternative modes of existence.

Jarman's embrace of the Docklands aligns him with a particular demographic, a bohemian scene that colonized certain of London's derelict areas.[29] Jarman's warehouse studios were artfully enough constructed to be profiled first in *Vogue*, and later in 1972 in a volume called *Underground Interiors: Decorating for Alternative Life Styles*, which praises his juxtaposition of decor: "furnishings that are not-quite-antiques, hammocks, large contemporary canvases, and a variety of primitive-looking objects."[30] The early films Jarman makes with the super-8 camera are intimately connected with this created space and its environs. The first of the super-8 films could be labeled psycho-geographical experiments. In *Studio Bankside* (1972), *One Last Walk, One Last Look* (1972), and fragments later incorporated into *Glitterbug* (1994), the camera attempts to record the ambience in and around the Dock-lands, looking at the life passing by on the Thames and in the streets and cafés of the area. Later films might be seen as following the pattern of the *dérive: Journey to Avebury* (1973),[31] for example, shows a journey structured by an arbitrary principle, and *Gerald's Film* (1975) is the product of a drift that produces unexpected results. Many of his films are explicit attempts to record or analyze the experience of a particular space, whether this is an artist's studio or a flat in Sloane Square.

The second area in which Situationist ideas become especially useful in understanding Jarman's aesthetic is the notion of the situation itself. As we noted, the constructed situation is "A moment of life concretely and deliberately constructed by the collective organization of a unitary ambiance and a game of events." This could hardly be bettered as a description of Jarman's directorial method. As a filmmaker, Jarman was highly collaborative, assembling around him a team of artists and actors, setting up the conditions for filming, and then letting things happen. As with the work of Jack Smith, the process was at least as important as the result. Of *The Last of England* he wrote: "I would never say I am making this film for an audience: that's very dishonest. It would be true to say I am making this film for myself with my collaborators, we are the community."[32] Some of the films record situations, such as *Ula's Fete* (1976), while others, such as *Jordan's Dance* (1977), constitute situations in themselves. Further, the earliest films were imagined primarily as elements to be used in further situations and not so much as works of art in their own right. They were shot to be screened at parties in Jarman's studio, shown in different orders at different speeds with different sound tracks, occasionally combined with other films such as *The Wizard of Oz*. They thus became détourned elements in larger situations, which from the widest perspective were the gatherings themselves. There is, of course, a more important point to be

Jarman's Bankside studio, 1970. Photograph by Ray Dean.

made about this. While play is obviously of central importance here, it is a meaningful play that involves an underlying belief in art's potential for transforming the everyday. The goal is for art to invade life, for the artistic spectacle to incorporate the spectator, so that through the incorporation of play into everyday life one can challenge the alienation of contemporary society. This would be a central and overriding goal of Jarman's aesthetic career from beginning to end.

To more fully understand the politics that informed the aesthetic of the early films, we have to back up a little. The Situationists were ultimately Marxists, and although Jarman had some leftist tendencies (one anecdote has him handing out Socialist Worker pamphlets with Vanessa Redgrave one New Year's Eve), a more pressing and fundamental interest was sexual politics. As already mentioned, the student riots of May '68 spurred on other identity-based movements, including the gay liberation movement, to which we will now turn.

The Gay Liberation Front

Although queer space discourse is a relatively new theoretical terrain, its concerns about the relations between space and sexuality were in fact central to the activities of the Gay Liberation Front. Although there had been public venues for socializing in the interwar period, in the postwar period spaces for gatherings of gay men and women in Britain were very rare and rarely safe. Matt Houlbrook writes that "In postwar London it seemed inconceivable that men had ever been able to dance together, to kiss, embrace, or be openly queer in commercial venues."[33] This situation did not substantially change during the sexual revolution. While gay men were central to many aspects of the swinging sixties, they found, as did women, that the revolution was more liberating for some than for others. Moreover, homosexual acts between consenting adults in private were not legalized in the United Kingdom until 1967. Although there had been homosexual advocacy groups in Britain operating for some time, most notably the Campaign for Homosexual Equality (CHE), the end of the 1960s saw the arrival of a new form of gay activism, no longer characterized by polite, largely apologetic requests, but rather by a more positive and aggressive insistence that "Gay is good."

The first meeting of the Gay Liberation Front was held at the London School of Economics on October 13, 1970.[34] Bob Mellers and Aubrey Walter organized the group, building on the example of similar organizations in New York and San Francisco. Many of the GLF's activities were centered on claiming a presence in the public world. This included the organization of gay dances (which they were astonished to find highly popular), as well as street theater, mass attendance at pubs, and "Gay Days." Gay Days were forays into public parks, where members of the GLF would meet, carry signs, kiss in public, and picnic. Claiming a presence in the parks during the day had a particular resonance given their role as nighttime cruising sites. An idea surfaced among some GLF members to perform missionary work in the parks after dark, encouraging closeted gay men to come out. They quickly realized that their youthful idealism was misdirected, and some abandoned the mission to take up cruising themselves.

Accompanying this interest in claiming public space for gays and lesbians was a utopian faith in the new possibilities for transformation. Keith Birch recalls that "We believed everything would change, even ourselves. Days and nights were an exhilarating turmoil of ideas, actions and experiments, about politics, sex and our whole lives."[35] One of the cornerstones of the GLF was the weekly consciousness-raising meetings; Birch notes that in the GLF context, "'consciousness-raising', while sounding like a term from the personal growth groups in the USA, had much more to do with building a collective sense of identity."[36] Out of these meetings arose various experiments in personal and social transformation, such as think-ins, radical drag, and communal living.[37] The communes in particular were aimed at reinventing or replacing the family with other affective relations, much, it could be argued, like Jarman's home movies. The GLF manifesto called for "the replacement of the family unit, with its rigid gender-role pattern, by new organic units such as the commune, where the development of children becomes the shared responsibility of a larger group of people who live together." To use Foucault's heterotopic discourse, the communes deformed the relations of emplacement of the home, partly by disregarding the almost sacred opposition between public and private. This, the inhabitants felt, would effect radical change at the level of subjectivity. The communes never evolved to the point of raising children, but radical transformation of self and society was at the heart of the GLF for as long as it continued to exist.

One of the key features of the gay liberation movement that is sometimes overlooked is how closely it identified its aims with the women's liberation movement. The GLF manifesto sharply distinguished gay liberation from gay activism, the latter defined as

> when gay males seek their full share of male privilege. . . . As opposed to gay activism, gay liberation starts from the recognition that male supremacy and the gender-role system has to be rooted out; that gay men can't be liberated except in the context of a radical transformation of the relationship between males and females in general—we thus support completely the women's liberation movement, as being in our vital interest.

We can see here an earlier version of the political and theoretical divide that would later surface between gay and queer activists, particularly in the queer critique of essentialist identity politics. According to the manifesto, gay activism is essentially assimilationist, whereas gay liberation is a revolutionary activity founded upon a radical critique of the gender system. From the evidence of the weekly meeting sheets

and articles in *Come Together,* the publication of the GLF's Media Work-
shop, the critique of masculinity was a topic of vigorous debate and
serious concern. The radical drag movement was one attempt to confront misogyny and to challenge gender stereotypes, and the GLF's
nonhierarchical structure was an attempt to challenge authoritarian
power structures. Ultimately, however, the GLF suffered the fate of
similar activist organizations. The lesbians split off to form their own
organization, the nonhierarchical structure proved too productive of
infighting and endless debate, and the GLF collapsed. Nonetheless, it is
important to remember that a vigorous and sustained critique of gender
was at the core of the movement.

The centrality of this critique of gender within gay liberationist
thought is particularly important to remember when discussing Jarman,
who is occasionally accused of conscious or unconscious misogyny,
generally on the basis of very little evidence. In an otherwise insightful discussion of *Edward II,* for example, Colin MacCabe writes that
"The film is much more unambiguous in its misogyny than any of his
other work. In that gay dialectic where identification with the position
of the woman is set against rejection of the woman's body, *Edward II*
is entirely, and without textual foundation, on the side of rejection."[38]
We will deal with this at greater length in discussing that film, but
here it is enough to note the two sweeping assertions made about the
nature of gay male sexuality and the current of misogyny that apparently runs through all of Jarman's films. For neither assertion is any
evidence offered, or assumed needed. In the context of an essay that is
sensitive to the history of sexuality, about an activist filmmaker very
much concerned with history, the ahistorical claim about a "gay dialectic" is particularly notable. Statements such as these tend to ignore
the very dramatic shifts in gay consciousness from the pre- to post-
GLF eras, and the pre- to post-AIDS eras, or the shifts in consciousness
implied in the changes of self-identification from homophile to homosexual to gay to queer. Such an approach also rules out the possibility
that an individual, while marked by his or her past, might experience
radical change in his or her own sense of self. On a less profound level,
it erases the possibility of political change, and the possibility that gay
men would somehow be affected by the ideas of the women's liberation movement or the GLF. I do not wish to claim here that particular

films by Jarman cannot be accused of misogyny, but rather to protest against the automatic assumption that gay men are predisposed to misogyny by virtue of their object choice.

In an interview in 1985, Jarman says, "I was at the first GLF meetings at the LSE. . . . It had a huge effect."[39] In her oral history of the movement, Lisa Power includes him among the "celebrity visitors" to the next regular venue at which GLF met, the basement of a disco in Covent Garden.[40] The first meeting of the Street Theatre group took place in Jarman's Bankside studio, although Jarman himself was not present.[41] In *At Your Own Risk* he briefly mentions his attendance at meetings, reprints sections of the GLF manifesto, and discusses the Bradford "zap" that was part of their antipsychiatry movement (71–74). Jarman was not centrally involved in the organization, and he did not seem to participate in the discussions of this incredibly garrulous organization; most of its core members were younger and less experienced in the world than he, and dedicated involvement in the GLF could mean meetings every night of the week.[42]

Moreover, as we have noted, Jarman had already found an accommodating world in the gay art scene of the sixties that included, most notably, Patrick Procktor and David Hockney; Hockney's public acknowledgment of his homosexuality was revolutionary, according to Jarman: "By example, he was a great liberating force, reaching far beyond the confines of the 'art world': his work paved the way for the gay liberation movement at the end of the decade."[43] In an unpublished section of the same interview, Jarman says, "Patrick said to me, 'It's not important what you paint it's the way you lead your life which is more important,'" advice that Jarman seems to have taken to heart. By the early 1970s, Jarman was a part of the largely gay bohemian scene circulating around Andrew Logan, who staged such events as the Alternative Miss World pageant, a highly theatrical radical drag party. This glam scene would later foster parts of the early punk movement, which, as we will see, went on to distance itself from these gay roots.

But in spite of the fact that Jarman had less need of the social world offered by the GLF, the attraction of the GLF and its ideas cannot be dismissed. He was certainly more predisposed to the central ideas of the GLF, particularly its call to invent new ways of being in the world, than he was to the ideas of the other dominant gay organi-

zation of the time, the CHE. In spite of its relatively short life, the
GLF had a huge impact on gay culture; as the editorial in the final
issue of *Come Together* noted, most of the major gay institutions and
organizations of London of the 1980s came out of the movement.
Whatever Jarman's participation in GLF activities actually was, he certainly shared the group's ideals, and although his thinking about community, art, and activism evolved, he remained true to the radical
spirit of the GLF even as the gay community itself became more and
more mainstream.

My aim in surveying these two different contexts for understanding
Jarman's early works is not to tie them (or him) firmly to particular
movements, but to establish some of the major currents of avant-garde
thought and practice that stimulated their emergence. No context can
ever fully explain or exhaust the meaning of an artwork, particularly
work by an artist as idiosyncratic as Jarman. But exploring what was
current or thinkable at a particular moment may help to establish
exactly how idiosyncratic a work is, and what the nature of its innovation is. And, for an artist as interested in history as Jarman, it can be
helpful to rehistoricize his work, in order not to read his works in light
of later political and cultural developments.

TWO

Liberation, Space, and the Early Films

ROWLAND WYMER HAS OBSERVED that "there is a critical consensus that Jarman's early short films were crucial to his development as a director, but there is less of a consensus about how valuable they are as autonomous works of art."[1] One answer to this conundrum is to argue that the films were not initially conceived as autonomous works of art, but rather only as elements of larger artistic productions, the countercultural events at which they were shown. The super-8s, which Jarman called his home movies, participated in a redefinition of home and family, documenting the new spaces and scenes in which Jarman moved. *Sebastiane,* which starts with a party similar to those at which the super-8s were shown, is Jarman's first use of the space of the past to challenge the construction of the present. He uses this space as a site on which to stage a countermythology, which has at its heart the liberation project of a revolutionary transformation of the gay self. As Wymer suggests, we can see in these early forays into filmmaking the beginnings of many of Jarman's preoccupations; it is important at the same time to see their embeddedness within their own historical moments, and the movements and ideas with which they were engaging.

Reconfiguring "Home" in the Super-8s

In the course of a discussion of his film *Sebastiane,* Jarman says, "The home movie is the bedrock, it records the landscape of leisure: the beach, the garden, the swimming pool. In all home movies is a longing for paradise. How have the victims prepared themselves for their brief immortality? Who smiles when they are told? Whose hair is brushed? Where is the serpent hiding?"[2] He notes that his grandfather was an enthusiastic proponent of home movies, making them as early as the 1920s, and his father continued this tradition, evidence of which we see in Jarman's apocalyptic feature, *The Last of England*. In that film, his family's home movies serve both as fragments of pastoral, juxtaposed against the decay of contemporary England, and, given their settings in Anglo-Indian compounds and army barracks, as the home movies of empire.

In calling his early super-8 films "home movies," Jarman lays claim to a family tradition and reconfigures it. The home movie is, even more than paint by numbers, the preeminent twentieth-century, middle-class, suburban art form, produced in and producing the "landscape of leisure."[3] In an interview around the release of *The Last of England* he says that all of his films are home movies, "because I try to keep everything very close to the concept of home, which is perhaps something which is difficult because I am gay. It is hard to establish 'home' being a gay man. My home movies therefore reported a very different world to that presented by my grandfather and my father."[4] The ideological function of the home movie is not just to document but to bring into being the family and home pictured on the screen, and Jarman's super-8s are no different, constituting the world of the Bankside parties as a new version of home. He says of these films: "What I discovered in film was community. I discovered my world in film. I wasn't the director in those Super-8 films in that sense. I merely directed the camera."[5]

Taking a form most often associated with conservative content and disrupting it is one of Jarman's most characteristic political and aesthetic gestures, and one that employs the Situationist strategy of *détournement*. By filming the denizens of the London counterculture in super-8 and calling the results home movies, Jarman is challenging the dominant understanding of home and family, one that is premised precisely on the exclusion of the people and scenes Jarman is filming; moreover, he does this through a medium that is, appropriately enough, heavily invested in reproducing precisely those ideologies being challenged. Although it would be too much to claim that he thereby ruins the potential of the home movie for reproducing repressive ideologies, he does at least make a powerful claim of ownership on those two terms, home and family. This, again, is also characteristic of his use of genres associated with national rather than familial belonging. Jarman doesn't reject the nation that is founded on his exclusion; instead, he uses its favorite ideological forms to insist upon his claim to belonging, the aesthetic equivalent to the GLF's strategy of invading and colonizing (and thereby transforming) public spaces. The home movies function to map out new territories of intersubjectivity and desire, ones that are continuous with and related to the initial spectatorial experience, where the lines between spectacle and spectator are deliberately and purposefully blurred. Thus, although the films may be viewed away from their initial moment of production and exhibition, they cannot adequately be considered apart from it.

In what follows, Jarman's early home movies will be roughly divided into three groups according to their treatment of space. I will discuss in some detail representative examples of each of these, not so much for their intrinsic merit (although, as O'Pray notes, in *Derek Jarman: Dreams of England*, some of them do hold up quite nicely), but rather for what they might establish for the films that follow. The first group is interested primarily in recording or exploring places, whether landscapes or built environments. This includes some of the very early super-8 films like *Journey to Avebury* (1973) or *The Siren and the Sailor* (1972), which offer literal landscapes, and others, like *Studio Bankside* (1972) or *Gerald's Film* (1975) that can be seen as psychogeographical explorations. One significant subgroup is a series of films documenting artists' studios, the best of which is *Duggie Fields* (1974). These artists' studio films can be seen as forerunners to later films such as *Imagining October* and *Caravaggio* that examine the studio as an alternative, experimental social space.

A second group of films, such as *Andrew Logan Kisses the Glitterati* (1973), *Ula's Fete* (1976), and *Picnic at Rae's* (1974) record the new world being created in the countercultural heterotopias in which Jarman traveled. They are, to paraphrase Laurie Anderson, both the time and the record of the time. Finally, the more experimental films, such as *Garden of Luxor* (1973), *The Devils at the Elgin* (1974), and *Fire Island* (1974), in which Jarman begins to develop a private mythology along the lines of Kenneth Anger, can be seen, as Jarman says of the later experimental feature *The Angelic Conversation,* to be "exploring a landscape I had never seen on film: areas of psyche that hadn't been projected before."[6] The films go from documenting space to exploring the potential for the creation of a purely cinematic space. In all three groups of films, what is crucial to note is the continuity between the new geographies or spatial regimes in the films, and the particular spectatorial experience of the initial viewing of these films. From the beginning of his career, Jarman can be seen to be interested in the potential of art to transform the world both on-screen and offscreen.

Although the primary context for the early films is avant-garde art rather than experimental film, Michael O'Pray points to some of the influences and echoes of American and British experimental filmmakers whose work Jarman had viewed as an art student at the Slade.[7] Films by Maya Deren such as *At Land* (1944) show a similar interest in the creation of imaginary geographies and the exploration of psychic terrains, as does, to take another prominent example, Stan Brakhage's *Dog Star Man* (1961–64). And while Andy Warhol and the Factory seem more of an influence in terms of production and exhibition rather than of aesthetics, in films like *Sloane Square* we can see an interest in time and duration that continued to develop in Jarman's more experimental work. Kenneth Anger, whose work was screened relatively frequently in London in the 1960s, was probably the most formative of these influences, both in his combination of occultism and homoerotic imagery and in his formal interest in montage.

We can also see a number of similarities between the early work of Jarman and the films of Jack Smith, a central figure in the New American Cinema, and in particular, in what Jonas Mekas dubbed the Baudelarean cinema, produced by a group of New York filmmakers including Smith, Ron Rice, Ken Jacobs, and Bob Fleischner (and who clearly inspired Susan Sontag's "Notes on Camp"). Mekas championed their cause in the *Village Voice,* highlighting their cheerful perversity, the films' homosexual content, their apparently improvisational technique, and their interest in contingency and accident in the filming process.[8] A number of these films found their way into distribution in Britain through the London Film-Makers' Co-op (LFMC) (founded in 1966).[9] In the latter half of the sixties there was an upsurge of interest in experimental, avant-garde and underground cinemas, as evidenced by the emergence of such things as the LFMC, venues like the UFO Club, New Cinema Club and the Electric, alternative distribution circuits, film magazines like *Cinem, Cinema,* and *Cinemantics,* and even commercial distributors for this material.[10]

Sarah Street notes that "some commentators were keen to stress the unique characteristics of the British avant-garde in this period, claiming the "structural" film as primarily British."[11] Some of Jarman's more formal explorations, in particular with the layering and manipulation of images, parallel what was happening at the LFMC in the seventies, where structuralist filmmakers like Malcolm Le Grice were experimenting with the optical printer. O'Pray points as well to the influence of David Larcher's drug-based aesthetic, particularly in the more experimental films.[12] But while Jarman was familiar with these artists and their work, he stated in an interview that "the gulf between myself and the people there was that they knew about filmmaking and were interested in the semantics of film, and that was the primary objective of the films that I tended to see in that period. . . . It seemed to me that what was important to them was film as itself."[13] For Jarman, the important thing was not the work of art, but what the work of art could accomplish. What differentiates Jarman from these early influences, and what places him in the camp of the underground filmmaker rather than the experimental or structuralist artists of the LFMC, is the way in which history and politics inevitably inflect his vision. Even at its most abstract, we can detect in Jarman's aesthetic an overriding interest in the world in which he moved, reflected at the most basic level in his interest in landscape and social space.

Films of Place

A number of the earliest films show an interest in the experience of particular spaces, as well as in time, which film, unlike painting, can explore. Jarman's first film, *Studio Bankside,* is an exploration of space that is at the same time interested in temporality, and the way that duration and history alter or condition spaces. The film works by first zooming in on objects in photographs of his studio, and then attempting to locate where those same objects are in the studio now. Like the Situationist *dérive,* the film traverses a space by following an arbitrary rule ("Where is the photographed object now?") and then reading the signs that consequently appear. The migration of objects highlights the passage of time and the evolution of the space. As noted earlier, this is one of a series of films,[14] including *One Last Walk, One Last Look,* that record the world of the studio and the area around it. Others offer images of the people that passed through the space, the boats on the Thames, and the views of London on the other side of the river.

A Journey to Avebury (1973), another very early film, consists almost exclusively of shots of a landscape from a stationary camera. These classically composed images resemble landscape paintings except for the occasional inclusion of cars, people, or cows, which disturb the stillness of the shots (not unlike the effect of the three-dimensional objects that were affixed to his stylized landscape paintings). The strange stasis of the journey, which has something of the rhythm of a slide show, is broken by the final shot, which slowly pans right and then begins to zoom in on the horizon, when the film abruptly stops. Around the same time that he made the film, Jarman painted his Avebury series, and in the posthumously edited *Glitterbug,* images of these paintings are cut into a sequence from the film. Avebury is the location of an ancient circle of standing stones, and Tony Peake argues that the film "shows Jarman's fascination with the past, how the past leaves traces of itself and how these traces—in this case, a circle of stones—have spiritual and mystical properties on a par with the landscape itself."[15] Here is a grander version of the game in *Studio Bankside,* exploring how the past inhabits or overlays the landscape of the present.

In an interview, Jarman said that "film enabled me to make a rapprochement with my real world. The world of the paintings was sterile, an empty world. . . . Although I didn't believe it at the time because I didn't have any confidence, I had been isolated by being gay in painting. Film restored that connection missing in my painting."[16] The turn to film is not so much a break from painting as it is an extension of some of the same aesthetic explorations in a medium more amenable to Jarman's political concerns, and in particular his sexual politics. Although Jarman's sexuality might seem to be more in evidence in a film like *Fire Island,* which films the dunes of New York's most famous gay resort, *Journey to Avebury* is nonetheless a crucial starting point. The film can be seen to be comparing the representational possibilities of painting and film, while at the same time exploring the relation between space and motion. Rather than portraying only the relations of objects in space, as in painting, the traveling eye of the camera (even in this stuttering journey) invokes the relation of the viewer to the space

Landscape with standing stones in *A Journey to Avebury* (Jarman, 1973).

portrayed. The film is interested not just in documenting space but in constructing a particular relation to it, through editing. History thus is introduced in a number of ways: most obviously in the subject matter, but also more subtly in the way that the audience is made conscious of its relation to the represented landscape and its imagined motion through it.

Jarman only rarely included images of landscape in his feature-length films. *The Garden* features the most sustained representations of natural space, and even there Jarman is most often interested in those spaces that reflect past or present human activity. This is the case in one of the most beautiful of the early super-8s, *Gerald's Film*. While on a trip through Essex, Jarman and Gerald Incandela stumbled across an abandoned and decaying Victorian boathouse on the edge of a dried-up lake, and Jarman decided to document it. The film starts at the top of the chimney and follows it down, taking in as many details as possible, and then pulling back to reveal the entire structure. The camera moves into the boathouse, picking out architectural details and patterns formed by the process of disintegration. After surveying the interior, the film shows us Gerald sitting on the floor, looking like a figure in a Modigliani painting with his dramatic hat and scarf. The camera then moves outside, looking back in through the window, with the glass somewhat distorting the image of Gerald. The film ends back inside the building, with the camera pulling back and then tilting up into the roof. The tone of the entire film is elegiac, with the beautiful ruins suggestive of the relationship between the director and the person being filmed. This use of a decaying structure as a metaphor for psychological space is a recurring feature in the later works.

The artist's studio films work in a parallel way. In *Duggie Fields,* the camera records everything within the studio in a long series of static shots, using essentially the same rhythm as *A Journey to Avebury.* This has the effect of rendering everything within the studio as equivalent. The paintings, furniture, props, photographs, and the artist himself all become interrelated elements of a larger experience of space, and at the same time, extensions of the artist, as the title of the film suggests. Space and subjectivity are seen to be mutually defining. But the film is also interested in a more particular examination of the space where art is created. Anticipating moments in later films where we see painters at work, here the film focuses in on details of paintings and on the photographs that serve as sources for them, as if attempting to isolate the work that painting accomplishes as it remakes elements of the world. The studio is seen as a laboratory, and the work of painting (and by extension filming) as both analytic and transformative.

Alternative Worlds

Sloane Square: A Room of One's Own (1974–76) is another exploration of space, but in this case the new worlds in which Jarman moved. It is more structured than films like *Ula's Fete* or *Picnic at Rae's,* which similarly act as explorations and records of a created situation, and the ambience of a particular social terrain. Those films, however, seem to begin and end arbitrarily, and are concerned mostly with making careful observations of events and, in particular, the people at them. The films are interested in constructing and relaying a more subjective experience of time and place. As is the case with many of the feature films that would follow, it is difficult to get a good sense of the actual space in which the events occurred; there is no super-8 equivalent of an establishing shot, which might serve to stabilize the relation of the audience to the represented space. What we have instead is a purposeful disorientation of the viewer as an attempt to stimulate a reorientation to these alternative spaces. Although these films bear a similarity to the early films of Warhol, which also apparently record real social situations as they unfold, here the camera is far more active in structuring the experience of viewing.

Sloane Square, which commemorates Jarman's eviction from Anthony Harwood's flat in the eponymous square, is the most Situationist of the early films, in terms of both content and structure. It is more artfully constructed than the other films of events, and it can be roughly divided into five sequences. In the first, an unmoving camera set up in the corner of the living room records in stop-motion photography the comings and goings in the room. Figures enter, lie on the floor, read, talk on the phone, remove paintings from the wall; at other times, the room remains empty, inviting us to contemplate it as a space. The time-lapse photography alerts us to the heterochronic dimension of this particular heterotopia.

The second sequence offers a series of quick shots of images within the flat, moving around and zooming in and out on jewels, books, flowers, people, body parts, records and a record player, and the view from the flat. A note from "Cat" (Jean-Marc Prouvier) to the audience alerts us to its self-consciousness as film, as do the images of Jarman filming himself in a mirror. The next section is something of a continuation of this, except that we are offered more or less stationary shots of roughly equal length of the inhabitants of the flat, body parts, and flowers. Here at the center of the film (and thus of the experience of the flat) we seem to be focused most clearly on objects of desire, obscure and otherwise, a sense reinforced by the slow, regular pace of the editing, which makes the film throb like a heartbeat. The fourth section is again dominated by stop-motion photography, this time observing a party going on in a now-altered flat with the walls spray-painted with Situationist graffiti.

The final sequence is something of a leave-taking, consisting of a series of rapidly photographed, sometimes blurry images, showing us a drawing of a young man, a copy of Mary Renault's homoerotic classic *The Persian Boy,* a picture of Rimbaud, an address, bills, political pins, plants, and other objects from the flat. As with other films, we read the space by reading objects encountered. While the first section establishes the film's interest in space, in particular the space of the flat, the following sections expand the experience of that space to include the objects within that space, the persons that pass through it, and the dimension of time itself. The film as a whole is interested in mapping out a psychic geography: attempting to convey the experience of this particular social and sexual milieu.

Imaginary Space

For Jarman, formal experimentation often came in the processing and reprocessing of images and, in particular, an exploration of the effects of projection. Films would be projected speeded up or slowed down and then refilmed. The texture of the resulting image becomes a focus of interest, which is connected, in films like *The Angelic Conversation* or *Sloane Square*, to an interest in the texture of recorded time. *Garden of Luxor*, an early work marked by Jarman's ongoing fascination with Egypt, is the first to experiment with the combination of détourned images. Different kinds of filmic images are layered onto each other by means of projection, including actions filmed by Jarman (a man, Christopher Hobbs, whips something at the bottom of the frame; a man with a fake or blackened nose looks at flies crawling on his glove; a young man reclines); postcards of pyramids and the Sphinx; and found footage of riders in the desert. All of these are filmed, projected onto the wall, and then refilmed. In the case of the early shot of the whipping, we see the resulting film projected and refilmed a little later, with the attendant alteration and decay of the image.

The film has a poetic rather than a narrative structure; the whipping establishes a beat that is occasionally echoed by the editing, and images recur and are recombined in various ways. The dreamy quality of the film is evocative of the surrealist (and Situationist) interest in the unconscious; the flies on the glove, in particular, echo the ants on the hand in *Un Chien Andalou*, and the repetitive action in the film resembles Maya Deren's surrealist *Meshes of the Afternoon*. The title provides some frame for interpretation: gardens for Jarman were always an alternative space, as was the exoticism of Ancient Egypt, functioning much like Jack Smith's delirious version of Baghdad. Kenneth Anger's

Lucifer Rising (1972) also features the Pyramids, although in an unironic way; Egypt, part of Richard Burton's Sotadic Zone, has long had a place in Western homoerotic fantasy. In the same vein, one of Jarman's most cherished unrealized projects was *Akenaten,* a film about the son of Amenhotep III and husband of Nefertiti, although Jarman's violent reimagining depends as much on William S. Burroughs's *Wild Boys* as it does on any historical source.

In the film, the garden of Luxor is created by projecting a film of the Pyramids (taken from a postcard) onto floral wallpaper. The screen thus becomes both entrance to the garden and the garden itself. The film thereby draws attention to the role of the screen in the creation of the projected space, and the evidently constructed nature of the filmic fantasy. This is underscored by the use of the found footage, which suggests how fantasy redeploys available material. But while the filmic space might be constructed, that does not mean that it is any less real, or that the resultant heterotopia is any less available to the viewer. By staging action in front of the screen, filming it, and projecting the result onto the wall, the film offers something of an allegory for the spectator's relation to cinema. The viewer moves from the spectatorial space into the heterotopic garden behind the screen, a space that allows for the exploration of homoerotic desire. The film seems to be exploring the potential for film itself to offer an alternative space of consciousness, to create a space that is entirely constructed via the filmmaker's art.

In the Shadow of the Sun (1974–80), a longer experimental work that combines footage from earlier shorts, also consists of layered images. For the most part, shots of landscapes are overlaid with symbolic images or actions: hooded figures, a maze of fire, persons dancing, a classical bust, someone walking holding an umbrella. The interest in the film is at least partially the interaction between the superimposed image tracks: how the landscape qualifies the symbolic images, how the figures alter the landscape, how each supplements or cancels the other. In one particularly interesting sequence (which also exists as a separate film, *The Devils at the Elgin*), Jarman refilms off the screen of the Elgin Cinema in New York the conclusion of Ken Russell's *The Devils,* "the final moment when Madeleine escapes from the claustrophobic city of Loudun into the world outside, over the great white walls; but

Layered and refilmed images in *Garden of Luxor* (Jarman, 1973).

now, in my version, she walks into a blizzard of ashes."[17] As with *Garden of Luxor*, the film explores how projection and reproduction can change not just the quality of the image but the very meaning of it: art inevitably transforms the real. In both films, the screen itself becomes a crucial site of experimentation and transformation.

The hallucinatory quality of *In the Shadow of the Sun* suggests that the experience of watching the film is, in a sense, what the film is about. Jarman notes that "The first film viewers wracked their brains for meaning instead of relaxing into the ambient tapestry of *random images.*... You can dream of lands far distant."[18] This again reflects the avant-garde interest in liberating the unconscious through play. Jarman's interest in transforming the experience of spectatorship is more directly apparent in *The Art of Mirrors* (1973), which features a stationary camera filming three figures: a hooded man in a suit, and a man and woman in evening dress. The man in evening dress carries a circular mirror, which he uses to flash sunlight into the camera. Direct light into the lens causes the camera's internal light meter to spike, and the screen to flash white and then go black. The film ends with the woman slowly approaching the camera, periodically flashing light into the lens.

This effect shows up in a number of Jarman's early works: an enigmatic figure in *The Angelic Conversation* holds a mirror toward the camera, and in *Jubilee* Ariel flashes light into the camera to transport us to the near future. In *The Art of Mirrors,* however, the repeated use of the effect draws attention to the physical dimension of the spectatorial experience. The blinding flashes of light from the screen remind us of the power of cinema to act upon us. This, I argued earlier, can be understood in relation to both Benjamin's interest in cinema's role in retraining our sensorium and Eisenstein's desire to virtually assault the audience. Closer to home, it fit in with the notion of "expanded cinema," which sought to dislodge the complacency of the audience by changing the experience of spectatorship; Jarman was among the filmmakers shown at the ICA in 1976 at the Festival of Expanded Cinema.[19]

The super-8 films are characterized by an exploration of the possibilities of film for the transformation of vision, the viewer, and the world, an exploration that would mark all of Jarman's films. At the same time, the spatial regimes established in the production and exhibition of the super-8s are also, arguably, foundational to the films that would follow. If, as Jarman says, "The home movie is the bedrock" of the films that follow, we have to understand this in relation to the ideological function of the home movie: how the experience of watching the film brings into being the home pictured. The particular spectatorial regime of the home movie can be seen, for example, in the riotous orgy scene that opens *Sebastiane,* which resembles the parties that would accompany the screenings of the super-8s at Butlers Wharf. The filmed party acts as a frame, reproducing for the audience the earlier spectatorial conditions of the Bankside screenings. We see the film through the party, in other words, and it serves to establish some of the appropriate questions to be directed at it. The main body of the film is, in the first instance, directed toward the partygoers, Jarman's community, who are recognizably part of the London scene. This pointed refusal of any claim to the universal appeal of art reflects his keen sense of historical specificity.

The super-8s, therefore, should be seen not as autonomous works of art, but rather as elements of larger works or situations aimed at transforming the audience. This belief in the power of art to transform the everyday, most crucially by altering the experience of space, puts

Jarman's work in the context of larger aesthetic and cultural movements. The Situationist International's use of structured play and *détourne-ment* to effect political revolution is the most obvious forerunner, but the emergence of a new gay political movement, which also stressed the importance of the transformation of the everyday, was likely a more immediate influence. Regardless of what led him to pick up the camera, in film Jarman had found the best medium for exploring the aesthetic and political concerns that most deeply mattered to him, and while he would continue to experiment with other forms, film would occupy him for the rest of his life.

Gay Liberation Theology in *Sebastiane*

Sebastiane starts with an orgy at the court of Diocletian, where Sebas-tian refuses to participate in the execution of a young man suspected of arson, and is subsequently banished to the military outpost where he will meet his demise. Although visually the sequence owes more to Ken Russell or Fellini than it does to Pasolini, the orgy scene does play a structural function similar to that of the opening scenes of Pasolini's *Oedipus Rex*, ultimately anchoring the film in the present.[20] The scene was shot in Andrew Logan's studio, and many of the actors who take part are recognizable figures in the largely gay demimonde that circu-lated around Logan, some of whom would go on to be central in the punk scene. It was Logan who organized the Alternative Miss World pageant, which Jarman won on his third try; the second Miss World plays the role of the executioner (part of a film of the 1975 pageant appears in *Glitterbug*). In the scene, Jarman observes, "Modern London winked at ancient Rome."[21] The costumes, many of which were pro-vided by the actors, are a fairly heterogeneous mix, including punk icon Jordan's decidedly contemporary take on the classical era; Jarman notes that "everyone was in fancy dress—not period at all—Magritte togas and the like."[22] The script had originally called for an even more obviously anachronistic approach than what appeared on film, with a gossip columnist named Vigilantia dispensing fashion tips and satiric comment, but this was abandoned under the pressures of limited time and film stock: "Our original intention of a cruel cocktail party where the glitterati met Oriental Rome disappeared—even the truncated version took till nine in the evening."[23]

At the orgy, Lindsay Kemp dances with a group of near-naked satyrs with enormous phalluses, who eventually cover him in a shower of simulated ejaculate. Lindsay Kemp Company had just had a West End success with a remount of *Flowers...a Pantomime for Jean Genet*, Kemp's adaptation of Genet's *Our Lady of the Flowers*. Kemp had also recently played the role of Polsky, the gay art dealer, in Ken Russell's *Savage Messiah*, for which Jarman had designed the sets. Jarman's association with Kemp's company continued after this film largely in the person of Jack Birkett, aka the Incredible Orlando, who played substantial roles in *Jubilee*, *The Tempest*, and *Caravaggio;* Kemp himself would appear briefly again in *Jubilee* in a similarly scandalous sequence. Jarman later identified Kemp as "one of the key gay figures to emerge from the sixties,"[24] and his appearance in the opening scene serves to position the film in relation to a particular artistic and political movement. More than just a series of inside jokes, the opening scene situates the film within a particular London culture, the members of which it takes for its principal audience. It announces, in other words, precisely on what grounds and from which perspective the story of Sebastian will be remythologized, and for whose benefit. By incorporating a representation of its own audience, the film raises the question of spectatorship and in particular the appropriate relation of the viewer to the film.

The opening orgy scene in *Sebastiane* thus acts as a bridge in a number of ways: not only as a temporal and geographic relay between the audience and the main body of the film, but also as a bridge between the world of the super-8s, and the world of the feature films, where Jarman would frequently turn to historical subject matter. Its flagrant breach of period realism establishes at the beginning of Jarman's feature-filmmaking career what would be his characteristic approach to the past, which Fredric Jameson identifies as a kind of magic realism, "a Nietzschean affirmation that there is no past, and thus, finally, no time at all."[25] Equally important, we see Jarman beginning to construct filmic genealogies. The orgy scene echoes the one in *Fellini Satyricon*, which is itself indebted to Jack Smith's *Flaming Creatures;*[26]

other possible precursors are Kenneth Anger's *Inauguration of the Pleasure Dome* (1954), featuring various ancient gods and goddesses, and the very sexualized biker party in *Scorpio Rising* (1964). The most important debt, however, is to Pier Paolo Pasolini, who would be a lasting influence on Jarman's film career.

In his book *The Last of England*, Jarman uses the occasion of watching a documentary about Pasolini's murder to reflect on the similarities between their two careers:

> Pier Paolo's enemies saw him as a radical, but in fact he fought for traditional values, he even wrote against the students of '68 throwing stones at the police. Why didn't these students, the fortunate ones, throw stones at the real source of repression: the bankers and the judges, rather than these simple boys from the south co-opted by the state?
>
> Pasolini got his targets right. I wonder if he would like my films; like his, they are made in an older tradition, and this is why they are misunderstood by TV execs from the fleshy world of advertising, co-opted by consumption.[27]

There are, in fact, numerous parallels between the two filmmakers, both trivial and profound. Both were children of middle-class families, with military fathers. Both adored their mothers and hated their fathers, although both, later in life, admitted to a grudging respect and even love for them. Like Jarman, Pasolini achieved success in a range of artistic media, starting his career as a poet and novelist, and entering filmmaking as a screenwriter for directors like Fellini. Both directors were eclectic readers and passionate if muddy thinkers, offering confident pronouncements on a variety of subjects, often contradicting or revising earlier statements in the process. Both became notorious public figures, for their sexuality and their unorthodox leftist politics, and their films were the targets of official government scrutiny and public controversy. Pasolini's passion for rough trade and Jarman's for cruising on Hampstead Heath made them controversial figures for certain sectors of the gay community, and well-nigh demonic for parts of the straight world. Their public personae tended to overshadow their films, so that the reception of the films, whether condemning or laudatory, was often more about the persona than the work. Both had deaths that were read as emblematic of their lives and sexual practices: Pasolini was purportedly murdered by a hustler, and Jarman died of AIDS.[28]

Jarman made no secret of his great admiration for Pasolini, which critics have duly noted.[29] In 1985, for example, he published an unrealized film script, *P.P.P. in the Garden of Earthly Delights,* which starts with the shooting of the final scene of *Salo* and ends with Pasolini's death.[30] Anticipating *Edward II,* it features a double ending in which Pasolini to some degree survives his own murder. Jarman even played Pasolini late in life, in Julian Cole's short film *Ostia* (1991) (Ostia was the site of Pasolini's murder). As Jarman's words indicate, there are profound sympathies between the directors that go beyond the biographical similarities, and indeed, it is difficult to name a film by Jarman that does not contain some echo of Pasolini, from *Sebastiane,* where Jarman comes closest to emulating Pasolini, to *Blue,* which calls to mind the all-blue painting made by the son in *Teorema,* after a homosexual affair has stripped away his bourgeois pretensions. Foremost among the sympathies between the directors, as Jarman indicates, is a radicalism that is at the same time a conservatism. In both cases, this leads to a frequent engagement with historical subject matter, and to repeated attempts to find the most effective way to film the past for the purposes of the present.

For Pasolini, the past was one of several sites of either resistance to or refuge from what he saw as the repressive conformism of a petit bourgeois society. His first films, *Accatone* (1961) and *Mamma Roma* (1962), remained in the present but retreated to the criminal fringes of Rome: the pimps and thieves and whores who consciously or unconsciously refused bourgeois values. A group of films that followed, *The Gospel According to St. Matthew* (1964), *Oedipus Rex* (1967), and *Medea* (1970), looks to the myths of the ancient world. In the latter two films especially, Pasolini creates a world of unsettling strangeness, a foreign world of the past where some version of peasant values still exists. A final group of films, often called the Trilogy of Life, filmed three classics from the preindustrial world: *The Decameron* (1970), *The Canterbury Tales* (1971), and *The Arabian Nights* (1974). These films imagine past societies characterized by the acceptance of the diverse pleasures of sexuality, and the films themselves celebrate the beauties of the flesh.

Although Jarman knew all of these films, it is the central group that he most obviously draws upon when making *Sebastiane*. Geoffrey Nowell-Smith characterizes the world of this group of films as "prehistory": "By pre-history I do not mean ancient times—tenth century BC or whatever—but a world about which all we can say for sure is that it is not the world of our known, measured, developing history. It is a world of indefinite time, separate from our world but clearly—and this is crucial—preceding it. It is a world prior to us, and not only to our present but to our past, a world prior to history."[31] In *Medea* and *Oedipus Rex*, the split between past and present is rendered in different ways. *Oedipus Rex* starts almost in the present, in Pasolini's childhood, before moving back to the past; Oedipus ultimately winds up back in present-day Italy, wandering through urban streets. In *Medea*, the split is located in the ancient world itself, both in the difference between Jason's Thessaly and Medea's more primitive, religious Colchis and in the difference between childhood, where centaurs are really centaurs, and adulthood, where centaurs are simply men. In all of these instances, the past functions somewhat like the Freudian unconscious: a place of primitive, archaic, animistic belief that lives on in the present in a diminished form.

In both *Medea* and *Oedipus Rex*, Pasolini renders the strangeness of the past in a number of ways. The characters wear (presumably) historically accurate costumes that are nonetheless bizarre and alienating, often including distorting masks, as they perform dances or rituals, the functions of which are only partially obvious. Like many Italian directors of his day, Pasolini does not use synchronized sound, so many scenes feel slightly unnatural both because of the expected noises that are missing and because of the added elements on the sound track, such as a constantly blowing wind or the keening of peasant women. The dubbing, which is frequently obvious, adds yet more distance, as if the characters were speaking a version of Italian close to, but not identical with, that spoken today. The disorientation is furthered by Pasolini's characteristic refusal to use sequence shots, which means that the viewer is not given the anchor of a single subjective or interpretative viewing position.[32] These and other formal elements work to make the past a foreign world, a world, as the Old Centaur observes in *Medea*, where reason works differently.

This particular relation of the past to present, as we will see, is one key difference in the way the two directors employ the space of the past. Neither director is interested in historical accuracy for its own sake, and neither conforms to the period film genre's preference for classic realist style. Nonetheless, both can be very attentive to historical difference and both use the space of the past as a place from which to implicitly or explicitly critique the present. For Pasolini, however, the past functions as a kind of utopian space from which the modern world has unfortunately drifted, but whose principles still live on in some real way in the cultural unconscious and which might be recovered. For Jarman, the past is more often seen as a collection of stories or myths that work to justify the dominant ideologies of the present, but which can equally be used to contest them.

It is Pasolini's *Gospel According to St. Matthew* to which *Sebastiane* is most obviously indebted, particularly for the way in which Jarman remythologizes the life of the Christian martyr and reimagines the outlines of Christian faith. *The Gospel According to St. Matthew,* like the other two films in the ancient world trilogy, idealizes an ancient peasant culture, in this case by examining the origins of the religion that grew out of it. Pasolini's Christ is an angry and at times unsympathetic figure, which relates to the leftist politics of the film. The film features handheld shots and other cinéma vérité techniques, although not, Pasolini argues, with an eye to demythologizing Christ:

> I did not want to do this, because I am not interested in deconsecrating: this is a fashion I hate, it is petit bourgeois. I want to re-consecrate things as much as possible, I want to remythologize them. I did not want to reconstruct the life of Christ as it really was, I wanted to do the story of Christ plus two thousand years of Christian history which have mythicized this biography, which would otherwise be an almost insignificant biography as such. My film is the life of Christ plus two thousand years of story-telling about the life of Christ.[33]

Jarman talks about the costumes in *The Tempest* in almost exactly the same terms, observing that they act as "a chronology of the 350 years of the play's existence, like a patina on old bronze."[34] In *The Gospel*

According to St. Matthew, this particular approach to remythicizing history is accomplished by balancing the elements of vérité style with the citation of religious iconography and art from the intervening two thousand years, including using the American folksinger Odetta's recording of "Motherless Child" and a Delta Blues song on the sound track. (Pasolini's use of Odetta can be seen as the forerunner of Jarman's more outrageous inclusions of Elisabeth Welch singing "Stormy Weather" in *The Tempest,* and Annie Lennox in *Edward II*).

As with *The Gospel According to St. Matthew, Sebastiane* cites iconic religious representations in order to foreground the nature of its engagement with the past, to make it clear that it is not offering a reconstruction of the past but rather engaging with the interpretive history of a legend. The dialogue makes reference to other Roman period films, both high art like *Fellini Satyricon* and down-market like DeMille's sword-and-sandals epics. Although the costumes and props are to some degree historically accurate, we also see the soldiers tossing around a golden frisbee. The Latin dialogue, similarly, is not used to promote the illusion of historical authenticity, but rather to dispel it. Publicity notes for the film state that "The film was made in colloquial Latin in order to eliminate the horrors of the normal English historical film that is epitomised by all English costume dramas and to allow the use of subtitling as an integral part of the film."[35] Jarman's career-long hostility to the mainstream period film evidently begins with his first feature. Not only does the Latin itself work against naturalism, the awkwardness of its delivery in the mouths of the actors further heightens its strangeness. The Latin dialogue and the subtitling thus function to some degree like Pasolini's use of dubbing, highlighting the self-conscious nature of the engagement with historical material.

The main body of the film provides a fairly stark contrast visually to the opening orgy sequence. Whereas the latter was filmed indoors, with vibrant colors and frantic energy, the rest of the film is shot outside, in brilliant sunlight that bleaches an already drab desert palette. The bored, buff soldiers resemble Jason's Argonauts in *Medea,* who alternate between lying around on the Argo and exploding into violent bursts of activity. Here, in a similar fashion, the soldiers in the isolated encampment practice their swordplay, swim, gamble, drink, and torment each other, and the pace of the film is at times as listless as they are. In an interview at the time of the film's release, Jarman said that "the isolated group of men are a laboratory in which it is possible to see a spectrum of relationships revolving around Sebastian."[36] Some of the relocated soldiers reproduce Rome's values in miniature, sometimes literally: Max stages a coliseum-style entertainment with a group of fighting beetles in the sand, naming them after various female figures (including, in an inside joke, Maria Domus Alba or Mary Whitehouse, the hated British guardian of public morals against whom the GLF struggled). This group is accepting of homosexual activity, although only if it is understood as a temporary substitute for heterosexual sex. The camp can also be, like Rome, notably violent and sadistic and, as might be expected, misogynist.

It is against this set of values that Sebastian defines himself, both in Rome and in the encampment. His rejection of the desire of his captain Severus reads more like a rejection of that world than a rejection of homosexuality per se. It is significant that Sebastian never actually refers to himself as Christian; the closest he comes is his affirmative answer to Severus's question "Are you still a Christian?" There is, in fact, almost nothing recognizably Christian about Sebastian; his friend Justin, by contrast, more than once identifies himself as such, and it is he who winds up occupying the position of Christ in the Pietà that the film later enacts.

Although Sebastian might nominally be Christian, the film empties that category of much of its content and, in effect, remythologizes it. As one early reviewer noted, Sebastian's religion "is really an updated form of Pantheism";[37] we see him several times offering prayers to a god who is, much like Medea's, associated with the sun. In a lyrical scene early in the film, Sebastian has a morning shower in the courtyard, while in a voice-over we hear:

Hail Messenger of Dawn
The young God has arisen.
The Chariot is prepared.
The horses of dawn fly forth to conquer the Goddess of night
The reeds sigh when the young God rises
The waters sing when the young God rises
Mankind awakens from sleep...

Although the voice-over is by the actor playing Sebastian (Leonardo Treviglio), it isn't entirely clear whether he is the young God arising or whether he's singing the praises of the young God, which underscores the narcissistic dimension of his worship.[38] The notably erotic quality of Sebastian's morning prayer is emphasized by the gaze of Severus, who watches, in his armor, from his room; the contrast between the openness of the courtyard and the closed-in space of Severus's stone hut acts as a visual commentary on Severus's constrained sexuality. Later we see Sebastian gazing into a pool of water, Narcissus-like, saying:

> Hail God of the golden sun
> The heavens and earth are united in gold
> . . . .
> Your body, your naked body.
> Initiated into the mysteries, step forth
> That beauty that made all colours different
> Comes forth into the world
> Hail God of the golden fire
> Your beauty holds my heart captive

This identification of beauty with diversity becomes in later films more explicitly associated with homosexuality, although the connection is hardly subtle here. As Richard Dyer notes, Sebastian's love for his god "is expressed in vividly homoerotic terms,"[39] resulting in what one mainstream review called "a gorgeously evangelistic vision of homosexuality."[40] If Pasolini's Christ is an angry Marxist, Jarman's Sebastian is the first gay liberationist, as Jarman himself suggested in a late interview with Colin MacCabe.[41]

The almost exclusively erotic content of Sebastian's religion takes on an ecstatic quality as the film progresses. When as punishment Sebastian is staked down in the blinding sun, he has an ecstatic vision. Justin attempts to shield him from the sun but Sebastian waves him away, saying: "the sun which caresses me is his burning desire. He is Phoebus Apollo. The sun is his burning kiss. His anger is divine." He occasionally sees a Bacchus figure in the wilderness, wearing an animal skin on his head and carrying a thyrsus-like branch. Sebastian's death is (at least in the script) envisioned as an erotic martyrdom, a longed-for sexual encounter with the god Sebastian has been worshipping throughout the film.

Sebastian's desire for an ecstatic communion with his god exists on a continuum in the film with the love of Anthony and Adrian, which is similarly distanced from the values of Rome; Sebastian's religion is, in a sense, the theory to their practice.[42] Max can understand why someone would have sex with a boy if there were no other alternative, but he cannot understand Anthony's love for Adrian. Severus's violent desire for Sebastian is paralleled with Max's indiscriminate heterosexual lust; not surprisingly, these characters are also the two most persistently associated with Rome. Rome, civilization, and heterosexuality thus stand in opposition to nature, spirituality, and homosexuality; homosexuality, far from being a crime against nature, is here seen as a pure expression of it. The film rewrites Christianity (to the extent that it is actually addressing Christianity at all) using the worship of the young sun god to infuse spirituality with sexual desire. This is consonant with most twentieth-century appropriations of the story: "Sebastian's fate in modern and contemporary representation is, above all else, the story of the mischievous appropriation of Christian symbolism and Renaissance imagery by homosexually identified men."[43] The myth of Saint Sebastian, the Christian soldier who emblematizes a narcissistic and suicidal self-denial, becomes instead the myth of an ecstatic homosexual spirituality, based on a rejection of civilized Roman heterosexual values.

These two modes of desire are differentiated visually in the film. The slow-motion photography of Adrian and Anthony's lovemaking in the water echoes the way that the camera lovingly moves across Sebastian's body during his early-morning shower. Jarman's frankly erotic gaze here is reminiscent of a similar approach to the bodies of young lovers in Pasolini's Trilogy of Life. In both cases, this gaze is connected to a lost chapter of civilization, one characterized by an earlier, more pagan religion and by what Pasolini calls an "ancient and real tolerance" that has been corrupted and lost in the face of "the petit bourgeois examples of consumerism and hypocritical tolerance."[44] One key difference is that in Jarman's film, the camera's gaze is exclusively homoerotic and hence more narrowly and pointedly political.

There are important differences to be noted, moreover, between the representation of the body in *Sebastiane* and, for example, in a film like the American gay feature *A Very Natural Thing* (1974), which offers similar soft-core beach romping, but in a kind of timeless present. Both films, it could be argued, offer nonpathological representations of homosexual desire, and a key strategy in both is to situate that desire in a pastoral setting. In Jarman's case, however, other bodies in the film work to promote an awareness of historical difference. In an early discussion of the limitations of historical films, Siegfried Kracauer writes that "What obstructs complete authenticity is the near-impossibility of making present-day actors fit into the costumes they wear. Conditioned by long-term environmental influences, their more subtle facial expressions and gestures are all but unadaptable. The costumes fully belong to the past, while the actors are still half in the present."[45] Kracauer's position is the reverse of the usual complaints about the historical film, which frequently draw attention to the inevitable anachronisms in the costumes;[46] at the same time, his comments challenge a common assumption about the ahistorical nature of the body. The cultural and historical specificity of the body is indeed one of the great problems of the realist historical film, a fundamental anachronism that costumes, makeup, and dialogue can only partially disguise. Styles of movement, proxemic codes, and other forms of bodily regulation are expressive of a range of historical differences, from social decorum to the meaning of the body: as Kaja Silverman argues, the sense of the body is one of the foundations of our sense of self, and thus one of the fundamental means through which subjectivity is ideologically determined.[47] The portrayal of the body is thus crucial to any attempt at conveying historical difference. In his "prehistorical" films, Pasolini addresses the historically different body partially through estrangement, by making the past foreign and disorienting; in *Sebastiane,* rather than trying to overcome the difficulties of historical realism, Jarman exploits this fundamental problem through heightening the disjunction.

For example, the specific problem that Kracauer identifies as the inability of the actors to fit their costumes is particularly productive in the case of Barney James's portrayal of Severus, who always looks awkward in his Roman garb, and never more so than when he is staring at the naked Sebastian. The artificiality of the costume works to sug-

Soft-core beach romping in *Sebastiane* (1976). Adrian (Ken Hicks) and Anthony (Janusz Romanov).

gest the constraining artificiality of Roman heterosexual values, as opposed to the liberated, natural nudity of Sebastian and the lovers. This artificiality is played more pointedly by the other character associated with Rome, Max, who sports a fake leather nose and occasionally a false penis. A similar disjuncture is at work in the early scene where Sebastian and Justin refuse to practice their sword fighting: the soldiers are practicing with wooden swords and shields, and this in combination with the awkwardness of the actors makes the whole scenario look like a game of dress-up. Their refusal to participate is a refusal to play along with a pointless charade. Given the film's critique of Roman masculinist values, this is very much to the point.

More crucial is the representation of Sebastian's body, which is, after all, at the center of the story. Jean-Louis Comolli has written of another dissonance that can result in historical films between the body of the actor and the historical figure portrayed, if the image of that figure is well known.[48] No representation of the historical Sebastian exists, but there is a rich history of iconography from the renaissance onward that stresses his youthful beauty.[49] Jarman's choice of Leonardo

Treviglio as Sebastian was greeted with some dismay by the film's producer: "James [Whaley] is completely thrown. He has an image of Sebastian which is out of *GQ*—sexy and muscle-bound."[50] Treviglio sports a patchy beard and, while not unattractive, he is by no means the most conventionally beautiful male on offer in the film. The dissonance between the expected *GQ* beauty and the slight and scruffy Treviglio is productive; it opens up a space between the received icon and Jarman's version, a space that allows Jarman to make the myth signify in substantially different ways. This is and isn't Saint Sebastian: this Sebastian is martyred not for renouncing homosexuality for Christianity, but rather for his embrace of a homosexual spirituality nominally identified as Christian.

This remaking of the meaning of Sebastian's martyrdom is at least partially accomplished by Jarman's focus on the masochistic dimensions of the Saint Sebastian legend. In a brief but stimulating reading of the film, Earl Jackson Jr. focuses on what he calls the "sadomasochistic logic" of the film, whereby the masochistic spectacle of Sebastian's torture positions the spectator as sadist.[51] Maria Wyke, however, notes

Playing with the iconic image in *Sebastiane*. Sebastian (Leonardo Treviglio).

that, quite unusually, the final shot is from the martyred saint's per-spective, looking out on his executioners, which aligns the spectator with the site of masochism.[52] Saint Sebastian has for some time been under-stood as a key representation of masochism, and focusing on this may allow us to see why a figure who was martyred for refusing homosexual advances has paradoxically become a homoerotic icon. I want to turn briefly to the theorization of masochism developed by Gilles Deleuze through his analysis of the novels of Leopold von Sacher-Masoch. Deleuze's reading is useful for explicating Jarman's film because it clari-fies the political logic of masochism, clarifying what, on the level of subjectivity, the masochistic fantasy is attempting to achieve or to bring into being. This focus will at the same time allow us to steer away from a biographical approach; whether or not Jarman was personally invested in masochism is largely immaterial to a reading of the film.

Deleuze starts by disengaging the logics of sadism and masochism. They are not reversible, he argues, nor are they complementary. A sadist would not want a masochist for his victim (the victim is not meant to experience pleasure), and a masochist would not want a sadist as his torturer. The masochist, writes Deleuze, enters into a con-tract with the woman, with the purpose of educating her so that she may assume the role of torturer. Whereas the Freudian account sug-gests that masochism results from a primary aggression being turned inward onto the ego by the superego, Deleuze argues instead that the ego of the masochist is strong and insolent: "If the masochist is lack-ing in anything, it would be a superego and not an ego at all. In pro-jecting the superego on to the beating woman, the masochist appears to externalize it merely in order to emphasize its derisory nature and make it serve the ends of the triumphant ego."[53] Deleuze thus rejects the idea that the father stands behind the figure of the cruel woman in the masochistic scenario. On the contrary, what is being beaten in the masochistic fantasy is in fact the father himself: "what is beaten, humil-iated and ridiculed in him is the image and the likeness of the father, and the possibility of the father's aggressive return. . . . The masochist thus liberates himself in preparation for a rebirth in which the father will have no part."[54] What the masochist is working toward is a rebirth accomplished through the contract with the torturer, a parthenogene-sis that does not involve the father. The masochist "abjures the father's likeness and the sexuality which it confers, and at the same time challenges the father-image as the repressive authority which regulates this sexuality and which is constitutive of the superego."[55] Viewing the investment in masochism this way helps to explain the "deliberate absence of the paternal figure" that Chrissie Iles notes characterizes much of Jarman's work.[56]

This revisionist reading of masochism clarifies certain dimensions of the radical political project of *Sebastiane,* in particular its differentiation between two versions of homosexuality on the basis of a rejection of patriarchal masculinity. This in turn involves an opposition to, and in a sense a denial of, the world of Rome. The masochist, writes Deleuze, "does not believe in negating or destroying the world nor in idealizing it: what he does is to disavow and thus to suspend it, in order to secure an ideal which is itself suspended in phantasy. He questions the value of existing reality in order to create a pure ideal reality."[57] The masochistic fantasy thus operates according to what I have been calling a heterotopic logic: for Jarman, the past is a space within the present that can be made to embody oppositional values. The heterotopia is complemented by the heterochronic dimension of the encampment, and indeed of the film; these correspond with the centrality of waiting and suspense that Deleuze argues characterizes the masochistic scenario, elements that John Paul Ricco says also define a particular version of queer space.[58] Sebastian coaches Severus into becoming his torturer in order to achieve the final ecstatic consummation with the Apollonian sun god, which will enable, in the realm of fantasy, his rebirth outside of the patriarchal regime of the father. According to this logic, there is no necessity of seeing Sebastian as rejecting Severus on the grounds of homosexuality, any more than we should see the heroes of Sacher-Masoch rejecting heterosexuality as such. What is being rejected in the film is a homosexuality that partakes of the father, or that reproduces in it the father's law.

The film's insistence on the spiritual component of homosexuality is reminiscent of the romantic idealism of gay liberation discourse, which saw homosexuality as a potentially revolutionary force, and one which, moreover, it similarly juxtaposed against a version of masculinity that could appear in both heterosexual and homosexual guises. Homosexuality, it was argued, could be a radical force in society by demonstrating an equality in sexual relations that was not possible for heterosexuals. This was possible, however, only if gay men were sufficiently vigilant about the residue of their heterosexual conditioning, and avoided reproducing in themselves either masculine or feminine stereotypes.[59] Pasolini was criticized from a gay liberationist perspective precisely on these grounds, for reproducing heterosexual power structures in the homosexual relations he depicts, and for the unreconstructed nature of the gaze in his films, even when looking at male bodies, "which reinforces the image of male-sexuality-as-activity just as relentlessly as the standard images of women enforce the concept of female-sexuality-as-passivity. That is to say, it reiterates heterosexual norms."[60] *Sebastiane* does seem to be taking seriously the liberationist project, at least insofar as it seems to be differentiating between two versions of homosexuality, one a simple reproduction of heterosexual structures and one liberated from them, through an ecstatic communion with the supernatural.

Jarman was criticized by some gay critics for producing pornography (even as the revolutionary force of pornography was beginning to be promoted in certain quarters). Thomas Waugh wrote in a review at the time that "the only thing that distinguishes *Sebastiane* from the realm of soft core is the honesty of the latter" (although he subsequently retracted this view),[61] which echoed the indignant complaints on the set that Jarman was making a pornographic film.[62] Jarman, however, insisted over the span of his career on the revolutionary potential of showing the nude male body, especially when engaged in homosexual sex, on the screen. In an interview around the time of the film's release he makes this argument: "The whole point about the film is that homosexuality is taken for granted, it is as natural as possible. The films that have dealt with homosexuality have either explained it away, ridiculed it or treated it in an abstract way. I hope *Sebastiane* is a real homosexual film."[63] Jarman clearly echoes both the GLF's "Gay is good" ethos and, more specifically, the efforts of its Counter-Psychiatry movement. Equally important, Jarman's comments push us to take seriously the intent of the sexual representations, and not to succumb too quickly to a cynical reading of the film that sees the soft-core elements as simply exploitation. The film does, after all, bring up the issue of pornography itself, in a scene where the soldiers ogle a drawing of a Roman whore and talk about various pornographic spectacles at Rome. However effective one deems this critique to be, the film does differentiate between kinds of sexualized looking, just as it differentiates between versions of homosexuality.

There is a further thing to note about Jarman's wish to make a "real homosexual film." He argued later that what was radical about the film was that "*Sebastiane* didn't present homosexuality as a problem and this was what made it different from all the British films that preceded it. It was also homoerotic. The film was historically important; no feature film had ventured here. There had been underground films, *Un Chant d'Amour* and *Fireworks,* but *Sebastiane* was in a public space."[64] The film had a long and successful run at The Gate Cinema in Notting Hill and Jarman is justified in pointing out the political importance of taking what was hitherto suitable only to an art house or a porn theater and moving it to a commercial venue: "The love scene was ecstatic. A generation went to see these nine minutes of a regular guy in a regular cinema."[65]

But I want to suggest that the film offers a further challenge to dominant notions of spatial propriety. This brings us back both to Jarman's use of the space of the past, and also to the spectatorial relations of the super-8 films. The super-8s, following in the tradition of the home movie, were explicitly performative, in J. L. Austin's terms, in the sense that they bring into being the "home" and the family that they picture. These films cannot sensibly be disconnected from a very particular spectatorial regime, and they work to establish as communities the communities pictured on the screen, the communities that were the films' principal audience. The super-8s thus challenge ideas about the spatial and temporal dimensions of the work of art, which is perhaps why they are occasionally dismissed as irredeemably private. I would argue that Jarman conceives of his feature films in a similarly performative manner: that the work of art is not in fact the finished seventy- or eighty-minute 35mm print, but rather that the work of art begins with the filming, and never really ends as long as the film is being screened. The print has to be seen both as the residue of a process and as the medium for the film's future work. This is the function of the opening framing sequence, which I have argued works to create a relay between audience and the main body of the film. For Jarman, the principal *work* of the work of art is the formation of community, which accounts for both the way in which he organizes the actual filming and what some critics have seen as the raw or unfinished nature of his films. It is the process that is the work of art, not the print.[66]

Sebastiane offers a fusion of homoerotic pleasure and an alternative history that is developed in opposition to Roman values, which are at the same time London values. The call by the gay liberation movement to reimagine gay sexuality and subjectivity is answered to some degree on the screen, through its offering of nonpathological representations of homosexual desire, and, equally importantly, new psychic terrains and structures of desire. The film offers a critique of contemporary heterosexual culture that is counterbalanced by the positing of a new homoerotic mythology, one that claims a homoerotic icon for a homosexual historical tradition. Once restored to its historical context, and, of course, with the benefit of hindsight, the truly radical nature of *Sebastiane* becomes clearer. It is important not just for its revisionist take on the Sebastian legend, or for its participation in the creation of an alternative film history, following in the path of Pasolini, that "most homosexual of filmmakers" according to Jarman.[67] It is also important for the way it reimagines homosexuality, within the context of a larger challenge to the dominant notions of cinematic space, and the spatial and temporal dimensions of the work of art. If it has never been judged as terribly successful (even by Jarman himself),[68] this is perhaps because the usual criteria are not in fact applicable to this film. However successful one deems it, the film clearly sets the direction for what would follow.

THREE

The Elizabethan Future

IF *SEBASTIANE* IS JARMAN'S VERSION of Pasolini's *Gospel According to St. Matthew,* then Jarman's next film, *Jubilee,* is perhaps his *Salo.* Pasolini's last feature, *Salo, or the 120 Days of Sodom* (1975), premiered at the Locarno festival alongside *Sebastiane.* In his final film Pasolini turned away from the sunny portrayal of sexuality in his Trilogy of Life to a violent, pessimistic view of human behavior, setting de Sade's infamous novel in Fascist Italy. *Jubilee,* similarly, is an angrier, darker, more violent film than its predecessor; in it, Jarman picks up the anarchic politics of punk to offer a critique of the corrosive effect of materialism on English culture. Jarman was disappointed that the political critique offered by the film was overlooked in the largely negative reviews,[1] although he did have the later satisfaction of declaring the film's commentary prophetic: "Dr. Dee's vision came true—the streets burned in Brixton and Toxteth, Adam [Ant] was Top of the Pops and signed up with Margaret Thatcher to sing at the Falklands Ball. They all sign up one way or another."[2]

Some of the mixed and negative reaction to the film, and the general failure to understand the political point Jarman was trying to make, are probably attributable to two central ambiguities in the film: the film's relation to the punk movement, and the particular use it makes of the Elizabethan past. Neither of these, I will argue, is as straightforward as is sometimes assumed. First of all, the film is neither an homage to nor a dismissal of punk. Although Jarman was certainly attracted to both the energy and the anarchic style of punk, he was ultimately suspicious of its political claims, which were, in any case, fairly murky. (*Sebastiane,* we might remember, is marked by a correspondingly ambivalent treatment of homosexuality, which caused some confusion among the critics.) Similarly, although there is a neoromantic element of Jarman's interest in the English Renaissance, the film's ironic title should indicate that he is taking a different approach to the period than the one summoned up in the Jubilee year celebrations. What has generally gone unnoticed is the traffic between the two periods in the film, and especially the way in which the Elizabethan past is made to embody positive aspects of the punk movement in order to critique the present nation. Jarman posits in the film a continuity between the punk movement, the Romantic tradition as embodied by William Blake, and marginal cultures of the English Renaissance.[3] In *The Tempest,* whose production is intertwined with *Jubilee,* Jarman goes one better and makes a punk heritage film with an essentially optimistic ending. By locating a version of punk in the English past, Jarman creates a genealogy of resistance for the present moment.

Jubilee and the Punk Nation

In an interview around the time of the film's release, Jarman says that *"Jubilee* is a cabaret, it's Dada, it's a docustated fanzine . . . it's a protest."[4] As Jarman's comments indicate, *Jubilee* is not just a film about punks, but rather one that adopts a punk aesthetic, an aesthetic that, it was noted even at the time, was at least as much associated with the art schools as it was with class struggle.[5] A very loose, largely unprogressive narrative exists more or less as a frame for a series of related vignettes. This collage structure is mirrored in the recording media used. In addition to 16mm, the film incorporates 8mm footage, both speeded up and slowed down, and it occasionally films images from off of a television screen. The central conceit of mixing the Elizabethan past with an apocalyptic near future is an early example of the postmodernist interest in combining and juxtaposing period styles (one of the first shots in the present is of graffiti reading "post modern"), but it is also part of the punk collage aesthetic. Within the British context, the film can also be seen to follow in the tradition of Lindsay Anderson's exuberant, antirealist satires of England in *If. . .* (1968) and *O Lucky Man!* (1973), as well as some of the darker, more absurdist strains in such Pressburger and Powell films as *A Canterbury Tale* (1944) and *The Life and Death of Colonel Blimp* (1943).

The spirited amateurism of punk, its celebration of an improvisational, anticommercial aesthetic, was obviously appealing to Jarman, and, as Michael O'Pray argues, it was formative in his filmmaking career.[6] Certainly, he never lost his delight in shock, often through images of apparently gratuitous violence or sexuality, or in cabaret-style musical numbers that pop up in later films such as *War Requiem* and *The Garden*. A connection can also be made between Jarman's interests in punk and in Eisenstein, to be seen particularly in the aggressive, rapid-fire editing of sequences of *The Last of England*, which assault the audience. Some of the problems with *Jubilee*'s reception may well have been because of the degree to which it embodied the anarchic, unpredictable, and hence uncomfortable nature of punk performance rather than the reassuring certainties of narrative cinema. As Julian Upton observes, "there is an outrageous, permissive abandon that serves to upset and unnerve the conventional cinemagoer."[7] This, of course, would be a hallmark of many of the films to follow.

It would appear that Jarman's principal interest in punk is as an art movement, and the exploration of various aspects of the punk aesthetic in filmic form. Simon Frith and Howard Horne usefully distinguish between the "punk-as-art movement" and the "punk-as-pub-rock movement," while noting how closely intertwined they were.[8] Certainly, Jarman had more connections to and affinity with the punk-as-art movement, including figures such as Genesis P-Orridge (with whom he would collaborate) and artists such as Gilbert and George. The film does make a surprising number of comments on art and its relation to the everyday. At one point, the punk musician Kid (Adam Ant) sits on the steps of the Albert Memorial and looks at the images of classical composers such as Beethoven, Mozart, and Bach, inviting a comparison between musical forms and their relevance to society. The character Viv is a painter, although she says that painting as a form is dead. Appropriately, she says she started her artistic career by tracing dinosaurs as a child. Amyl Nitrate announces early in the film that art is for those who lack imagination, and that the real artists are those who can make their fantasies reality, quoting *The Rocky Horror Show* on this point ("don't dream it, be it"). As an example of such an artist, she cites the serial child murderer Myra Hindley (a portrait of whom would later cause much consternation in Saatchi's *Sensation* show at the Royal Academy). In a similar punk gesture, Hitler shows up at the end of the film claiming to be one of the greatest painters ever.

Viv says that while artists offer the world their lifeblood, art has been sequestered away by the rich and the powerful. Now, she argues, "our only hope is to re-create ourselves as artists or anarchists and release the energy for all." As the character that comes closest to representing Jarman's view, Viv voices the most productive understanding of the potential of punk and thus clarifies the film's interest in it. Traditional art forms have become marginal or irrelevant, and what punk can offer is an embodied form of art. It recognizes that the work of art may be carried on outside of the traditional institutions of culture, and outside of commerce. More than being simply a style of dress or of music, punk offers a radical challenge to thinking about art's relation to the world, and the work it can perform.

Here is perhaps where we can intuit a connection between *Sebastiane* and *Jubilee*. In spite of the vast differences in tone, setting, and period, there are nonetheless parallels between Jarman's first two films. In retrospect, one can identify in *Sebastiane*'s postmodernist opening sequence, the combination of sex and violence in the film, and the overall desire to shock a clear precursor to the spirit of punk. There is also a political parallel. At the center of the gay liberation movement was a call to radical transformation: of the self, of society, of ways of being together. This was expressed in alternative ways of dressing, ways of living, and a confrontational approach to polite society. *Jubilee* takes certain aspects of this radical program and explores it within a radical aesthetic. We can thus see this film as the first of many attempts to explore the potential of an art movement or form for expressing or encouraging alternative ways of being or thinking. Of the films that would shortly follow, *Imagining October* and *Caravaggio* are the most obvious continuations of this exploration with their central interest in painting, but virtually all of Jarman's films are marked by it in some way.

Another parallel between the films, and one that might be less obvious from the perspective of the present, is in the two films' sexual politics. *Sebastiane* takes up the arguments of the gay liberation movement, and in particular its critique of gender norms. *Jubilee* continues this critique in a near-contemporary setting. Although it is difficult to make definitive statements about the punk movement (and in particular about its politics), punk was arguably the first popular music trend to allow for anything approaching an equality of participation to women and gays. Central to punk's assault on propriety was an assault on gender stereotypes, and at the forefront of this were prominent female punks, artists, and style-makers like Jordan, Siouxsie Sioux, Sue Catwoman, Poly Styrene, Helen Wallington-Lloyd, Linder, and Vivienne Westwood. Whereas the hippie movement of the 1960s had a presumptive heterosexuality, punk "was curiously asexual . . . punk choices to be asexual, gay, androgynous or celibate were usually accepted without comment."[9] Thus the character Mad pronounces in the film that "love snuffed it with the hippies" and that "sex is for geriatrics." Punk allowed female musicians to experiment with a whole new range of possible identities, whether aggressive, sexual, asexual, or violent.

Punk is most often remembered as a movement consisting of angry white working-class youths, but Jon Savage notes that it didn't start that way: "Throughout 1975 and 1976, a large, amorphous group of teenage stylists of all ages, sexes and sexual persuasions had gathered around the Sex Pistols and Sex, and around the other groups and shops on the King's Road strip as well. This was a milieu of some complexity, reduced within the twenty seconds of the Grundy interview to white, male Rock."[10] A lengthy article in the February 1978 issue of *Gay News* titled "Punk: Wot's in It for Us?" details the quite surprising number of gay musicians and bands in the punk movement, as well as the fact that punk had roots within the gay community (the lesbian bar Louise's, for example, was an early punk hangout).[11] The most successful of the out gay punks, the Tom Robinson Band, had as its anthem "Glad to Be Gay"; Andy Medhurst notes that while "few songs sound less 'punk' than 'Glad to be Gay' . . . such a song would never have been so widely known without the cultural climate punk had made possible."[12] The song is one of the clearest links between punk and the earlier gay liberation movement, and Robinson would be one of the key links between these and the antiracist groups such as Rock Against Racism that emerged to protest the association of punk with the neofascist National Front. The phenomenon of the gay punk would continue past 1977, emerging in such contexts as the New Romantics and activist groups like Homocore, and would be highly evident in the visual style of queer and AIDS activism.

More immediately for Jarman, punk had early connections with the group that appeared in the opening sequence of *Sebastiane*, the group that Jarman would later dub the Andrew Logan All-Stars, and which included Jordan, one of the stars of *Jubilee*. Jarman, in fact, shot some of the earliest footage of the Sex Pistols at Jordan's urging, when the Pistols played at a party in Andrew Logan's studio on Valentine's Day, 1976, using some of the scenery from *Sebastiane* as a backdrop.[13] The glam world that gravitated around Logan was to some degree the last remnant of the sixties' avant-garde and the sexual revolution, and *Jubilee* offers evidence of the continuity and the connection between the earlier and later movements.

It is this polymorphously perverse version of punk that Jarman shows us in the film, offering up sexually aggressive and aggressively asexual female punks, incestuous gay brothers, transvestite singers, and more. *Jubilee* reverses the usual temporal structure of the period film, starting in the Elizabethan past and then moving forward to an apocalyptic present or near future.[14] In *Jubilee*, writes Jarman, "the past dreamed the future present."[15] The dual structure functions in a similar manner to the split between Rome and the encampment in *Sebastiane*, offering two different visions of community anchored in radically different spatial regimes. Here, however, the citation of the English Renaissance allows Jarman to make a more pointed critique of specifically English values. The Elizabethan era is a key site for English nationalist mythologies; certainly, in the year of Elizabeth II's Jubilee, 1977, the year the film was made, there was much made of the queen's glorious predecessor.[16]

The film starts in the gardens of the Mortlake estate of John Dee, the Elizabethan scholar and necromancer. Jarman worked on the scripts for *Jubilee* and *The Tempest* at the same time, and the use he makes of the Elizabethan past in the two films is similar, placing John Dee and his alchemical practices at the center of a countermythology of the period. This opening section probably has its origins in an earlier film script titled *The Art of Mirrors/A Summoning of Angels* dated November 1975.[17] That script featured a dialogue between Dee, Elizabeth, and the angel Ariel, "In which Dr. John Dee unfolds the mechanics of the universe with the aid of his scrying mirror and intervention of the angel Ariel." In *Jubilee*, Queen Elizabeth is visiting Mortlake, and she asks that

John Dee summon one of his angelic interlocutors to give her a vision of the future. The angel that appears is a combination of the historical Dee's Uriel and Prospero's Ariel from *The Tempest* (his first lines in the film are the first lines spoken by Ariel in Shakespeare's play).

The vision Dee's angel Ariel offers Elizabeth comprises the central dystopian section of the film. Elizabeth and her retinue wander through the apocalyptic landscape of the near future, wondering at the chaos they see and questioning its meaning. In contrast to the most usual dynamic in the heritage film, the past here is not a source of nostalgic consolation for lost empire, or a refuge from the problems of the present. Nostalgia, the film argues, is the result of the commodification of history and is the opposite of historical understanding. Here the past serves rather to highlight and question the incomprehensibility, strangeness, or savagery of the present nation. The past does not explain or justify the present, but offers instead a potential site of resistance.

In the England of the near future, law and order has been abolished, everything has been commodified, and a murderous gang of female punks roams the streets: Bod (short for Boadicea), Amyl Nitrate, Crabs, Mad Medusa, and their French au pair, Chaos. Associated with this group are two incestuous gay brothers, Angel and Sphinx, and their female lover, the artist Viv. This band of outsiders occupies a squalid space in what appears to be an abandoned warehouse with mattresses on the floor and graffiti on the walls. (There is clearly something of an echo to Jarman's own Bankside studio.) Outside are dystopic urban scapes, marked by grim high-rise apartment buildings, barbed-wire fences, burning rubble, and harshly lit cafés. The queen of the punks, Bod, is to some degree a demonic double of Elizabeth I; the two characters are played by the same actress (Jenny Runacre, who had earlier appeared in Pasolini's *The Canterbury Tales*), and early on in the film we see her chasing down a very suburban-looking Elizabeth II (played by the punk icon Jordan, who also plays Amyl Nitrate), killing her and stealing her crown. The largely episodic narrative contains a number of assaults and murders: the gang kills a transvestite pop star, suffocates one of Crabs's one-night stands, bombs a policeman's house, and castrates one of the policeman who gunned down their friends. By the end of the film, however, most of the punks have signed up with the entertainment mogul Borgia Ginz, and they retreat with him to a

country house in Dorset. The film ends back in the Elizabethan period, with Elizabeth and Dee walking the cliffs of Dancing Ledge.

Like the punk movement itself, the film is critical of the contemporary state of England, which is emblematized by the various dystopian
urban spaces it shows. Mark Sladen argues that "the notion of social
crisis, and in particular the embodiment of social crisis in the image of
the traumatized city... [is] extremely punk,"[18] which shows a continuity between Situationist and punk urbanisms. The terrain of *Jubilee* is
for the most part devoid of life and hostile to it; the sterility of the culture is summed up in a kitsch suburban garden made entirely of plastic
flowers. Time has become stalled and unprogressive, exemplified by the
older ladies in the squalid bingo parlor who carry on with their game
in spite of the destruction around them. This unprogressive time is
mirrored on one level in the film's largely unprogressive narrative, and
on another in the punk's boredom, a temporality different from the
suspended time of *Sebastiane*, which is characterized by anticipation.
Here, as the Sex Pistols observed and as Mad screams at one point, the
characters can see "no future," which is partially the consequence of a
failed relation to the past.

The allegorical use of space in the film is much the same as in *The
Last of England*, where ruined landscapes also signal a failed national
community. The Special Branch officers in the film are agents of a
corrupt state, practicing a form of state-sponsored terrorism that is
largely indistinguishable from the crimes of the punks, and in no way
productive of law and order. All of the major institutions of society
now seem to be in the service of capitalism, embodied in the film by
the impresario Borgia Ginz. In the face of such a perceived societal
breakdown, the punks' call for a radical reinvention of the self and the
world can be seen as a productive response. The anarchist space of
the punks' headquarters becomes a version of the artist's studio, a
possible site of Situationist analysis and invention. But as with *Sebastiane*, the film insists on registering the violence, whether real or psychic,
that is involved in such reimaginings.

A key aspect of punk is the centrality of the body within its aesthetic. In common with many of the counter- or subcultural movements
that immediately preceded and followed it, punk was characterized
by a strong emphasis on fashion and masquerade. The vision of the

punk historian Amyl Nitrate, for example, wearing spiked hair and geometric makeup along with a twin set and pearls, is a desecration of a central icon of matronliness, a desecration at least as radical as her later punk makeover of the personification of Britannia. But while the antisocial anti-aesthetic of punk clothing was offensive to society at large, what was more disturbing about punk culture was the way this extended to the alteration of the body itself, an alteration that involved symbolic or actual violence, from safety pins in ears to self-mutilation, punk's "earnest insistence upon the body as a canvas for self-expression-cum-visual-terrorism."[19] In the film, this ranges from the usual self-destructive flailing about characteristic of punk performance, to more focused alterations of the body, as when we see Mad using a knife to carve the word *love* into Bod's back (in real life, Adam Ant had *fuck* carved into his). This speaks, on one level, to punk culture's "wish to offer up the body as a jumble of meanings."[20] At other times, this body alteration acts as fairly direct social critique. In an early version of the script, the punks murder a policeman using makeup applicators and other devices used in the creation of mainstream femininity: lipsticks up the nose, a powder puff in the mouth, a silicone injection in the chest, and so on. In the film, a less gruesome version of this scene is played out when Bod attacks a waitress who has earlier been seen applying makeup; she pulls off the waitress's curly blond wig and squirts ketchup on her face, the ketchup signifying simultaneously as blood and lipstick. Both scenes work as a rough commentary on the symbolic violence inherent in the creation of a consumerist, mainstream femininity. Punk acts out a literally violent rejection of mainstream models of identity, as expressed through dominant ideals of bodily decorum.

The violent inscription on the body, punk's extension of masquerade to the level of the body itself, challenged the status of the body and gender as natural and ahistorical, going one step further than glam rock's blurring of gender boundaries. The punk body becomes the site of history, signification, and revolt. Dressing up is no longer just masquerade, as with earlier subcultures like the mods and the rockers, but signifies instead a dangerous psychic mutilation, or worse, mutation. According to Freud, the outlines of the body are the foundations of the bodily ego and hence the sense of the self. In punk culture, the

The punk fracturing of history in *Jubilee* (1978). Amyl Nitrate (Jordan).

outlines of the body are no longer stable. The violence and anarchy embraced by the punk movement were terrifying to the mainstream in part because they were ultimately directed at the dominant conception of selfhood. Punk threatened not the dissolution of society but, more radically, the dissolution of the self, and this, presumably, was at the heart of the terror it inspired. It was also, of course, its central appeal, particularly for those who felt that the suburbanization of England had deformed the English soul. For gay youths and unconventional women, punk was at least initially the triumph of the freakish outsider.

The punk critique of the commodification of England is put forward most directly in the film by Amyl Nitrate, described in the script as a "historian of the void." She is engaged in writing a new history of England titled *Teach Yourself History*:

> History still fascinates me—it's so intangible. You can weave facts any way you like. Good guys can swap places with bad guys. You might think Richard III of England was bad, but you'd be wrong. What separates Hitler from Napoleon or even Alexander? The size of the destruction? Or was he closer to us in time? Was Churchill a hero? Did he alter history for the better? Now my friend Mad on the sofa is a pyromaniac, but

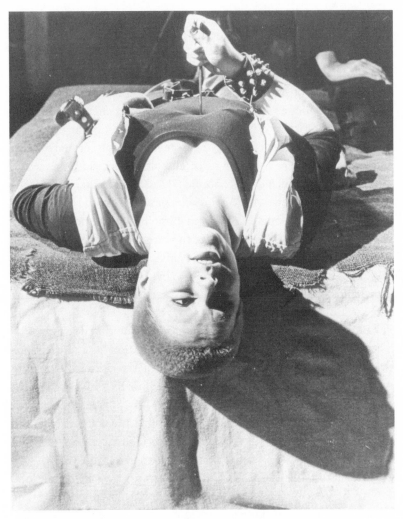

The punk body in *Jubilee*. Mad (Toyah Willcox). Production still.

she thinks she's a revolutionary out to better the world. I'm
not so sure.

Amyl extends the stalled time of the present to encompass all of history. This radical leveling of the past is reflective of the stance taken
by punk culture generally, rejecting any consensus on the past, particularly about the Second World War. The punk use of Nazi signifiers,
argues Jon Savage, had less to do with anti-Semitism than with a desire

to offend the majority; moreover, "There was one final point to the swastika that goes to the heart of punk polysemy: the erosion of meaning itself."[21] For Walter Benjamin, this was one of the negative aspects of the loss of the aura inherent in the mechanical reproduction of art: "if the destruction of the aura threatened the transmissibility of culture, Benjamin came to see the very ability to have coherent experience being eroded as well."[22] The film is less sanguine about the erosion of meaning and historical difference than Amyl, although certainly it does not disagree entirely with her revisionist history of England, which turns out to be principally economic ("It all began with William the Conqueror, who screwed the Anglo-Saxons into the ground, carving the land into theirs and ours"). Amyl's main point, which the film agrees with, is that once everything has been commodified, it becomes impossible to make distinctions based on any other scheme of values.

Amyl's view of history is exemplified by the career of Borgia Ginz. Ginz figures as the avatar of the capitalist recording industry that punk raged against. In spite of his contempt for them ("What are we going to call you? SCUM . . . That's commercial. It's all they deserve."), he quickly co-opts the punks and sells their revolution back to them, exemplifying the Frankfurt School's critique of the culture industry in general. Ginz's cynicism illustrates Fred Vermorel's observation that, "Far from being a dadaist assault on high culture, punk was a dadaist assault on popular culture. Thus the notion that 'anyone can do it' was also the idea that it's all crap anyway."[23] Ginz's radical commercialism is, however, ecumenical: he buys up Buckingham Palace and turns it into a recording studio. History, the film seems to argue, is easily commodified by the media industry, and sold back to us as harmless entertainment; this is part of *Jubilee*'s pointed critique of the heritage industry, to which we will return. Ginz explains:

> You wanna know my story, babe, it's easy. This is the generation who grew up and forgot to lead their lives. They were so busy watching my endless movie. It's power, babe, Power! . . . The media became their only reality and I owned their world of flickering shadows. BBC, TUC, ATV, ABC, ITV, CIA, CBA, NFT, MGM, KGB, C of E. You name it, I bought them all and rearranged the alphabet. Without me they don't exist.

Through Ginz's ruthless leveling strategy, all institutions become inter-changeable, stripped of all history, specificity, and difference.

Many of the punk characters in the film, Ginz's constituency, show the consequences of this policy. They are caught up in a world of facile politics, mindless entertainment, and boredom, a conjunction that re-sults in violence and murder. Law and order have been abolished, and the result seems to be, as Ginz indicates, that we have all become con-sumers rather than citizens. This, indeed, is another of the lessons in Amyl Nitrate's *Teach Yourself History*, from the chapter on human rights, in which she expatiates on the difference between political rights and material rights and on how we lost interest in the former:

> On human rights: human beings have no rights, but some
> dumb fuck told them that they had them. First, political rights.
> Freedom of speech and things like that. And if that wasn't
> enough they were told they had material rights too. They
> forgot about the political ones soon enough, but they got
> hooked on the material ones. One desolate suburban acre
> and a car. And then a TV, fridge, and another car. That was
> by right, mind you, and the habit demanded more and more.
> The day came when the expectations couldn't be fulfilled
> any longer, and everyone felt cheated. So here we are in the
> present, with civilisation destroyed by resentment, but since
> civilisation itself was always fucking awful for everyone, who
> gives a shit? We're better off without it.

The combination of analysis and nihilism is pure punk, reminiscent of the Situationist pronouncements of Vivienne Westwood and Malcolm McLaren, Jordan's real-life employers. Indeed, in the presentation of Amyl Nitrate as a verbose, schoolmarmy autodidact, it is hard not to see a satire of Westwood, who was originally a teacher.

Although the film identifies with punk's anarchic spirit, its gender critique, its gritty urbanist orientation, and its anticonsumerist ethos, it is by no means a straightforward celebration of punk. For one thing, Jarman was under no illusions about the political integrity of most members of the movement: "in reality the instigators of punk are the same old petit bourgeois art students, who a few months ago were David Bowie and Bryan Ferry look-alikes—who've read a little art history and adopted Dadaist typography and bad manners, and are now in the business of reproducing a fake street credibility. No one will admit that in a generation brought up on the consensus values of TV there is no longer such a thing as working-class 'culture.'"[24] An early version of the script makes clear that at least two of the central punks, Mad and Bod, are daughters of the gentry; the country house they retire to at the end of the film belongs to Mad's mother Bunny, who is married to Hitler.

Thus, if the punks in the film are reacting against the sterile, consumerist culture of England, it is also clear that they are a product of it. The happy-go-lucky Crabs works as something of a talent scout for Borgia Ginz, and Amyl cannot wait to get a recording contract with him. Her song, a punk version of "Rule, Brittania!" very obviously echoes the Sex Pistols' commercially successful, Jubilee-year single *God Save the Queen*. Peddling anticonsumerism can be lucrative, the film recognizes, and politics easily slide into style. Crabs admires a policeman's blood-soaked shirt, commenting that it must have cost a fortune; the shirt she is wearing she says she nicked from Seditionaries, one of the punk fashion boutiques run by McLaren and Westwood. The punks are not always, in other words, a politically radical alternative to the life-destroying consumerism of contemporary English life, a point made clear by the escape to the Little England of Dorset.

At the end of the film, Bod, Amyl, and Mad pile into Ginz's Rolls-Royce and they all drive off for a weekend in the country. Ginz has bought the entire county of Dorset as his retreat. Just as in the period film, the past is a foreign country, in this case with an elaborate border crossing. The border guard announces that "Blacks, homosexuals and Jews are banned in Dorset." Amyl remarks, "My God, the English customs are deplorable. It used to be just the colour of your skin." They then arrive at Ginz's country house, where they have tea with an aging Hitler and watch footage of a Nazi rally on TV. The country house, it should be noted, is virtually emblematic of the heritage film and the heritage industry. It is, as Jarman writes, "the indispensable prop for the English way of life. The soap operas of our lives demand them— anyway, they're big at the box office. Any film or TV series that has one is half-way to success."[25] In Jarman's film, we get what is one of the most familiar shots of the heritage genre, a traveling shot that approaches the country house and offers it as visual spectacle to the viewer. Crabs, voicing the typical reaction of the spectator, squeals, "It's wonderful, Borgia. Is it all yours?" The retreat to the country house, free of blacks, Jews, and homosexuals, is an obvious rebuke to the heritage film's construction of the nation; the incongruous spectacle of the punks in the drawing room highlights the heritage film's retreat to a fantasy of the past. In the printed version of the script, Jarman labels the sequence "Nostalgia." The country house is just a grander version of the bingo parlor: nostalgia is a stalled or unproductive version of the past that is clotting the present, corresponding to the stalled time of punk.

The problem, as stated earlier, is that once history has been leveled, life becomes unusually susceptible to commodification. While punk's questioning of history can work well to challenge the dominant nationalist mythologies and to unsettle versions of the nations based on such mythologies, it cannot offer any kind of alternative. Here is where *Jubilee* picks up on punk's unorthodox appropriation of history and makes it productive. The film is careful to distinguish between two different kinds of history. One is the fake, heritage-film past, ultimately symbolized by the country house in Dorset, where the worst elements of the present find refuge and justification. This version of history is seen throughout the film in various forms, such as Amyl's Winston Churchill mug (which gets smashed) or the punk makeovers of the nationalist anthems "Rule, Brittania!" and "Jerusalem." In this version, history is in the service of nationalism, and is reduced to a consumer good.

The other version of history is used to challenge rather than to support the present, and may in fact have a therapeutic dimension. The Elizabethan past in *Jubilee* is characterized as a space of life, diversity, and desire. Elizabeth is not portrayed here as the triumphant Gloriana, and the alchemist John Dee has never featured in any pageant of Elizabethan worthies. If the country house is, in the British film industry, the most common signifier of heritage, it is significant that the Elizabethan portions of the film do not feature the familiar establishing shot of a heritage property. The interiors, similarly, are shot with murky lighting, so that we are never invited to look at the past as a glittering diorama of heritage objects. Instead, we are led into the past, and into the film itself, through a garden maze, and most of the Elizabethan scenes take place outdoors in garden spaces.

Gardens are, for Jarman, the space of life, diversity, and desire, hetero-topias that operate in opposition to the mainstream. In the dystopian section of the film, the only garden we see is that of Max, the bingo caller and mercenary, who has replaced all of his plants with plastic ones. "My idea of a perfect garden is a remembrance poppy field," he says. The cyclical, productive time of a living garden opposes the stalled or dead time of the remembrance field. The angel Ariel, who shows Elizabeth the future, says in a later sequence in an Elizabethan garden: "Consider the world's diversity and worship it, by denying its multi-plicity you deny your own true nature. Equality prevails not for the gods, but for man. Men are weak and cannot endure their manifold nature." Equality, suggests Ariel, is the opposite of uniformity or same-ness, a life-destroying impulse that is most obviously represented by the capitalist Borgia Ginz.

In the present, the characters of Angel, Sphinx, and Viv are connected with this alternative heritage. At one point, we see them plucking a rose from a hedge, one of the rare manifestations of the natural world in the punk section of the film. This group, as Viv's name might indi-cate, is associated with life rather than death; the names of the broth-ers, Angel and Sphinx, echo familiar preoccupations of Jarman. In an early interview, Jarman said: "Viv is based on myself: rather sad, slightly ridiculous . . . a slightly failed artist, who has dreams but ends up in a black room because that's the truest thing she could do."[26] Viv's stu-dio, an empty black space, is something of a precursor to the produc-tive void of *Blue;* here it is not used for the production of conventional art but for an embodied practice. Although the particular conjunction of art and desire that they represent may be in this instance ineffec-tual, they do nonetheless represent an alternative within the punk world to the group that ends up in the country house at the end of the film, one that encodes a different version of the nation, a different tem-porality, and a different kind of political subject.

The final sequence of the film features Elizabeth and Dee walking along the coast at Dancing Ledge, reminiscing about their youth: "Oh John Dee, do you remember those days? The whispered secrets at Ox-ford like the sweet sea breezes the codes and counter-codes, the secret language of flowers." Dee's "secret language of flowers" can be connected to the garland of flowers swung between the two cell windows in Genet's *Un Chant d'Amour,* which will be discussed in a later chapter. Jarman explains that "Part of my interest in the magician John Dee was his pre-occupation with secrets and ciphers. Why this obsession with the language of closed structures, the ritual of the closet and the sanctuary? the prison cells of Genet's *Un Chant d'Amour,* the desert encampment of *Sebastiane;* Anger, insulating himself with magick, screening himself off."[27] Jarman's comments here bring us back to the Foucauldian heterotopia; the closet is, in a sense, a psychological or behavioral heterotopia, a very limited kind of sanctuary.

Cinema, for the gay filmmaker, becomes, like Dee's secret languages, a space of alternative knowledge, potentially either the closet or the sanctuary or both. In a 1985 interview Jarman remarked: "I think of the area of magic as a metaphor for the homosexual situation. You know, magic which is banned and dangerous, difficult and mysterious. I can see that use of magic in the Cocteau films, in Kenneth Anger and very much in Eisenstein. Maybe it is an uncomfortable, banned area which is disruptive and maybe it is a metaphor for the gay situation."[28] What Jarman's comments make clear is the connection in the film between the truly radical aspects of the punk aesthetic and marginal or disreputable practices of the past. Punk's colonization of the abandoned spaces of the city is mirrored in Jarman's embrace of the dead ends of history. Both of these become connected to a gay tradition of filmmaking. Anger's films, we might note, had been influential within the punk movement,[29] and Anger's *Scorpio Rising* was part of the program with *Sebastiane* when it played at the Scene 2. The actors in the Elizabethan section, moreover, solidify these punk connections: John Dee is played by Richard O'Brien, who had written and acted in *The Rocky Horror Show* (and later *The Rocky Horror Picture Show*); David Haughton, a dancer in the Lindsay Kemp Company, played the angel Ariel; and Elizabeth's lady-in-waiting was played by Helen Wallington-Lloyd, Malcolm McLaren's sometime lover and collaborator. Elizabeth, as I have said, is played by the same actress who plays the queen of the punks. In an early version of the script, Ariel is described as "a glistening punk rock messenger in a diamond crash helmet."[30] In the film, this costume changes, but he is nonetheless a figure of the future in his black body suit, black fingernails, and black contacts. The version of punk represented here is not the violent and aggressively hetero-sexual one that appeared in the media in the latter days of the move-ment (and in Vivienne Westwood's critique of the film),[31] but rather one that reflects more the sexually polymorphous subcultures and trends that fed into punk.

When we recognize that John Dee's magic is for Jarman a metaphor for an oppositional gay filmmaking tradition, we can see the political potential of the masquerade employed by the period sequences of the film. *Jubilee* relocates (or identifies) a version of punk values in the Elizabethan period as a way of contesting the dominant version of the period as reproduced and deployed in the present. Having the same actress play Elizabeth and Bod highlights the inevitable mas-querade involved in filmed history, and it connects with the destabiliz-ing potential found in the punk culture of body alteration. Having the punk version of Elizabeth hunt down her dowdy suburban successor acts as a dramatic refusal of the suggested equivalence between the two reigns. The film continues *Sebastiane*'s investigation of the relations between spaces, psychologies, and intersubjective possibilities, con-trasting the dystopic urban zones, the productive potential of the artist's studio (Viv's and to some degree the punks' lair), and the hetero-topia of the garden. *Jubilee* goes further, however, in its investigation of the very material ways in which history exists within the present, and its assertion that the creation of an alternative future depends upon making productive use of the past.

Punk Heritage in *The Tempest*

The Tempest, released in 1979, was to be Jarman's last feature film com-pleted for some time, and it can be seen as a continuation and culmi-nation of the thematic and formal concerns of the preceding films. All three features, for example, focus on a band of exiles or outsiders iso-lated from the mainstream, and all three feature some engagement with history. In fact, these two elements become increasingly linked, as the films more and more explicitly explore the usefulness of cine-matic representations of the past for the political ends of marginal communities. It is to *Jubilee*, however, that *The Tempest* is most closely related. Jarman worked on the scripts for the two films at the same time, completing the script for *The Tempest* before filming *Jubilee*, and a number of actors (Toyah Willcox, Helen Wallington-Lloyd, Jack Birkett, Karl Johnson, and Claire Davenport) appear in both films. But whereas the earlier film oscillates between the Renaissance and a postmodern punk apocalypse, *The Tempest* goes one step further by combining the two periods, offering a punk version of Shakespeare's play. The punk aesthetic can be seen in the film's key formal strategy, taking William S. Burroughs's cut-up technique to the play and extending it to both time and space in the film, and to history itself.

The more visible punk features of the film are the performers themselves. Toyah Willcox was by this point a well-known punk musician, so her casting as Miranda moved the film in a particular direction. This works rather differently than, for example, Marianne Faithfull playing Ophelia in Tony Richardson's 1969 film version of *Hamlet*. Faithfull's public image at that point harmonized well with the vulnerable and put-upon character of the play, while Willcox's loud and aggressive musical persona, however softened for the film, is nonetheless a real departure for the character of Miranda. The incongruity is to some degree heightened by the costumes, which do not allow Willcox to disappear into a period fantasy (of whatever era). Jarman wrote that the costumes "are a chronology of the 350 years of the play's existence, like the patina on an old bronze."[32] Willcox appears for the most part in a decaying ball gown, with beads and feathers woven into her hair; the costume clearly evokes the punk aesthetic of ripped and mismatched clothes, and in particular the mixing of various styles. But whereas in the punk aesthetic this mixing served "to offer up the body as a jumble of meanings,"[33] in the film it also works to signal a particular approach to the past. The historical range of costumes suggests that the film's real interest is not just in the play or its historical moment, but also in the history of the play's transmission and thus the play's historical and cultural significance, thereby making visible or manifest in a productive way the Benjaminian aura. As with *Sebastiane,* or with Pasolini's *Gospel According to St. Matthew,* the film is interested both in the cultural history of the story and in remythologizing it. What we get, then, is a palimpsestic or layered historical space that includes multiple temporalities, much like the opening scene of *Sebastiane.*

While the performers are the most obvious element of continuity with *Jubilee*, it is in the film's particular engagement with the English Renaissance that we can see the closest connection. In *Jubilee*, Jarman located a version of punk culture in Elizabethan England, particularly in the figure of hermetic scholar and alchemist John Dee. It is clear that Jarman follows the scholar Frances Yates in associating Prospero and Dee; in *The Tempest*, for example, Prospero has on his staff a reproduction of Dee's "hieroglyph monas," a symbol that encapsulated the wisdom of the universe. On the walls and floors of his study are what appear to be alchemical drawings and formulas, although some of them are actually images of cameras: "On the floor the artist Simon Reade drew out the magic circles that were blueprints of the pinhole cameras he constructed in his studio next to mine at Butler's Wharf."[34] Alchemy interested Jarman both as a system of thought that emphasized the diversity and interconnectedness of creation and as an example of a demonized practice that produced alternative knowledges. Hence the connection of the alchemists in Jarman's imagination with early-modern sexual minorities: "In the cities, people must have identified in underground groups; leading to rumours of covens, celebrating 'wild' sexual acts."[35] Alchemy, as the substitution of pinhole camera designs for alchemical circles in this film indicates, becomes for Jarman something of an analogy for his own cinematic art, as well as for queer filmmakers in general: "Film is the wedding of light and matter—an alchemical conjunction. My readings in the Renaissance magi—Dee, Bruno, Paracelsus, Fludd and Cornelius Agrippa—helped to conjure the film of *The Tempest*."[36]

In Jarman's early career, Dee thus figures in a similar fashion to the way that Aleister Crowley does for Kenneth Anger, as the center of an arcane, oppositional system of knowledge. This brings into question Tony Rayns's observation that "the alchemical equations and symbols that pepper [Jarman's] paintings and films co-exist rather awkwardly with the overtly gay elements, as if they were secretly intended to dignify what would otherwise be straightforward carnal representations."[37] John Collick is a bit more judicious in his assessment: "The rediscovery of ancient myths and belief systems like alchemy during the 1960s and 1970s was one of the many nostalgic attempts to create a homogeneous and liberating counter-culture in the face of an alienating mass cul-

Prospero (Heathcote Williams) and Ariel (Karl Johnson) in *The Tempest* (1979). Production still.

ture."[38] While this would account to some degree for both Jarman's and Anger's interest in arcana, the key difference is that because of the centrality of the Renaissance in English national mythologies, the choice of Dee is potentially more political. And while Anger's use of the near-contemporary figure of Crowley is unironic, Jarman's self-conscious engagement with the past rules out viewing his interest in alchemy as purely nostalgic.

The particular approach to the past is signaled in the opening sequence of the film. Prospero is asleep on his bed, evidently dreaming. Intercut with shots of him tossing and turning in his sleep is the dream itself, which consists of found footage of a ship in a storm, with the original black-and-white images tinted blue. The first lines of the play we hear, spoken by the sailors—"We split, we split!"—are now muttered by Prospero in his disturbed sleep. This opening sets up the frame of interpretation for what will follow; because the end of the film returns us to a sleeping Prospero, the whole film is readable as Prospero's dream. The terrain of the film is thus a psychological one, and one that, by virtue of the found footage, is identified as essentially cinematic, much like the terrain of the experimental super-8s. This is borne out by the particular geography of the film. Almost all of the action is set inside a decaying country house, which Prospero and Miranda are never seen to leave. Outdoor scenes are shot through a blue filter, which flattens the images and lends them an otherworldliness, while at the same time connecting them to the found footage of the storm. This is reminiscent of the use of both found footage and color filters in *Garden of Luxor,* which uses them to create a fantasy space that is purely cinematic.

Indoors, as Colin MacCabe observes, the house appears to be in a state of extreme disorder and disrepair. Jarman accentuates this by fracturing any sense of spatial coherence, in something of a reverse of Lev Kuleshov's filmic experiments with creative geography. MacCabe writes that "It is the fracturing of that representational space which makes *The Tempest* such a subversive film, for it sets itself not on an island but in a ruined aristocratic house, an imperial monument. If the viewer grasps that this is a house, there is no way in which he or she can organise the space that is presented."[39] As with the garden of Luxor, the viewer is aware that the space is only available on the screen; there is no correspondence to a real space that exists elsewhere. MacCabe's comments further highlight the political effect of relocating the action to an aristocratic house; the play is, after all, generally seen to be one of the first literary examinations of the English colonialist project. But as with the Dorset estate in *Jubilee,* there is also a more pointed filmic reference: the country house is emblematic of the heritage film, which has a nostalgic investment in the lost glories of the imperialist past, and one of the genre's chief sites is, of course, the Renaissance. The ruined house thus comments on the rot at the heart of the nationalist imagination and its investment in nostalgia, which in the film (and the play) is most centrally associated with Prospero. English nationalism, the film suggests, is a nightmare from which Prospero is trying to wake.

The film can thus be said to be interested not so much in history, but in how history works in the national imagination, the means through which it is reproduced (literature and film), and its favorite stories, all with an eye to disrupting the smooth reproduction of the present. This is combined with a punk-like interest in rummaging through the detritus of the past for things that might be salvaged for other purposes, such as alchemy, or the Renaissance masque. The masque form in particular is crucial to Jarman's project. In *Dancing Ledge,* he writes that the masque "seems to have been lost, not only in the English theatre (Lindsay Kemp is in exile) but also in everyday life—it's such a vital element and so distrusted by chapel and Eng. Lit. *The Tempest* is a masque; what it lacks, in the theatre productions I've seen, is a sense of fun."[40]

Like the Bankside parties or the Alternative Miss World pageants, the masque worked to transform the everyday through intense theatricality. However, as David Bevington and Peter Holbrook point out, "as 'the most inherently topical of all seventeenth-century art forms,' the masque was unavoidably and consciously political."[41] Although frequently dismissed as frivolous (as, indeed, was this film),[42] the masque was an art form that aimed directly at intervening in the production or reproduction of the community. As such, the masque was crucially involved in the establishment of cultural difference, and so many masques featured cultural others who were positioned as threats to order or as disorder itself: Africans, Gypsies, masterless men. Jarman's version of *The Tempest* takes up these crucial aspects of the masque in order to comment both on *The Tempest*'s cultural history and on the current state of England. His aim, as with the early-modern masque, is to create through spectacle the grounds for a new community. But he does this by turning the masque against its own original historical moment, a *détournement* that disrupts the smooth reproduction of certain narratives that have played a significant role in structuring the present nation.

A Renaissance masque was a combination of dance, spectacle, and a fairly minimal script. Usually designed to be performed only once, generally for a special court occasion, masques featured extravagant costumes, perspective sets, and expensive stage machinery used to work astonishing visual effects: rocks that opened to reveal castles, goddesses descending on clouds or swans. Characters were often a mix of allegorical, mythical, and historical figures, and the story was generally a Neoplatonic allegory involving a conflict between order and disorder that would be resolved in a dance that joined audience and actors. The masque generally began with the antimasque: figures of disorder, such as satyrs or witches or racial others, would perform a disordered dance, and then the figure of the sovereign or the god would descend to banish them and restore order. The most notorious anti-masquers appear in the two spectacles Ben Jonson staged for Queen Anne, *The Masque of Blacknesse* and *The Masque of Beauty,* although there were a number of masques in which Gypsies, Moors, Egyptians, Irishmen, and Indians embodied the principle of disorder.[43] Whether or not the figures of disorder were racial others, however, there is a sense in which the masque was always about the staging of the white European body, which embodied order through its control of desire. The range of figures who could embody disorder reminds us of John Gillies's argument regarding the generic nature of exotic others in the early-modern period; it should also alert us to the fact that were internal others, such as masterless men and the Irish, who could also fill that role. Indeed, as Stephen Orgel has remarked, in 1606 "the language of racism was being principally applied to the Irish, where it obviously had little to do with skin colour."[44]

Orgel argues that the masque as a genre "attempted from the beginning to break the barrier between spectators and actors, so that in effect the viewer became a part of the spectacle. The end toward which the masque moved was to destroy any sense of theatre and to include the whole court in the mimesis."[45] The masque encourages the audience to participate in the ideology of the masque both by offering it wonder-inducing spectacle and by including it in the spectacle itself, in the final dance that joined audience and actors. Thus the potentially disorderly bodies of the spectators are disciplined and assimilated by the ordered world of the dance. This physical inclusion was linked to a thematic one, as the end of the masque was usually about social order and social harmony, which depends, of course, on securing agreement to create an ideological community. Any possibility of dissent is banished along with the antimasquers.

In *The Tempest,* it could be argued that the opening storm is in some way the antimasque, introducing us to a chaos that will be tamed by Prospero (and that is in fact produced by him). The storm is answered at the end of the film by Elisabeth Welch singing "Stormy Weather," which tames the disorder and converts it into rich pleasure. The disorder is connected with sexual and racial disorder, because of the linkage between the tempest and the marriage of Claribel and the King of

Tunis, a marriage that no one in the play seems to approve of (least of all Claribel) and that almost destroys the ruling family of Naples. The storm and the racially mixed marriage are clearly paralleled as forces of disorder and destruction, and we can see echoes of this disordered marriage elsewhere in the play. It is fleetingly conjured up within the masque by Iris's banishment of Cupid and Venus, who helped "dusky Dis" abduct Ceres's daughter (4.1.89), and who were on their way to wreak havoc on the betrothed. Outside the masque, we have the attempted rape of Miranda by Caliban and his dream of peopling the island with Calibans, which functions as a disordered version of the eventual marriage. The masque thus echoes the connection between racial otherness and disordered sexuality that informed other court masques, and that is most monstrously summoned up in the union of Sycorax and the devil.

In the play, the masque starts with the goddesses Iris, Ceres, and Juno, who banish disorderly desire. They are joined by nymphs and reapers just before the masque breaks off, when Prospero suddenly remembers the plot by Caliban, Stephano, and Trinculo, who are among the major candidates for antimasquers in the play. One threat to Prospero's rule and property (premarital sex) thus gives way to another (class rebellion). These threats are at the same time clearly linked, at least in the mind of Prospero, and both are concerned with the ownership of Miranda. In *The Tempest*, the masque is staged as an allegorical justification of Prospero's insistence on premarital chastity, and it achieves its purpose primarily through inducing wonder in its audience. "This is a most majestic vision, / And harmoniously charming," says Ferdinand in response to the spectacle,

> Let me live here ever.
> So rare a wondered father and a wise
> Makes this place paradise. (4.1.118–19, 122–24)

The memories of Prospero's arbitrary punishments and violent temper melt away in the heat and light of the theatrical vision, and Prospero becomes in Ferdinand's eyes the ideal father and sovereign.

It is important to note that although *The Tempest* is in many ways masque-like, it is not a masque, and so the play is more ambiguous in its political valences than the masques generally were. Like Shakespeare,

Jarman seizes on the masque form and addresses it to a different audience, and, as in the play, the masque in the film spills out to encompass the work as a whole. Instead of staging the masque as it stands, Jarman has elements of it appear at various points throughout the film. At one point, for example, Ariel stands on a rocking chair and delivers to Miranda one of the goddesses' blessings from the masque:

> Honour, riches, marriage-blessing,
> Long continuance, and increasing,
> Hourly joys be still upon you!
> Juno sings her blessings on you. (4.1.106–9)

Later in the film, Miranda stands on the rocking chair and repeats these lines to herself, as a way, perhaps, of taking for herself the goddess's power. Most notably, however, Jarman moves the masque out of the fourth act and makes it the climax of the film, which changes both its significance and its function. Welch sings "Stormy Weather" in the final glorious scene after the sailors, having been fetched from their ship, dance a Busby Berkeley–style number for the assembled wedding guests. Casting a black, glamorous, aging cabaret singer as a classical goddess is a recognizably campy gesture, one that displays the potentially rich and subversive historical vision that camp employs.

Susan Bennett begins her discussion of productions of *The Tempest* by noting that "No Western text has played a more visible role in the representation and reconstruction of the colonial body than Shakespeare's *The Tempest*." She argues that in spite of the intense scrutiny the text has recently received, critics have been less than attentive to "the intervention of the performing body" in the performance text.[46] In the case of a historical text, this intervention can work in a number of ways: to resist the text, as Bennett points out, but also (perhaps unconsciously) to dehistoricize it. Recent studies of early-modern culture have emphasized that the body is a historically and culturally constructed artifact, but this awareness has not been fully extended to consider what happens when an actor embodies a historical text. This, as we noted in the discussion of *Sebastiane,* is a crucial problem for the period film. In both films, however, the temporal disjunction works to Jarman's advantage: in *The Tempest,* it helps to frustrate a sense of the historical body as completely familiar or knowable.

The role of the actor's body has been central to many discussions of Jarman's version of *The Tempest*, especially with regard to the body of the actor playing Caliban, Jack Birkett. Both he and Claire Davenport, who plays Sycorax, are white. Sympathetic critics of Jarman's film often note with some regret that it does not seem interested in the now-dominant reading of the play as one of the first literary treatments of colonialism, forgetting, perhaps, that the principal object of colonialism at the time was the Irish.[47] For example, Colin MacCabe observes that "From this point of view Jarman's *Tempest* is an embarrassment, for his Caliban is white and the concerns of colonialism are largely absent from his film."[48] Chantal Zabus and Kevin A. Dwyer write that Jarman's "cultural conservatism inevitably goes hand in hand with a professed lack of concern for the post-colonial potentialities of the play."[49] Kate Chedgzoy argues that

> Jarman explicitly eschewed the interest in colonialism which
> has loomed so large in reproductions of *The Tempest* in recent
> decades, telling one interviewer, 'it was very possible to make
> Caliban black, but I rejected it because I thought it would load
> the whole film in one way, make it more specific than general'.
> Jarman's phrasing here reproduces a racist paradigm which sets
> whiteness up as neutral and universal, blackness as a 'marked',
> deviant condition.[50]

Although Jarman's comments may well imply the racism that Chedgzoy reads there, I want to suggest that there are other, more productive, ways of reading Jarman's wish to avoid making the film "more specific than general." One obvious question that arises here is whether there might be reasons not to be too specific about Caliban's (or Sycorax's) race and whether a historical understanding of race might involve more than the specific matter of skin color. It may well be that "the concerns of colonialism" are not in fact absent from the film, in spite of Caliban's and Sycorax's apparent whiteness.

To turn the question around for a moment: would it necessarily have been better, as Jarman originally planned, to have had "a black, beautiful, sympathetic Caliban, wearing a mother-of-pearl necklace to symbolize the loveliness of the world he had shared with Sycorax"?[51] Present-day viewers and readers of *The Tempest* are predisposed to see

Caliban in sympathetic terms, and so familiar with the spectacle of his slavery that it generally fails to raise either questions or outrage. We are all too ready to read the character specifically in terms of contemporary notions of race, forgetting that the "various histories" of white racism "indicate interlinking situations of oppression rather than a trans-historical colour consciousness."[52] Indeed, as Lynda E. Boose argues, "race as contemporary Anglo-American culture understands it was quite probably just on the horizon by the end of the sixteenth century, just beginning to displace the notion of divine necessity as antecedent rationale for principles of difference. But it was also a moment when several systems of meaning were clearly still in competition."[53] John Gillies offers one example of this historical distance in his discussion of "the promiscuous or 'pandemic' quality of Othello's exoticism, the way in which his Africanness is constantly being telescoped into other notorious forms of exoticism: Turkish, Egyptian and Indian." The same is also clearly true for Caliban, who has links with Africa, the Caribbean, North America, and Ireland. Gillies explains that, "For Shakespeare and Marlowe there is no geographical incongruity. Turk and African, ancient 'Thracian' and Renaissance 'moor', all share a generic identity as 'erring barbarians'. . . . It is for this reason that the sharper, more elaborately differentiated and more hierarchical character of post-Elizabethan constructions of racial difference are inappropriate to the problems posed by the Elizabethan other."[54] A black Caliban is thus an invitation to unwitting anachronisms, and although these anachronisms may well prove productive, we might consider whether there are other ways of playing Caliban's alterity that could unveil in less expected ways the origins and dimensions of British racialist thinking and disrupt our own unconscious naturalization of the very concept of race.

Caliban is, after all, still referred to in the film as a "thing of darkness" and a "monster." As played by Jack Birkett he is a large, vulgar, sloppy Northerner, older than Prospero and dressed in what appears to be a tattered butler's outfit. He is also recognizably working-class, which adds a further dimension to the rebellion he stages with Stephano and Trinculo, who are the other serving-class characters in the play.[55] As Kim F. Hall and a host of others have argued, race has always been connected with economic issues, most obviously property. Property claims are, of course, at the center of this play, with Caliban arguing that "This island's mine, by Sycorax my mother / Which thou tak'st from me" (1.2.331–32).[56] Caliban has two solid legal claims: prior possession and inheritance. Prospero never manages to contradict either of these, countering instead that Caliban is the progeny of a witch and the devil. Caliban's race is the only argument Prospero can successfully mount against Caliban's claim to ownership of the island, or the only claim that he bothers to mount: it is clear that he holds the island through force. Here Prospero's body comes crucially into play. Because Jarman's version has a "strikingly young Prospero . . . the powers he exercises seem to have little to do with either patriarchal authority or avuncular benevolence,"[57] and so some of the usual rationalizations of Caliban's enslavement vanish. Caliban does not pose the threat to the settlers that was often used to justify a repressive colonial regime. Caliban's body also works against the usual reading at this moment. Portraying Caliban as an appetitive, physically excessive, working-class Northerner reminds us that "most tropes of blackness operate within a larger discursive network"[58] and that race has very little to do with the slight biological difference that naturalizes a whole array of cultural codings. Caliban, in other words, might still be functioning as a racial other in the film, in spite of the actor's color.

Hall notes that race, gender, and sexuality were already intertwined in the first works to deal with race in early-modern England.[59] Using the unruliness of women to suggest the unruliness of foreign lands was a familiar strategy in the period, one that at the same time demonstrates the necessity of imposing a patriarchal European order upon them. Johannes Leo Africanus's *Geographical Historie of Africa* is particularly interesting in this regard, which, as Hall observes, loses its composure whenever it contemplates the spectacle of female misrule in Africa. Female misrule in Leo Africanus's text figures much like sodomy in accounts of the New World. As Jonathan Goldberg notes, the "discovery" of sodomites in the New World gave colonial conquest a moral dimension, "righting a wrong against the hierarchies of gender."[60] The unruly women of Africa, like the sodomites at home and abroad, are a danger to the family, gender hierarchies, order, economy, and the nation.[61]

Whether or not he read Africanus, Shakespeare is certainly drawing upon the same discourse in which race and sexually unruly women are intertwined. Prospero, like Leo Africanus, can barely control his disgust and outrage when describing the African witch who was banished "For mischiefs manifold and sorceries terrible / To enter human hearing" (1.2.264–65). Sycorax's crimes, like those of the sodomite, are terrible to hear and not proper to speak. Prospero once again hints at the nature of Sycorax's monstrosity when recounting the story of Ariel's imprisonment, for being "a spirit too delicate / To act her earthy and abhorred commands" (1.2.271–72). Jarman picks up on these hints of Sycorax's sexual monstrosity and offers a rare on-screen representation of a character who otherwise seems only to exist in the realm of Prospero's overheated imagination. In this representation, the film makes clear the threat that Sycorax poses to Prospero's order, showing us a naked adult Caliban suckling at Sycorax's breast. A naked Ariel wears a collar attached to a chain, which Sycorax uses to haul the unwilling spirit closer. This portrayal of Sycorax with her nonnormative body and her bondage gear ahistorically evokes the rebellious femininity of the punk movement, while at the same time signaling the character's geographic origins. Rather than being marked by skin tone, Sycorax's racial otherness is signified by the European signs of oriental depravity, right down to the hookah she smokes. Sycorax is thus coded exotic and North African, but more importantly, as unruly, perverse, and grotesque, making her the perfect foil to the European woman's submissive white body. Thus, Chedgzoy's comment that "Jarman's depiction of Sycorax does nothing to query the misogyny and racism of Shakespeare's text in this respect"[62] misses the point. In fact, by making Sycorax white but North African, physically "disordered" and, moreover, sexually threatening, the film foregrounds the interconnections of racism and misogyny in colonialist discourse and the means by which this discourse constructed racial otherness, without at the same time reforging these links in the film's visual economy.

If we focus in this way on how the grotesque bodies and monstrous desires of Caliban and Sycorax are being deployed in the film, we can begin to see how the film may in fact be making a complicated point about the historical construction of race in early-modern colonialist discourse. This introduces an important qualification to MacCabe's reading of the film:

Ariel (Karl Johnson), Caliban (Jack Birkett), and Sycorax (Claire Davenport) in *The Tempest*.

> Jarman's *Tempest* concentrates on the relationship between
> Prospero and Ariel with its barely suppressed sexual under-
> tones. Jarman's homosexuality is what leads him to concen-
> trate on the repression at the heart of the English state from
> which all other repressions follow. The complete containment
> of sexuality within sanctified heterosexual marriage, the
> rigorous policing of desire and excess, the focusing of male
> sexuality and the denial of female sexuality. These are the
> fundamental themes of *The Tempest,* the sexual politics which
> underpin the birth of capitalism as it appropriates its colonial
> surplus.[63]

MacCabe's argument that the film is about the foundation of the nation is productive, but it needlessly downplays the film's interest in
race and gratuitously plays up the issue of Jarman's sexuality, or rather,
it too easily separates race, sexuality, and economics. The relationship
between Prospero and Ariel does not in fact seem to be particularly

sexualized in the film (in *Dancing Ledge,* Jarman notes that he explicitly rejected this approach as too predictable), although Ariel does seem to be coded gay at various points. MacCabe is, however, correct to insist that Jarman's work continually interrogates current definitions of the nation, by interrogating some of its foundational texts. This questioning is vital because, as Ania Loomba suggests, "contemporary colour prejudices are interlinked [with those of the past]; they draw upon and rework this earlier history."[64] The film's interruption of this historical process works in tandem with its fracturings of other narratives it sees as informing and structuring the present nation.

As with those of Sycorax and Caliban, the bodies of the other characters often work to disrupt familiar readings. Miranda is in general given far more agency in this film than in other versions, and her tiny rebellions against her father are given more prominence. As played by the punk Willcox, Miranda is an active, sexual subject rather than the passive, sexual object that the play, the masque, and her father typically render her. (By contrast, in Peter Greenaway's *Prospero's Books,* Miranda seems to spend much of the film asleep.) This shift in the presentation of the character is most apparent in Miranda's relation to her own body. Ferdinand's nakedness in the film renders him vulnerable, both to the gaze of the viewer and to the on-screen characters: most significantly Miranda, who is enchanted by the sight of this brave new world, but also Prospero, who views Ferdinand's nakedness as humiliation. It is Ferdinand's body, rather than Miranda's, that is offered to the viewer as erotic spectacle, as Ferdinand stumbles naked from the waves like a homoerotic Venus, wanders across the dunes, and then decorously falls asleep by a fireplace in Prospero's home.

By contrast, Miranda's partial nakedness leaves her neither vulnerable nor a sexual object; the scene of her vigorously scrubbing herself by the fire is notably unerotic. When the lecherous Caliban wanders in on the scene and makes obscene gestures at her, she throws a wet sponge at him, boots him out of the room, and then collapses in a fit of giggling. His hooting laughter can be heard accompanying hers off-screen. It is as if they were playing out a drama the point of which they no longer can remember, and whose absurdity suddenly strikes them. The scene disrupts or defuses to some degree the dynamic Jyotsna Singh locates between these two characters in the play: "interpellated within Prospero's narrative of sexual and racial control, the identities of both Caliban and Miranda must constantly be *produced* in terms of sexual struggle in which, as Prospero's subjects, their sexuality comes under constant surveillance, even as one enables the repression of the other."[65] In the film, the characters' laughter at the end of the scene works to undermine any possibility of mutual repression. Willcox's off-screen identity is also a factor in the presentation of Miranda: "Connected to a movement whose identification was with aberrant, often violent social behaviors as a rejection of mainstream values, her body (as primary site for her designation as a punk artist) works against the romanticization of Miranda."[66] Significantly, then, Miranda's body can no longer participate in the racist dynamic that plays off the passive European woman against the sexually unruly racial other, whether this is Caliban or Sycorax.

Although Jarman has not given us a black Sycorax or a black Caliban, the film is not in fact all-white. The unexpected racial coding of Caliban and Sycorax is countered by the appearance of Elisabeth Welch in the masque, who replaces the usual goddesses. This most spectacular intrusion of the masque form into the play, which is also the most showy rearrangement of the text, is the emotional climax of the film. One effect of moving this finale out of the masque and into the play is that the masque is staged not just for Ferdinand and Miranda, but rather for the whole community assembled at the end of the film (which now includes Caliban and the other rebels, who react with pleasure to the spectacle). The masque is thus no longer about the importance of Miranda's virginity as exchangeable commodity. On one level, it now works both to symbolize and to consolidate the new community or the new nation that has been formed by the political reconciliations, a community that is further symbolized and consolidated by the union of the young couple. Placing the conclusion of the masque at the end of the film has the further effect of turning the film itself into a masque. In this regard, the glaring anachronisms of the sailors' uniforms and Welch's song are crucial. The fictional frame is fractured here by the entrance of a cabaret singer playing both a goddess and herself. Welch's appearance is the precursor to Annie Lennox's similar role in *Edward II,* which can also be read in relation to the masque. Characters in a Renaissance masque functioned both inside and outside the spectacle, their real identities visible to the audience. The scene thus functions in much the same way as the opening sequence of *Sebastiane,* which establishes an identificatory relay between the space of the audience and the space of the film. Welch's performance here works to bridge or break down the gap between spectator and spectacle that, as MacCabe argues, had always been one of the goals of Jarman's artistic productions.[67] The film at this moment engulfs the viewer in an intensely pleasurable spectacle.

If the masque's aim is to manufacture an ideological community, what, then, are the grounds of this community in the film? Jarman stated that he was interested in the play because of its interest in redemption and forgiveness: "The concept of forgiveness in *The Tempest* attracted me; it's a rare enough quality and almost absent in our world. To know who your enemies are, but to accept them for what they are, befriend them, and plan for a happier future is something we sorely need."[68] This should not be read, however, as an endorsement of the current British nation; if nothing else, the decaying country house in

Elisabeth Welch as the Goddess in *The Tempest.*

which the action takes place should steer us away from such a conclusion. In determining how the masque scene is functioning to reconstruct this fractured nation, we need to attend to the various discourses at work in this final spectacle. The first is alchemy, which for Jarman functioned as an alternative knowledge, one connected, moreover, with a more humane set of values than those currently operative in what he calls the "heterosoc" of contemporary England. On the level of the fiction, Prospero's alchemical arts are responsible for the production of the spectacle and the appearance of Welch.

The entrance of the sailors draws on a more contemporary discourse, camp. Camp is the modern equivalent of alchemy: practiced by a marginalized group, dependent on a specialized knowledge, and representative of an entire philosophical outlook. As Andrew Ross argues, "camp involves a rediscovery of history's waste."[69] Like alchemy, camp transmutes substances, taking the dross of contemporary society and turning it into gold, as in Jack Smith's ecstatic reinterpretations of the 1940s Hollywood Orientalist fantasies starring Maria Montez. Like Ariel, camp performs salvage operations, and it does so in spectacular ways, by turning the British navy, one of the prime agents and symbols of British imperial glory, into benign and vaguely silly entertainment, partly through directing at it an improper desire.

The drag in this scene (involving Caliban and his conspirators) is working closely with this. Drag also implies a relation to dominant culture and history, often by performing styles of femininity that are recognizably outmoded. Drag draws attention to the history of the body without fully inhabiting that history, fracturing any sense of the natural body in the process. Moreover, the film's version of drag is that of the radical drag of the GLF and the Alternative Miss World pageants, a highly theatrical, satiric, and self-conscious form of performance. By including the conspirators, wearing drag, and now included in the final vision of community, the film reverses the masque's historical role in representing the white European body as the incarnation of order. A final thing to note about camp, and one that is crucial in this film, is its utopian impulse, as evidenced in its faith in the transformative power of spectacle. It is the use of the masque that allows Jarman to recuperate the strain of utopian discourse that runs through the play, largely associated there with the ineffectual character of Gonzalo. In the film, this scene becomes a realizable vision of utopia, the "brave new world" of Miranda's imagining.

A third major element in this scene is the blues. As Harris and Jackson note, "A blues number is the ideal twentieth-century song form to encompass love and hate, vengeance and forgiveness, estrangement and reconciliation; to acknowledge how hard it is to limit desire, proscribe sexuality, exact penitence, or contain suffering."[70] The blues, like camp or alchemy, is a marginal discourse invested in transformation, one that displays a faith in the transformational power of art. The history of the blues is of course bound up with the history of slavery, racism, and colonialism, a history in which The Tempest played an early and significant role, particularly in the sphere of representation. The song acts, then, as a pointed intervention in the climax of the film, putting at the center of order a voice from the other side of that history. We might also note that "Stormy Weather" has a significant performance history, associated primarily with black divas. The song, by Harold Arlen and Ted Koehler, was first performed by Ethel Waters in a 1933 Cotton Club review; it revived Waters's career and became her signature song.[71] Later, in 1943, it became the centerpiece of an all-black musical film by Fox. Lena Horne sang what was the title song, and it became a signature tune for her as well.[72] The musical-comedy origins of the song are clearly signaled in the film through the 1930s production values; musical comedy is the camp genre nonpareil (as Caliban might say) and one whose aesthetic principles are strikingly similar to those of the masque.

The combination of camp and blues in the final number combines the two communities continually read as threats to British nationhood in the postwar era, queers and blacks. The connections between the perverse and the racial other as threats to the English nation, which seem to have their origins (or at least parallels) in the early-modern period, gained new force in postwar Britain. The 1950s were marked by antihomosexual witch hunts, where, according to the Cold War discourse, gay men became threats to national security. The 1960s saw the rise of Enoch Powell's inflammatory racist rhetoric, through which black immigrants became the threat to a more traditional (white) version of the nation.[73] In the 1970s, punk's use of Nazi iconography led to an association in the popular mind-set with the National Front, the largest of England's fascist organizations and in the late 1970s the fourth-largest political party in Britain. This association was repudiated by a number of punks through the Rock Against Racism and Anti-Nazi League concerts, although the National Front countered with Rock Against Communism.[74]

The rise of punk rock coincided with the rise of Thatcherism in England (Thatcher became leader of the Conservatives in 1975), and both were to a large degree a reaction against dire economic times. Thatcher exploited anti-immigrant sentiment of the era, writes Greil Marcus, and effectively "buried the National Front by coopting much of its program"[75] in the 1979 general election. Anna Marie Smith documents the interdependencies of homophobia and racism through the late seventies and eighties: "Thatcherite homophobia ... borrows its structure from Powellian / Thatcherite racism in the sense that it reconstitutes the Powellian image of the nation under siege through the substitution of the dangerous queer for the black immigrant."[76] One of the products of this monstrous union in the 1980s was the specter of the black lesbian, who for conservatives functioned as the symbol of the "loony Left" and the negative of traditional British values: "the figure of ... the black lesbian [was] used to invalidate the Labour Party's support for a whole range of feminist, black, disabled and lesbian and gay projects."[77] Ann Tobin similarly notes that "the phrase 'Black lesbians' was ... central to the right-wing press attacks on Labour Councils. Indeed some papers when referring to Labour Councils, never seemed to use the word 'lesbian' without preceding it by the word 'Black.'"[78] It might be argued that the black lesbian in the late 1970s and 1980s functioned as the symbolic heir to Shakespeare's Sycorax. In one way, then, Welch's appearance is a salvaging of Sycorax, and all her demonized sisters. Sycorax, via Welch, becomes the avenue of reconciliation and transcendence in the play, rather than Prospero, or at least they share in the production of this final triumph. The links in the play between Sycorax and Prospero have often been noted, in their parallel histories, their use of sorcery, and their common literary predecessor, Medea, another troublesome North African woman.[79] In

Jarman's version, Sycorax and Medea are no longer conquered or sub-sumed by Prospero as a means of achieving this final vision of order, but rather are represented at the center of the film's final vision of community.

It is the masque, then, that becomes the most important moment of forgiveness or redemption in the film, rather than Prospero's rec-onciliation with his brother and his political foes. In the play, the politi-cal reconciliation looks more like revenge and power mongering, at least insofar as Prospero's relation to his brother is concerned, and the carefully stage-managed romance and marriage is to a large degree the capstone to Prospero's triumph. In the film, it is not as clear that Prospero has manipulated the lovers, and it is Ariel who opens the doors onto the masque and presents it to both on-screen and offscreen audience. All attention is thereby focused on the spectacle, and the political question of who will rule Milan becomes secondary to the larger question of the values of the resultant community. These values come largely from the margins of the play and are expressed through minority aesthetic practices. They are practices, moreover, that share a faith in the redeeming power of art and spectacle. It is not Prospero's forgiveness that matters, in other words, but rather Sycorax's or Cali-ban's or Ariel's or Miranda's, as well as the communities that will take up the heritage of these characters. Which is to say, Jarman's most radical intervention into the masque form is to make the antimasque into the masque. The disorderly bodies of blacks, Gypsies, witches, which like punks bear "the inscription of otherness on the body,"[80] are moved from the margins of the world to its center, reversing the masque's tendency toward differentiation in the name of order. Jar-man's masque aims at undoing a historical process that began in the early-modern period and in which the early-modern masque actively participated.

And this is of a piece with the rest of the film's punk-inspired sub-versions, from the cut-up of a text by one of the very avatars of Eng-lishness to the fracturing of time and space in the film that make the psychology of English nationalism one of the central subjects of the film. The masque is a perfect vehicle to hijack for such purposes, be-cause of its anti- or nonrealist aesthetic, its faith in theatricality, and its ultimately political ends. Most interesting, however, is the relation it structures between spectacle and audience. The actors are simultaneously inside and outside the spectacle, and the culmination of the spectacle is to expand and incorporate or co-opt the audience in its final vision of community.

The punk history that Jarman constructs in *Jubilee* and *The Tempest* is ultimately more productive than the nihilist version written by Amyl Nitrate. Through these films we can see a lineage of avant-garde thought and practice that connects Situationism, gay activism, glam, and punk, putting them in opposition to the rise of Powellian racism, the National Front, and Thatcherism. These films also allow us to look forward to some of the inheritors of punk—not just the New Romantics of the early 1980s, with whom Jarman would be associated, but more importantly queer activism and anti-AIDS organizations, which would draw on both punk's visual style and its aggressive self-presentation.[81]

FOUR

The Caravaggio Years

AFTER THE EARLY SUCCESSES in independent film, making three features in four years, came a period of relative quiet. Jarman started writing the script for *Caravaggio* in Rome, in May 1978, following the premiere of *Jubilee* at Cannes. There would be about sixteen subsequent drafts of the screenplay, with at least three substantially different approaches to the story. *Caravaggio* would not be released until 1986, although two other films of note, *Imagining October* (1984) and *The Angelic Conversation* (1985), would appear in the intervening years. There was also a renewed interest in painting, including shows at the B2 Gallery in the Docklands (1981), the Edward Totah Gallery (1982), and the ICA (1984), and another collaboration with Ken Russell, this time doing the sets for Stravinsky's *The Rake's Progress* in Florence, in 1982. The other major artistic production was his first volume of writing, *Dancing Ledge,* which appeared in 1984. To pay the bills, Jarman started working in a newly emergent genre, the music video. The most notable were a series of three produced for Marianne Faithfull's *Broken English* album in 1979, which were followed in the early 1980s with videos for Lords of the New Church, Wang Chung, and Marc Almond, among others.[1]

In formal terms, the three major films produced in this period— *Caravaggio, Imagining October,* and *The Angelic Conversation*—could not be more distinct. *Imagining October* is a highly political film that set the stage for many of the activist videos of the 1980s. *The Angelic Conversation,* on the other hand, returns to Jarman's super-8 experiments, offering a dreamlike narrative of gay love set against a vaguely Elizabethan backdrop. *Caravaggio,* by contrast again, is in some ways Jarman's most conventional film, a lush if low-budget biopic shot on 35mm. What one learns from reading the many different rewrites of the *Caravaggio* script, however, is that these three films, as well as other unmade scripts (including two meditations on gay artists: *P.P.P. in the Garden of Earthly Delights* and *Nijinsky's Last Dance*) and *Dancing Ledge,* are a sustained attempt to work through a series of issues: the interconnections between sexuality, politics and commerce, and art. They constitute an early, perhaps unprecedented, reflection by a mature, gay artist on the possibilities and limitations faced by this new generation.

Jarman was, at this point, in a unique position to explore these issues. The idealism of the gay liberation movement had by this point begun to fade. One could already speak of a gay establishment, gay institutions, and a gay mainstream. This is not to say that all of the battles had been fought and won: there was a furor that made it all the way to the House of Commons when Channel 4 broadcast Jarman's films, and while the fight over Section 28 was still in the future, Thatcher's government was actively hostile to gay and minority issues. As one of the first major gay directors of the post-Stonewall gay liberation era, Jarman was quite cognizant of the ways in which his sexuality both hurt and helped his career, and the Caravaggio scripts reflect this clearly. For example, an early version quotes Allen Ginsberg's "Howl," a copy of which Jarman purchased on a pilgrimage to City Lights Bookstore in San Francisco in the summer of 1964.[2] "Howl" might be seen as an aesthetic precursor to a film that would follow soon after, *The Last of England*. Like that film, Ginsberg's poem is a highly personal, angry rant from a canonical gay oppositional figure, one who himself actively forged a longer gay tradition through his citations of Walt Whitman, the nineteenth-century poet of lusty male friendship.

Jarman addresses some of his frustrations during this period in *Dancing Ledge,* his first major foray into publication. The book starts with an account of the origins of the Caravaggio script, but turns into a highly fragmented memoir. It ranges over Jarman's childhood in England, India, and Italy, his education, his coming to terms with his sexuality, and offers accounts of the making of his various films. It ends with a fairly bleak inventory of his life at the age of forty, followed by a more optimistic postscript, an excerpt of the final sequence from the script of *Jubilee,* where Elizabeth and Dee wander along the coast. The book is a provocative blend of personal history, family mythology, social history, diary, and artistic reflection, employing what might be seen as a montage aesthetic transferred into the literary realm. Although it is technically an autobiography, it is hardly a conventional one: its fragmentary, hybrid structure might suggest that the particular subjectivity formed by this history does not yet have a narrative form suitable for its exploration. It is less interested in outlining the private, interior world of its subject than in exploring the mutual interpenetrations of self and world. It is also, as befits its subject, more alive to the advantages as well as the occasional necessities of self-invention for the generation that spanned Stonewall. Bearing this in mind, the various attempts to sort out where Jarman invented stories, rearranged details, or changed the facts in his memoirs miss the point entirely. Historians, argued the Renaissance poet Sir Philip Sidney, often get things wrong because they are "captived to the truth of a foolish world,"[3] and Jarman would likely have agreed.

The form established in *Dancing Ledge* would be followed in two later books, *The Last of England* (aka *Kicking the Pricks*) and his literary masterwork, *Modern Nature*. The book published to accompany *Caravaggio* is also a hybrid work, although it moves in a different direction. *Derek Jarman's Caravaggio* (1986) combines the script with photos taken during the production by Gerald Incandela. The photos are a mix of standard production stills, shots of the crew, lush color photos, and black-and-white photos on which Incandela has painted. Some of the photos of the tableaux are accompanied by small reproductions of the paintings they reenact. The script itself (which is different from that of the finished film) is interspersed with accounts of the filmmaking process and reflections by Jarman on Caravaggio's life and art, along with reflections on his own career, including a brief comment on the scandal that followed the screening of *Jubilee* on Channel 4. In another typeface we are given excerpts from different contemporary or near-contemporary accounts of Caravaggio. What we get here is a remarkable mix of versions of Caravaggio, a collage of different media that emphasize the degree to which the resulting film, like any other version of Caravaggio's life, is a construction. This is not to say that all constructions are equal: the book, like the film, uses the occasion of Caravaggio to meditate on the interconnections between sexuality, art, and economics, which, as I have said, was an ongoing preoccupation of the long period during which he wrote the various versions of the script. Before looking at the development of the script, and the film itself, we will turn to the two films that were completed in the meantime, *Imagining October* and *The Angelic Conversation*.

Imagining Change: Imagining October

Michael O'Pray writes that *"Imagining October,* which cost £4,700, was for many a turning point in Jarman's career. A critical success, it transcended its home-movie roots to become a brilliant merging of sexuality, politics and history in a form that was to be influential."[4] The film would be influential not just for the next generation of activist filmmakers; many of the concerns of this film would show up in the films that would follow. The investigation of art and politics would show up almost immediately in *Caravaggio,* the protest against the spiritual sickness of England in *The Last of England,* and the working out of a gay ethics in *War Requiem.* Formally, it is interesting not just for its hybrid form (combining super-8, 16mm, and video intertitles), but for the way that these media become thematized: the super-8 gauge becomes associated here, as it would remain in Jarman's films, with what might be called the human. In *The Last of England,* for example, Jarman includes home movies of his childhood as a bucolic contrast to the ruined state of England; in *The War Requiem,* the home movie works as the memory of childhood for both English and German soldiers, emphasizing their shared humanity (an Eisensteinian gesture). Of this period in his career he says that he "took up my Super 8 camera, deciding to develop a parallel cinema based on the home movie which would free me. A space where I could paint my garden."[5]

The film originated in a trip taken in October 1984. Jarman went to Moscow with filmmakers Sally Potter and Peter Wollen at the invitation of Peter Sainsbury, to screen some of their films. According to Tony Peake, "Jarman later said that with the single exception of his first trip to America in 1964, his visit to Russia 'had more effect on me that any other journey I've made out of this country.'"[6] He took with him ten rolls of super-8 film, and these became the foundation of *Imagining October.* The first referent of the title is a visit to the study of Sergei Eisenstein, one of Jarman's heroes. Jarman writes that "Among the books Peter Wollen discovered a copy of Reed's *Ten Days That Shook the World*, signed 'Eisenstein, Moscow 1920'. It had been crudely censored: Trotsky's name blocked out in black ink; on this Eisenstein had based the official film of the Revolution *October* [released in the West as *Ten Days That Shook the World*]. I had been filming the flat, with the consent of Mr. Kleeman, the curator; I filmed Peter turning the pages of this book, nearly all my ten reels were now exposed."[7] If the title indicates that the film is something of a meditation on the possibilities of revolutionary art, this early moment in the film certainly limits the optimism. (Ironically, this footage led to *Imagining October* itself having an extremely limited circulation, and so, because of its relative unavailability, I will be describing the film in some detail.)[8]

The film starts with this super-8 footage. Titles locate the film precisely: "Sitting on Eisenstein's chair, Moscow 1984, October," and the first image is a dark, chiaroscuro shot of Jarman himself (anticipating some of the lighting in *Caravaggio*). The camera tilts up, and there is a lap dissolve to a shot of an eternal flame. The subsequent shots in this section are principally of huge Stalinist-era buildings, both exteriors and interiors, and monumental squares, reminiscent of the recurring use of the huge statue of Alexander III and the Winter Palace in *October*. This section ends in Eisenstein's study, with Peter Wollen holding Reed's book. He shows us the blacked-out name, and then titles announce: "EISENSTEIN CENSORED! TROTSKY ERASED!" These titles are partially obscured by flickering lines, as if they were themselves being censored. The flickering lines and the exclamation points are evocative of silent-film conventions, drawing a link between the film *October* (where many of the intertitles are excited exclamations) and its censored source.

At this point we have a long series of computer-generated intertitles on a flat video background, starting with "HOME THOUGHTS," which pushes the viewer toward a comparison of social and political conditions in the Soviet Union and the United Kingdom. These titles begin with questions about social conditions and political repression in England, bringing up in particular recent acts of repression against the gay community (seizures of books at the border, and the raid on the bookstore Gay's the Word) but also against workers, in allusions to the government's brutal response to the miners' strike. The titles move on to emphasize the insidious collusion of government and the forces of capitalism (and in particular the ethos of the advertising world, which was seen as crucial to Thatcher's election victories). Quotations from the poetry of William Blake about the evils of nineteenth-century England ("The harlot's cry in each high street, / Weaves old England's winding sheet")[9] are juxtaposed with evocations of the newly reenergized heritage industry ("Step forward into the past that is not / Into the Merrie Olde Land of Was"), against whose promotion of nationalist nostalgia Jarman had battled in *Jubilee* and *The Tempest*.

The subsequent titles work to suggest a connection between Thatcherite nostalgia, the heritage industry, the advertising industry, and mainstream British cinema, which at this point had been reinvigorated by the international success of films like *Chariots of Fire* and *A Passage to India*. The title "ADMEN FALSE IMAGING THE NEW BRITISH CINEMA SUCCESS!!" reflects Jarman's anger at the celebration of commercial filmmakers (both David Puttnam, producer of *Chariots of Fire*, and Hugh Hudson, the director, had worked in advertising) at the expense of more innovative directors like himself, Sally Potter, Ron Peck, and Terence Davies. In particular, it cites James Park's book *Learning to Dream: The New British Cinema*, published in 1984, which fails to mention those directors at all, except for Jarman. Jarman would continue throughout his writings to pour acid on this self-proclaimed British Film Renaissance, later pointing with some glee to the ironically titled *Revolution*, which led to the collapse of Goldcrest Studios: "some of your chums sponsored a *Revolution* and lost the *renaissance* with it. That hurt a little, but who cares, it was another little fiasco over the garden wall, and you were busy re-writing history, far away in Hollywood."[10]

The early juxtaposition of Blake and the heritage industry becomes quite pointed in the last series of titles: "ROLL ON THE CHARIOTS OF FIRE." The radical visionary poet (to whom *Jubilee* was dedicated) is co-opted for the title of a film that Jarman elsewhere called a "damp British *Triumph of the Will*."[11] The section ends with titles remarking on "CRIMES AGAINST GENIUS AND HUMANITY / HISTORY RANSACKED," which draws a further parallel between the art of Blake and Jarman and his fellow filmmakers, and opposes that to the baneful effect of the heritage cinema. This is followed by the full text of Blake's poem "The Sick Rose." Given the preceding titles, it is clear that the poem acts as a commentary on the sick spiritual condition of England, which will be more savagely anatomized in *The Last of England*.

With the Blake poem, the color of the titles changes from white to red, and the next short series of intertitles shifts the film from a critique of the current situation in Britain to a meditation on the possibilities for the alternative artist. The titles read: "PRIVATE SOLUTION. SITTING IN EISENSTEIN'S STUDY WITH A HOME MOVIE CAMERA. IMAGINING OCTOBER. A CINEMA OF SMALL GESTURES." The "cinema of small gestures" refers most immediately to the gauge of the film at this point and to the centrality of the home movie in Jarman's filmmaking aesthetic. It also perhaps reflects a new, more tempered, political understanding.

The sequence that follows, which is roughly two-thirds of the film, shows an artist, played by the painter John Watkiss, painting a picture of five soldiers, centered on the embrace of two of them. As is inevitable with Jarman, the figure of the painter is to some degree a stand-in for the director, and the artist's studio is at the same time a film studio. The soldiers are dressed in British army uniforms, but the style of the painting strongly echoes the heroic style of socialist-realist art that we see elsewhere in the film. A few times we get close-up shots of individual soldiers looking directly into the camera, framed by a poppy wreath. The shots of the soldiers framed by the poppy wreath invoke most immediately the sacrifice of young men for national causes, which will later be the central concern of *War Requiem*. Here, in the context of the studio, but also in the larger political context of the film, the shots are more concerned with the way that art participates in the perpetuation of repression or social injustice, whether the system is communist or capitalist (and, of course, at the same time imagining the possibility of art that actively opposes this). These are not soldiers, after all, but artists' models, and the film spends considerable time looking at the artist looking at the models, concentrating on the transformation that occurs in the act of representation: in an abstract way, art also sacrifices the being of its models in the service of its aims. This is juxtaposed with reminders of the uses to which art is put. The studio scenes, shot in 16mm, are intercut with super-8 footage from the Russian trip. We get images of Red Square and Lenin's Tomb, along with other shots of a socialist-realist mural on the side of a two-story building.

The painting scene seems to shift when the soldiers break the pose, one removes his sweater, and the two central soldiers then resume their embrace. The absence of the uniform changes the meaning of the embrace to some degree, at the very least drawing attention to the man beneath the uniform and to the way that a uniform molds or transforms the person wearing it (much as the act of painting transforms the model). The scene switches to a more formal shot of a meal, arranged as a tableau: the five soldiers all sit on one side of a long table, facing the camera, with a wreath in the center of the wall behind them flanked by two flags on flagpoles, and two portraits of Lenin. The construction of space here is much different, with a single plane of action, which alerts us to a shift in subject matter. While this setup resembles the arrangements of models in the studio that Jarman will later film in *Caravaggio,* it is not possible to easily assimilate this sequence back into the earlier one of the painter painting. For one thing, the painter isn't present here, and we never see a painted representation of this meal. More important, it is clear that the men in this scene are in fact soldiers, and not artists' models dressed as soldiers as they were in the previous sequence. This central scene takes place in the mind of either the painter or Jarman (whom we see at the beginning and the end of the film, leaning back with eyes closed) or both, and it clarifies what it means for him, or for the film, to imagine October: the values on which a revolution can or should be founded.[12] The tableau takes place in the world of art itself. We pass through the painting into what might be seen as the imaginary of the painting: the pure space of art and, by extension, of cinema.

This long series of shots of the soldiers eating, drinking, and talking is intercut with super-8 shots from the Soviet Union. In contrast to the earlier shots of Russia, these are almost all of individual persons: an old woman gesturing at the camera and smiling, a street vendor offering something to the camera, an older man in overalls pointing to something and explaining it to us, a good-looking younger man who smiles in a wolfishly seductive way, and finally a group of children playing on the street with a length of rope. These shots, which are evocative of home movies, clearly work in parallel with the shots of the soldiers sharing fellowship. Both of these scenes work in contrast to the earlier, more monumental shots of Stalinist architecture or heroic painting, a gesture that is reminiscent of Eisenstein's frequent juxtapositions of the human and the monumental. What they work to emphasize here is the necessity of art to answer to the human dimension, which includes, but is not limited to, sexuality and desire.

To make this argument is not to downplay the centrality of sexuality in Jarman's vision of art and of politics. On the contrary: the film reflects a far more complex thinking about sexuality and the ethics of representation than had previously been present in his work. There is no direct reflection on sexuality per se, and very little in the film that could be considered homoerotic: although some critics draw attention to the inevitable eroticism of power in the soldiers and their uniforms,[13] for the most part the pose of the soldiers evokes tenderness and fellowship more than anything else. State repression of sexuality is briefly evoked in some of the intertitles, but within the context of a larger argument about the state's use of coercion generally, whether physical or ideological, and the extent to which art colludes with or resists that process. This in turn will be one of the major themes of *Caravaggio*. The most consistent evocation of homosexuality is more abstract: the connections made in the film between gay artists such as Eisenstein, Benjamin Britten (in his setting of Blake's poem "The Sick Rose"), and Jarman himself. It is within this tradition (which he extends to include the heterosexual but hardly straight William Blake) that we can see Jarman beginning to posit an ethics (which includes an ethics of representation) that arises out of the particularities of gay experience, but that is not necessarily limited to it. In particular, it is an ethics that is attentive to the body and resists its sacrifice, and that is ultimately founded on the values of friendship or fellowship.[14]

The film returns to the scenes of painting, and then finally takes us out of the realm of art and back to the world: we see the models removing their uniforms and putting their own clothes back on, and the painter cleaning his brushes. We return to the footage of Russia, now mostly traveling shots that evoke a leave-taking. We then see the artist laying down the brushes, and we return to the shot of Wollen in Eisenstein's study, pointing to the erased name in the book. A shot of a figure in a heroic pose behind a rippling piece of red fabric dissolves into a shot of a flickering flame. We return to the shot with which the film began, a shot of Jarman smiling, then leaning back with his eyes closed, which dissolves again into the shot of the flame, and then black.

Beginning and ending the film with a shot of the director looking directly into the camera pushes us toward seeing the film as something of a personal, filmic essay, somewhat in the mode of Jean-Luc Godard. However, in spite of the polemical intertitles, this film is less overtly didactic than those of Godard, preferring instead to make its point through juxtaposition. The film is a tightly structured meditation on the relation between art and politics, a meditation that advances largely through a series of contrasts. The initial contrast is between England and the Soviet Union, and it suggests that in spite of the differences, each society is repressive in its own way, for its own reasons. This gives way to a more pressing concern of the film, a comparison of art in the service of larger politics, whether socialist or capitalist, and art that arises out of, and is attentive to, the human. The monumental architecture and sculpture of the first part of the film gives way to smaller, quirkier pieces of folk art in the second half (including, most poignantly, a father's bizarrely constructed memorial garden to his daughter),[15] where the film begins to emphasize the human dimension of its subjects. This is echoed in the contrast between the two gauges of film used: the 16mm sequences are obviously shot in a studio, whereas the 8mm sequences conjure up the feel of the home movie. This contrast is implicitly linked to the contrast evoked in the sequence of polemical intertitles: a filmmaking that is in the service of commercial interests, as opposed to filmmaking interested in art and the common good. The film thus explores the possibilities of different media for political engagement, and particularly different filmic modes of presentation: from pure language, conveyed by computer-generated type on a flat screen, to the textured, bodily inflected documentary footage of the super-8, to the more dimensional and illusionistic, but more impersonally rendered spaces in 16mm.

The extended sequences of the painter at work push us to think about the impulses at work in the creation of art, and the relations between art and the world. This is, of course, a subject that Jarman would soon explore at much greater length in *Caravaggio;* we see here the same interest in the relation between artist and models, and the same attention to the work of painting. The work of imagining October that the painter undertakes is the difficulty of representing revolution in order to effect further change. What the film suggests is that small gestures, like the home movie, are the most responsible way for the alternative artist to intervene. Only small gestures are capable of being responsive to the human dimension, such as the fellowship represented in the tableau scenes, or the individual gestures to the camera made by the Russian figures in the second half of the film. Larger gestures, such as the Soviet realist mural, Eisenstein's *October,* or *Chariots of Fire,* inevitably get caught up in larger systems of power, whether these are economic or political. The result is the inevitable compromise: Eisenstein crossing out Trotsky's name.

Homoerotic Countermythologies in *The Angelic Conversation*

The film following *Imagining October* takes up some of the same issues, using the more intimate gauge of super-8 to explore the terrain of gay desire. Using a technique similar to that used for his early home movies, Jarman shot *The Angelic Conversation* at very high speed, projected it slow, and refilmed the result using a video camera connected to a U-matic deck.[16] Initially, this method was simply a means of extending three minutes of film to almost twenty, but Jarman quickly recognized its aesthetic possibilities. The result, as Jarman said of his short film "*Sebastiane* Wrap," is that "they work rather like a slide show, you're always pulled back to the image."[17] The images in the film appear to trace out a very loose narrative of desire, and are held together by the sound track, on which Judi Dench reads fourteen of Shakespeare's sonnets. Morgan Michael Holmes discusses the film's "quintessentially 'New Romantic' rendering of male beauty and erotic allure,"[18] which provides a link to the pop music videos Jarman was making at the time. New Romanticism's emergence from the punk movement points as well to a continuity between this film and Jarman's work in the 1970s.

One should perhaps begin a consideration of *The Angelic Conversation* by reflecting on the choice of the sonnets themselves. The most

Looking through the past in *The Angelic Conversation* (1985). Philip Williamson. Production still.

obvious reason to choose Shakespeare's *Sonnets* is that they are the most famous of the Renaissance sonnet sequences, written by the central icon of the age. They represent cultural capital and can act therefore as a site of cultural contestation. Moreover, given the homoerotic nature of the first part of the sequence, the sonnets addressed to the young man, the choice makes sense for a film that is to some degree concerned with building or asserting a gay tradition. Indeed, it is largely on the basis of these sonnets, rather than other literary works or historical evidence, that Shakespeare has been claimed for a tradition of gay artists, in spite of the fact that the final sonnets in the sequence address the poet's love for the duplicitous Dark Lady, who simultaneously disgusts him and incites his lust. Although the film is by no means a simplistic claiming of Shakespeare for a gay tradition, using the *Sonnets* as the backbone of a reverie on gay desire is nonetheless a provocative political gesture, one that resists a long history of heterosexualizing the crown jewel of the English literary tradition.

A related but less remarked upon reason for choosing the sonnets is the particular portrait of desire that they offer. Unlike Edmund Spenser's *Amoretti,* which traces out a Neoplatonic idealization of love, or Philip Sidney's *Astrophil and Stella,* which idealizes the cruel Petrarchan mistress Stella, Shakespeare's *Sonnets* offer a more complex and less idealized examination of what can be seen as heterodox desires. In her commentaries on the sequence Helen Vendler remarks that "the sonnets show the cycle of idealization, infatuation, and inevitable disillusion twice over, once with a male love-object and once with a female."[19] Shakespeare's sequence is both a development of and a break with the earlier traditions of sonneteering; in spite of the dreamy quality of the film, Jarman's use of these sonnets might similarly be seen as a break with, or at least a distancing from, an earlier utopian strain in gay discourse.

It is significant that in selecting the fourteen sonnets he includes in the film, Jarman does not simply take those from the beginning of the sequence that idealize the young man, which would have made the film a more straightforward celebration of gay romance. Instead, he ignores for the most part the early sonnets (which, in any case, frequently urge the young man to marry and reproduce), and ranges over the entire sequence, using as an epigraph lines from one of the final sonnets (#151) that reflects on the inevitability, but also the value, of romantic disillusionment. Isolated by themselves, however, the lines register differently: "Love is too young to know what conscience is, / Yet who knows not conscience is born of love?" (151.1–2). These lines suggest that desire is itself amoral (and thus object choice is not a matter of morality), but the experience of love (any experience of love) is the foundation of morality. In this poem, argues Vendler, Shakespeare "admits the libidinal base of adult consciousness itself."[20] This is not the same as the Neoplatonic insistence on the essentially moral nature of desire, which lifts us up out of carnality and moves us toward heavenly understanding. In these poems, disgust as much as delight is what breaks us out of egoism and leads us to both self-consciousness and a recognition of the other (the foundation of ethics), and this is a desire that is always solidly rooted in the flesh. This is a highly appropriate sentiment for a film whose politics are grounded upon an insistence on the centrality of sexual expression in human experience, and also, of course, on an insistence that certain sexual practices traditionally regarded as degraded are equally an avenue to greater self-consciousness.

Both the *Sonnets* and *The Angelic Conversation* can thus be seen to be charting new ground. Joel Fineman argues that by shifting away from the idealizing poetry of praise previously associated with sonnets, Shakespeare moves from a poetics of homogeneity to a poetics of heterogeneity. In so doing, argues Fineman, "Shakespeare in his sonnets invents the poetics of heterosexuality."[21] Jarman can be seen in this film to be exploring new psychic terrain, a post-Stonewall gay consciousness, while at the same time inventing a filmic poetics that would allow such an exploration. The inclusion of the *Sonnets* in the film is thus something of a strategic reclamation. The homoeroticism of the early sonnets is underlined, and the poet's despair at the heterodox nature of his heterosexual desire for the Dark Lady in the latter part of the sequence is redeployed for other purposes.

The film selects a group of sonnets from across the sequence (57, 90, 43, 53, 148, 126, 29, 94, 30, 55, 27, 61, 56, and 104) and rearranges them to construct (or suggest) a new narrative. Jarman described the film as "A series of slow-moving sequences through a landscape seen from the windows of an Elizabethan house. Two young men find and lose each other. The film ends in a garden."[22] This skimpy outline is similar to what one gets when one tries to describe the narrative in a sonnet sequence ("A poet is infatuated with a young man, who disappoints him. He winds up infatuated with an unfaithful woman."). The interest of a sonnet sequence lies not in the narrative complexity of the story it tells, but rather in the way it registers a series of lyrical moments of consciousness that are related to or that arise from the implied story. This is the most productive way of viewing the film as well. The slight narrative that it offers does not bear (or indeed, reward) as much examination as what might be called the experience of the film, the series of images, sounds, and textures that act as meditations on certain themes.

Jarman starts with a poem of cheerily masochistic longing: "Being your slave, what should I do but tend / Upon the hours and times of your desire?" (57.1–2). The poems that follow trace out an arc that is suggestive of a particularly gay experience of desire. We move from poems of longing and anxiety (57, 90, 43) to a poem marveling at the beauty of the beloved (sonnet 53), which is juxtaposed with another (sonnet 148) about finding something beautiful that the rest of the world deems inappropriate: "If that be fair whereon my false eyes dote, / What means the world to say it is not so?" (148.5–6). The central poem of this new sequence, from which came the title of a pioneering gay play,[23] meditates on what it means to be an outcast, and how love compensates for the world's scorn: "When in disgrace with Fortune and men's eyes ... Haply I think on thee ... For thy sweet love rememb'red such wealth brings / That then I scorn to change my state with kings" (29.1, 10, 13–4). Sonnet 94 thinks about the power of the beautiful, sonnet 30 returns to the contrast between worldly disappointment and the private joy taken in contemplation of the beloved, and sonnet 55 continues this thought by contrasting worldly monuments with this more intimate tribute to the beloved (reminiscent of the small gestures of *Imagining October*): "Not marble nor the gilded monuments / Of princes shall outlive this pow'rful rhyme" (55.1–2). Two poems originally about sleeplessess caused by thinking on the beloved (27, 61) become, via the imagery, poems about staying awake after sex, looking in wonder at the beloved sleeping. This is followed by a sonnet of parting, in which, argues Vendler, "the yearning of a heterodox form of attachment to be a socially sanctioned one is visible" (272). Finally, the sequence ends with an elegiac tone, offering reassurances that the beloved's beauty will not fade, at least not in memory: "To me, fair friend, you never can be old" (104.1). This sentiment is reminiscent of C. P. Cavafy's homoerotic elegies, memorably illustrated by David Hockney in a 1960s edition that Jarman identified as groundbreaking.

As can be seen even in this brief overview, the film is strategic in its use of the sonnets, neither completely faithful nor completely anachronistic. Some of the dominant themes are retained (erotic obsession, longing, heterodox desires, alienation), others from the sonnets do not show up (sexual disgust, misogyny, reproduction), while others, as we have seen, are to some degree reconfigured by the imagery that accompanies them, or their placement in the new sequence. Other elements of the sound track work in a similarly multivalent way: the music is a mix of jarring, discordant themes written for the film by Coil, interspersed with the more romantic Sea Interludes from Benjamin Britten's modernist opera *Peter Grimes*. The choice of this latter music is significant for both its content and its author. The opera concerns itself with a tormented outsider, and Britten's homosexuality was an open secret that was the barely concealed subject of a number of his works.

If the sound track constructs at least a couple of different gay lineages for the film via the voice-over and the music, the image track constructs yet more. The Renaissance imagery of the film is an obvious match for the sonnets, and connects with Jarman's earlier films of the past. A number of images in particular recur: a young man in vaguely Elizabethan dress uses a circular mirror to flash light into a camera, much like Ariel in *Jubilee*. Other images are reminiscent of *The Tempest*: a young man on a beach performs a variety of enigmatic tasks, including carrying alternately a barrel and a large log on his shoulders, which is suggestive of both Caliban and Ferdinand. More generally, we get the recurrent images of flowers and gardens, which Jarman frequently associates with the Renaissance.

Steven Dillon places *The Angelic Conversation* in the genre of the poetic film, a genre that frequently explores themes of sexuality and subjectivity.[24] The film locates itself more narrowly in a tradition of gay filmmakers working within this genre, which includes Cocteau's Orpheus trilogy (and especially *The Blood of a Poet* [1930–32]), Kenneth Anger's *Fireworks* (1947), and Jean Genet's *Un Chant d'Amour* (1950). In particular, *The Angelic Conversation* recalls Cocteau in its suggestion of an Orphic journey to the underworld and it draws on some of Anger's favorite biker imagery in its underworld sequence. Genet's film can be seen as a reaction to the earlier films by Cocteau and Anger,[25] and Jarman's film, I would argue, can be seen as development of Genet's.

Un Chant d'Amour is a tightly structured film about a literally closeted desire. Set in a prison, it juxtaposes actual attempts at metaphoric intercourse (prisoners swinging a garland of flowers between two barred windows, one prisoner blowing smoke through a straw into another prisoner's mouth, a guard forcing a gun into a prisoner's mouth) with sequences of a prisoner and a guard's fantasies of sexual intercourse. Desire in the film can only be consummated metaphorically, or via displacement. Genet more or less disowned the film later in life, and its producer dismissed it as a romantic, immature work.[26] It is certainly true that the tightly schematic imagery leaves little room for complexity or depth, and the fantasy sequences are highly (but no doubt purposefully) pastoral. It is at least partly by virtue of the intervening years that Jarman's film can be seen as a response to and further development of Genet's and, of course, as an advance on his own film Sebastiane, which can be seen as an intermediate point between the two. Sebastiane is set in a similar terrain as Un Chant d'Amour[27] (prison versus isolated army encampment) and offers similarly lyrical, pastoral treatments of gay desire. Sebastiane's treatment of homosexual desire, however, is indebted to gay liberation discourse, attempting to disengage it from pathology and criminality by inventing what amounts to a gay spirituality, or at the very least, by insisting on the utopian possibilities of a liberated sexuality.

What in turn distinguishes The Angelic Conversation from Jarman's earlier film is a retreat from (or advance beyond) the idealism of the gay liberation years. The film still offers lyric portrayals of gay desire, but it does this within the context of an exploration of gay psychology. It is one of the functions of the sonnets he chooses to offer a complex, nonidealized portrait of desire. What distinguishes the film from others in the genre of poetic or lyric film, gay or otherwise, is its insistence on placing this exploration of subjectivity in relation to the outside world. Here is where we might see the influence of another, earlier gay filmmaker working in a much different tradition: Eisenstein, the subject of Imagining October. Echoes of Eisenstein occur visually in a couple of places, most notably in a repeated side-angle shot of a young man kneeling on a beach, holding up a shell, looking much like a statue. More crucially, however, Jarman uses Eisensteinian montage to place the psychological exploration within a political context. The most obvious examples of this are the repeated images of a chain-link fence and a radar tower. As Jarman states, "Destruction hovers in the background of *The Angelic Conversation;* the radar, the surveillance, the feeling one is under psychic attack; of course we are under attack at the moment."[28] The first time we see the radar tower it is crosscut with images of the young man with the flashing mirror, which in earlier films is associated with alternative desire. The crosscut echoes the juxtaposition in the sonnets of the private, heterodox desire with the hostile outside world. What is notable here and in *Imagining October,* and what is largely absent from the earlier films, is the clear emphasis placed on the interconnections of sexuality, subjectivity, and history.

The development of themes and images from his earlier films is matched by the film's reinvestigation of certain formal techniques he used in the 1970s. *The Angelic Conversation* returns to the experimental super-8 format of the earlier "home movies," only now combined

The flowers and the radar tower in *The Angelic Conversation.*

with video, which was emerging at this point as the next home-movie format. Jarman says of *Sebastiane* that "The home movie is the bedrock, it records the landscape of leisure: the beach, the garden, the swimming pool."[29] The super-8s of the 1970s documented a newly emergent social terrain, alongside their more formal experiments with filmic space. Both of these pursuits are taken up again in *The Angelic Conversation;* Jarman notes that "All the things that happen in that film were things that happen in 'home movies', like down on the beach swimming, walking through the landscape, going to the stately home."[30] The home movie as a form is particularly suitable for Jarman's version of the Renaissance, or at the very least for this particular Renaissance exploration.

If the home movie records the "landscape of leisure," *The Angelic Conversation* alerts us to the fact that the landscape of leisure is, not surprisingly, also the landscape of desire. This is generally effaced in the home movie, which is almost by definition a chaste genre, its chastity underscored by its demonic doubles, the stag film and the amateur sex video. Desire is banished from the home movie, but homoerotic desire in particular is the true serpent lurking in the grass, given that the familial ideology that the home movie reproduces is specifically premised on its exclusion. But at the same time that they attempt to banish desire, home movies are nonetheless strongly marked by it: as Jarman notes, "In all home movies is a longing for paradise."[31] They record real gardens, in other words, but long for ideal ones. In both the sonnets and in Jarman's film, this longing is connected in the first instance to homoerotic desire: it is a longing for its immediate object, the beautiful young man, but more importantly for the time and space of that desire. For Jarman, this is always connected with the garden, or, as he says elsewhere, "our corner of Paradise, the part of the garden the Lord forgot to mention."[32] This is why, presumably, the film ends in the space of the Elizabethan garden.

Daniel O'Quinn argues in his essay on *Modern Nature* that Jarman associated what O'Quinn calls the sacred "sodomitical" space of the garden with a different apprehension of time. Time in the garden is opposed to what might be called monumental time. O'Quinn locates in Jarman's work a critique of "an imperial allegory in which time and knowledge colonize history such that access to paradise has become prohibited."[33] Imperial time or monumental time is linked both to the experience of time that Benedict Anderson argues characterizes the modern nation and, of course, to our modern sense of narrative, which both the home movie and *The Angelic Conversation* eschew.

The home-movie format is well suited formally to the sonnet sequence, particularly Shakespeare's, which is so centrally concerned with time and with longing: as we have seen, the first lines of the film are from sonnet 57: "Being your slave, what should I do but tend / Upon the hours and times of your desire?" On the sound track, we hear the heavy tick of an old clock, which accentuates the stuttering pace of the images. The rhythm of the images, says Jarman, is like that of a heartbeat; we might note as well that it comes close to the beat of iambic pentameter (the meter of a sonnet). What we get, then, is an entirely different experience of temporality: a series of discrete moments in which the texture of time becomes evident. Like the sonnet sequence itself, the film becomes a concatenation of individual moments of apprehension, taking place in an eternal present: in lyric time, in other words, rather than monumental time. This different experience of time is connected to a different experience of space. The graininess of the image draws attention to its texture, and although they are not entirely dispelled, we become aware of the how the illusions of depth and motion are created on the screen. Like the super-8s of the 1970s, the film's reprocessing of the images draws attention to the screen as a space: like the garden in *Garden of Luxor*, the space of *The Angelic Conversation* is a purely cinematic one. Moreover, the experience of watching the film lulls us into a particular mental space, a dreamy receptivity, where the succession of images works on our imagination, and the boundary between self and film becomes blurred. This apprehension of a different kind of time and a different experience of space is crucial to the project; the film, we might say, inhabits the space of the garden in order to resist the monumental time of the nation. The return to this particular space and time in the Renaissance is a way of returning to the point where this particular version of nationhood was being newly consolidated, and most importantly, the film resists a particular construction of time, narrative, and nationhood in the present.

To what extent, we might wonder, is the home movie a Renaissance genre? Social historians argue that the Renaissance was marked by the establishment of a clear separation between the public and private spheres, which accompanied both the emergence of what would become the middle class and the invention of the nuclear family. It is in very real ways, then, the ideological home of the home movie. But the Renaissance is also a prime site for the contestation of ownership of England. Shakespeare, Elizabeth, and the English Renaissance were—and of course still are—potent sources of meaning for nationalist ideologies. As Jarman notes, "Elizabethan England is our cultural Arcadia, as Shakespeare is the essential pivot of our culture."³⁴ For English nationalist ideologies, then, the Renaissance *is* home, and a cursory glance at the production of the British film industry from its origins to the present would suggest that the Renaissance period film is the nationalist equivalent of the home movie. Each new example is an attempt to capture, or perhaps inhabit anew, the cultural Arcadia. By returning to this Arcadia, these films reimagine the national home and family. How this cultural home is pictured, then, and who makes it into the frame, have an obvious importance.

When questioned about the politics of *The Angelic Conversation*, Jarman immediately remarked upon the effort "to reclaim Shakespeare for a homoerotic tradition."³⁵ One need only reflect on the complete effacement of the homoerotic themes in the *Sonnets* in John Madden's film *Shakespeare in Love* (UK, 1996) to see that this is not some quaint project from the early days of gay liberation. The heteronormative conceit of *Shakespeare in Love* is that, as the character of Viola de Lessups puts it, "stage love will never be true love while the law of the land has our heroines being played by pipsqueak boys in petticoats." Consequently, the sonnets that were originally addressed to the young man now turn out to be written to a young woman. In essence, the film suggests that the only authentic desire is heterosexual; everything else is just dressing up. This film, which is only one example of a centuries-long tradition of heterosexualizing Shakespeare, is a particularly apt demonstration of Jarman's claims about the politics and the problems of period films. Costume drama, he wrote, is "a delusion based on a collective amnesia, ignorance and furnishing fabrics. (Lurex for an

Oscar)."[36] (It is something of an irony that Sandy Powell, Jarman's longtime costume designer from *Caravaggio* onward, won an Oscar for *Shakespeare in Love*.)

The problem is not just the familiar one of under- or misrepresentation, writing blacks or gays or women out of history. *Shakespeare in Love* would not have been a more historically accurate film had the Gwyneth Paltrow role been played by Leonardo DiCaprio. It has to do as well with the texture of that representation itself, with an understanding of the psychic dimensions of cultural memory. Here is where *The Angelic Conversation* differs from some of Jarman's other Renaissance films, such as *Caravaggio* or *Edward II*, in spite of the historical self-reflexivity that is signaled in their use of creative anachronism. *The Angelic Conversation* uses the resources and especially the affective pull of the home movie in order to intervene at the level of fantasy, at one of the key sites of English nationalist fantasy. It is not enough, in other words, to rewrite or correct history, which might imply that history was stable, knowable, and real. *The Angelic Conversation* understands that the history involved in nationalist imaginings offers itself as an answer to the longing for home. The strategy the film employs is not to critique the longing, but to shift the grounds; what Jarman offers is not so much a corrective as an alternative mythology. Through the dreamlike time and texture of the film, Jarman offers a countermemory, a memory of homoerotic desire. What makes this peculiarly effective is precisely the choice of form: by invading the grounds of the home movie, which records the alternative time of leisure, and the alternative space of the garden, Jarman challenges the production of the nationalist present by intervening in the representation of its past.

Caravaggio: Gay History and the Scripts

The long development of the Caravaggio script offers an interesting insight in the evolution of Jarman's thinking over an extended period of time. As noted earlier, work for the script began in 1978, and more than sixteen versions would be written before the film finally appeared. This was a subject close to Jarman's heart: all of the scripts, and indeed the film, are premised on an identification of one artist with the other. The various attempts to think through the life of Caravaggio are simultaneously reflections on Jarman's own artistic career, and in particular the situation of an artist working outside the mainstream.

The earliest version of the script in the British Film Institute archive, written long before either *Imagining October* or *The Angelic Conversation* appeared, tells the life of Michelangelo Merisi da Caravaggio in a more or less straightforward way. It starts with the teenaged Michele working in a studio in Rome as a copyist, with a couple of other friends who are also streetwise painters. Michele attracts the attention and becomes the protégé of Cardinal del Monte, a cultured churchman with an interest in art and Neoplatonic philosophy. The central dilemma, as in many versions of the script, comes when Caravaggio wins his first major public commission to paint *The Martyrdom of St. Matthew*. He finds himself unable to complete the painting, until he meets and falls in love with Ranuccio ("the thief that unlocked the soul of his art," as the script has it), and Ranuccio becomes the executioner in the painting, an equivocal figure of attraction and danger. Ranuccio is a thief and hustler who is attached to Lena, a prostitute. He and Cara-vaggio nonetheless fall in love and consummate their passion in a moonlight scene in the water, in what sounds like a counterpart to the highly romanticized gay sex scenes in *Sebastiane*. Lena subsequently becomes Scipione Borghese's mistress and is murdered by him when she becomes pregnant. Ranuccio is jailed for the crime. To set his lover free, Caravaggio paints a portrait for the pope. Ranuccio, on his release, is incensed that Caravaggio has apparently colluded with Lena's murderers. In an ensuing struggle, Caravaggio accidentally kills him. The film ends here, with an epilogue featuring Cardinal del Monte re-counting the final acts of Caravaggio's life at a dinner party.

As written, this early script picks up on some of the elements of Jarman's first three feature films. It claims Caravaggio for a gay histori-cal tradition, putting his sexuality at the center of his artistic genius, and putting that at the center of an aesthetic revolution that is opposed by the critic Baglione, described in the script as a "critic and artist who is preoccupied with old fashioned academic theory." It connects this story of an alternative aesthetics with a fairly romantic gay love narra-tive (perhaps the most romantic of all: the conversion of the straight man). Interspersed with the central narrative is the story of the trial and execution of Giordano Bruno, which it characterizes as a key turning point in the Renaissance. Bruno figures as an Italian equivalent to John Dee in *Jubilee* and *The Tempest,* as the representative of an alternative, marginal knowledge. The Bruno narrative will be reduced to little more than a mention in the final script, as del Monte educates the young Michele. (Howard Hibbard notes that the historical del Monte "was a serious practitioner of alchemy.")[37] One final thing to note is that the film would have featured a dream sequence in super-8, featuring Caravaggio as Goliath and as David a young shepherd named Jerusaleme, who earlier "screws Caravaggio in the darkness against a tree." This is interesting for a couple of reasons: for the psychological narrative it offers for Caravaggio's famous self-portrait, and for the way it insists on including in the film a range of portraits of gay relationships. Thus we see the camaraderie of the young friends in the atelier, del Monte's mentoring relationship with the young painter, the romanticized affair with Ranuccio, and the casual sex with Jerusaleme.

A subsequent version of the script, dated 1981, differs markedly from this one. It starts in the present, with "Derek Jarman" talking on the phone to an American producer named Chase Manhattan III. In the background, "a young artist photographer is shooting naked boys" in the style of Caravaggio. In rather leaden satiric dialogue, the producer tries to coax Derek into making a pornographic video based on the life of Caravaggio: "It's perfect for the video market: Sex and violence, like Joe Orton. There's a huge gay audience here in the States for the film. We saw 'Sebastian' the other day and thought you might take it on; the idea is to make the film on location in Italy." When the producer tells him they need it to appeal to a heterosexual audience as well as a gay one, Derek (ploddingly) responds: "But he was gay although it's never mentioned in the art books, like Leonardo or Michelangelo nearly all the greatest painters of the Renaissance, like film-makers now: Murnau, Ei[se]nstein, our whole culture's gay, Jesus Christ, Plato, Shakespeare and Caravaggio, he was very narcissistic you can tell it by the early paintings, but obviously fell out of love with himself. I think his death was a sort of suicide. He was immensely controversial, violent, but also the most popular painter of his day. I can't see how you can put a life like that on film without trivialising it."

The structure of the film is much more interesting than the opening dialogue would indicate. Derek and the young photographer travel to Italy to do research for the film, and the past and the present become intertwined in complex ways. Visits to churches to view the paintings initiate temporal crossovers, and at one point Derek and his friend visit a bathhouse at the same time as the sixteenth-century characters Borghese and Giustiniani. The critic Baglione's condemnations of Caravaggio are juxtaposed with reviews of Jarman's work, including Vincent Canby's poisonous review of The Tempest in the New York Times. In a later draft of this version of the script "Derek" mentions at the beginning of the film that he once picked up a beautiful boy on the beach at Porto Ercole, where Caravaggio died. The final image of this version is Derek holding the hand of the young Caravaggio.

While all versions of the script depend to some degree on an identification of Jarman with Caravaggio, in this version it is the clearest. The opening section reflects on the kinds of pressures, both economic and ideological, that Jarman was now encountering, as a market for gay-themed material was becoming more obvious, and more obviously exploitable. The films of Jarman and other gay directors of the 1970s had made Caravaggio "a totally commercial life story" even if, according to the producer in the script, "'Sebastian' disappointed the queens in San Francisco." (The Village Voice review of Caravaggio subsequently and similarly noted that "those members of the rabble hoping for 93 minutes of lavender hubba-hubba" will be disappointed.)[38]

The pressures on the gay artist of the early 1980s are paralleled with those faced by the homosexual artist of the Renaissance. One of the key dangers facing both, the script would suggest, is the compromising complicity that comes with the funding agencies, whether these happen to be the Catholic Church or Channel 4. In a speech that would find its way only slightly altered into the filmed version, the pope explains why the church turns a blind eye to Michele and Ranuccio's various crimes, and why "scandalous" art of the seventeenth or twentieth centuries is tolerated: "Revolutionary gestures in art are a great help for us. Bet you hadn't thought of that, you little bugger. Keeps the quo in the status. Never heard of a revolution made with brushes. The 'Spirit' must be expressed and you have the keys. Scipione says the paintings are very popular, very useful, so useful we will absolve the most equivocal actions" (120). It is noteworthy that in the film Jarman is onscreen throughout much of this speech, playing a minor papal official; the pope is speaking as much to Jarman as he is to Caravaggio.

On the other hand, this version of the script is also clear about the necessity, or at least the advantages, of such complicity. It does allow for the kind of assertions that Derek makes early in the script for the existence of a tradition of gay artists and philosophers, for an examination of the corrosive effects of homophobia in the creation of self-hatred, and for an interesting and at times poetic exploration of the relations between minority artists and intellectuals over the centuries. The interest in a gay tradition was an ongoing preoccupation throughout Jarman's career that would find its most immediate voice in *The Angelic Conversation*, and its most complex statement in *War Requiem*. Most remarkably, the final image of Jarman and Caravaggio holding hands imagines artistic influence within this gay tradition not as an antagonistic relation, as it is often figured in the mainstream tradition, but rather as a kind of cruising, which insists on the centrality of sexuality in the artistic process.[39] In that regard, Jarman offers an updated version of the account of the relation of philosopher and pupil in Plato's *Symposium*, which similarly places desire at the center of the learning process.

The next major version of the script would, over a lengthy series of revisions, become the final one. In a script dated April 1983, we find that the present-day frame narrative has been abandoned. Like the realized film, this script begins and ends with Caravaggio's death, and it introduces the figure of a mute boy, Gianni, who will become in later versions Jerusaleme. Some of the key scenes of the realized film appear in this script, including the sequence where Caravaggio keeps Ranuccio posing for him through the night by periodically tossing him gold coins, which Ranuccio pops into his mouth. The most remarkable change to the main narrative, however, is that in this version it is Ranuccio who murders Lena, not Scipione Borghese. He is pictured with the body in the river, and the murder assumes more prominence in the script. There is also a major addition at the end of the script, which works like a dream sequence. We see a gardener pushing a wheelbarrow in which a young boy sits with a pile of scarlet flowers. They come to the mouth of cave and the gardener opens it by rolling back a huge rock. The child wanders in and sees a *tableau vivant* of Caravaggio's painting of the raising of Lazarus, with Ranuccio as Lazarus and Caravaggio as the gravedigger lifting him up. This rather enigmatic sequence will be replaced by a different but equally enigmatic one in the final film, with Caravaggio as a boy coming upon a *tableau vivant* of Caravaggio's *Crucified Christ,* with the adult Caravaggio in the role of Christ.

The relationship between Caravaggio and Ranuccio continued to shift in the ongoing revisions to this version of the script. Ranuccio remains central to unblocking Caravaggio's art, but the relationship is no longer a physical one. The version titled "Blue is Poison," dated December 1984, contains the scene from the film where, at the end of the night of posing, Caravaggio places a final gold piece in Ranuccio's mouth and kisses him. A voice-over tells us: "that kiss was as near as Michele ever got to Ranuccio Thomasoni the hustler who provided the key which unlocked the masochistic soul of his art. . . . Michele painted himself gazing sadly at his ecstatic murderer who deep in his heart he knew he could never possess, who had stolen half his soul." Ranuccio remains the murderer of Lena, although Caravaggio believes the culprit was Scipione Borghese, and works to have Ranuccio freed. When Ranuccio confesses upon his release that it was he who murdered Lena, Caravaggio kills him deliberately, rather than accidentally as earlier.

The changes in the Caravaggio/Ranuccio relationship shift the interest of the film quite dramatically. No longer is there a romantic story of gay love at the center of the film, a love melodramatically cut short by a frame-up job and an accidental killing. Instead we have a more severe and psychologically complex narrative about self-hatred and self-delusion, masochistic attachment, and the painful necessity of certain renunciations and acceptances. It is important that Caravaggio's killing of Ranuccio is a conscious rather than an accidental act; it comes after a final stripping away of the veils of romantic illusion, and a conscious acceptance of the outsider's, indeed outlaw's, position in society. Michele's renunciation of the heterosexual Ranuccio, and his recognition of the price of his own self-delusion, are something of a development of Sebastian's rejection of Severus, stripped of all the religious and mystical overtones. Whereas the early scripts were focused on artistic inspiration and the breakthrough to artistic genius, the film is about artistic maturity, as is signaled, perhaps, by putting the Saint Matthew painting, Caravaggio's first mature work, at the center of it.

Taken together, the scripts for *Caravaggio* can be seen as a sustained reflection by Jarman on his own artistic practice, and in particular the ways in which politics, sexuality, and economics were intertwined with it. What we can see by looking at the development of the script alongside the work that was produced is that the particular approaches that were left behind were not abandoned, but rather emerged in different and more satisfying forms in other projects. The central romantic narrative of the earliest version emerges in a far more interesting and abstract way in *The Angelic Conversation*. The angry and somewhat cynical postmodernism of the second version of the script winds up in the more direct political critique of *Imagining October*. While they have different emphases, all three films are interested in looking at the same set of questions, partly by drawing on what was coming to be seen as a tradition of gay artists; *Imagining October* uses the political difficulties of Eisenstein to address the situation of a gay filmmaker working in the hostile climate of Thatcherite politics; *The Angelic Conversation* mines the homoerotic sonnets of Shakespeare for a contemporary exploration of the psychological landscape of gay desire, which does not, at the same time, ignore the hostility of the dominant culture.

Caravaggio and the Art of the Past

The years of work on the Caravaggio project left indelible effects on Jarman's aesthetic practice. Just as there is scarcely a film of Jarman's in which one cannot see a conscious or unconscious homage to Pasolini, the same is true of the painter. In the films that follow, this influence is evident particularly with regard to his visual style, but more generally with the way he engages with and represents the past. In fact, Jarman continually pairs these two important forerunners in *Dancing Ledge*: "Had Caravaggio been reincarnated in this century it would have been as a film-maker, Pasolini"; Caravaggio's David is "a rough little number, one of those Roman street boys in whom, like Pasolini, C. continually sought 'perfection'"; Caravaggio "brought the lofty ideals down to earth, and became the most homosexual of painters, in the way that Pasolini became the most homosexual of film-makers."[40] Even Jarman's anachronistic treatment of Caravaggio's sexuality, evident in these comments, can be seen as indebted to Caravaggio. Jarman figures Caravaggio in the same way that Caravaggio remakes his historical subjects, making them embody the relation between two historical moments. Genevieve Warwick writes that Caravaggio "conceived of his subject as a performance of history staged in the present. . . . Caravaggio demonstrated the relevance of the past to his contemporaries by enacting it within the framework of the present."[41]

David Gardner argues that this connection between artist and director carries into the film itself: "Caravaggio allowed Jarman to insert his own life into Caravaggio's story in further homage to Pasolini."[42] The twinning of the two artists in Jarman's imagination is also signaled by the fact that in the lengthy period while Jarman worked on the Caravaggio script, he also produced the scenario for the unmade film *P.P.P. in the Garden of Earthly Delights*. That scenario takes a similar approach to Pasolini's life as the former does with its subject, purposefully mixing the life and the art in such a way that the art both predicates and extends the life, rather than simply reflecting it. Both explore, as does much of the work of this period, the links between sexuality, art, and power.

As with Pasolini, there are a number of biographical parallels that might begin to account for the profound identification that Jarman felt with his subject, particularly at this point in his career. The most obvious is, of course, Caravaggio's presumed homosexuality, which was the basis of Donald Posner's groundbreaking 1971 study of homosexual themes in Caravaggio's early paintings,[43] and which had since become an increasingly accepted part of the biography.[44] Caravaggio's status as scandalous outsider was partly cemented by his various runins with the law. In the mid-1980s, Jarman's name and reputation were being used in the House of Commons to put forward new obscenity legislation (excerpts from *Jubilee* were shown in the debates around the "Video Nasties Bill").[45] Caravaggio's oppositional stance to the artworld establishment of his day might have been seen by Jarman to echo his own stormy relationship with the British film industry (detailed in *Dancing Ledge, Kicking the Pricks,* and alluded to in *Imagining October*), and his conflicted engagement with the work of Michelangelo mirrors that of Jarman's engagement with filmmakers he saw as important forerunners. Bersani and Dutoit argue that "It is . . . generally agreed that when Caravaggio quotes Michelangelo (in such works as *Victorious Cupid* and *St. John the Baptist with a Ram*) he seeks, as Hibbard puts it, 'to tear away [Michelangelo's] idealizing mask' and to expose 'the true source' of his devotion to male nudes."[46] Jarman's more explicit representations of homosexual desire might be seen to be doing the same thing to Cocteau and Pasolini. We might even see in Caravaggio's early mentorship by Cardinal del Monte and his older, homosocial milieu[47] an echo of early patrons of Jarman such as Frederic Ashton and John Gielgud. But if the biographical echoes caught Jarman's attention, it is the artistic similarities that are clearly most important, in the shared formal and thematic concerns.

In terms of form, the most obvious similarity or debt is the use of light. Caravaggio, Jarman provocatively stated, invented cinematic light, and he notes that he and the lighting designer strove to reproduce as closely as possible the lighting in Caravaggio's paintings. Caravaggio's chiaroscuro is for many the most readily identifiable feature of his artwork, one remarked upon by his contemporaries and imitated by many who came after him. Bellori, one of the chief historical sources, reports: "He never made his figures emerge into the open light of the sun; instead, he invented a method whereby he placed them in the brown air of a closed room. Then he chose a light placed high above, which falls in a plumb line on the principal parts of the body, leaving others in the shadow. In this way he attains a great force through the vehemence of his light and shade."[48] The effect is occasionally called "cellar light," and Bellori's description of the method calls to mind immediately *Edward II*, which gives the impression of being shot underground. Bracketing off the two experimental features (*The Last of England* and *The Garden*), one can see this use of stark lighting and indoor settings as a characteristic of the feature films that will follow.

Caravaggio's lighting, in contrast to that of many of his contemporaries, does not uniformly illuminate the pictorial space. One immediate consequence of this is the relative paucity of objects in his paintings, and a relative lack of interest in settings. Walter Friedlaender remarks on "Caravaggio's warm feeling for the material value of the single object,"[49] which is characteristic of the almost fetishistic quality of certain of Jarman's props, and in particular the knife that Caravaggio carries with him throughout the film. In *Dancing Ledge,* Jarman talks about the importance of getting right the few props they used, and in the notes accompanying the *War Requiem* script he states: "I have developed an intense feeling for what, I think, is mistaken as the 'object' world. I hope this can be seen in my films."[50] Caravaggio's restricted use of props means that the significance of the objects that remain in the paintings is necessarily heightened. In the case of the early painting of the penitent Mary Magdelan, for example, it is only the objects at her feet—the broken string of pearls and the jar of perfume—that identify her as the biblical figure, because she is dressed in late-sixteenth-century clothing. This is precisely the reverse of the way that Jarman uses anachronistic props to solicit our attention: the poisonous critic (and rival painter) Baglione uses a typewriter in order to enforce the connection between Renaissance and modern critics, and the bath in which he sits creates a further, more complicated set of historical connections.

Baglione's voice-over at this point connects Caravaggio's lighting with his morality, complaining of a "conspiracy between Church and gutter. Those who love art must be alerted to this poison that seeps into our Renaissance, as insidious as the dark shadows that permeate his paintings, cloaking his ignorance and depravity." The critic's pairing of aesthetics and morals is apposite. His excoriating comments echo the Thatcherite historian Norman Stone's infamous attack on Jarman in the *Sunday Times* ("Sick Scenes of English Life"), as well as a host of other reviews that thinly veiled their homophobia with aesthetic objections.[51] Further parallels arise in relation to Baglione's pose in the tub, which reproduces Jacques-Louis David's *Death of Marat.* Jarman associates David with a school of historical representation that is in direct opposition to both his and Caravaggio's: "The 'scientific', archaeological method forged by Poussin became a war cry in the late eighteenth century with the painter David; then in the nineteenth century it became a neurosis, as painting turned into an obsessive catalogue of detail."[52] The bathtub pose is not so much anachronism as the vehicle for a series of analogous comparisons. Caravaggio's approach to history opposes Baglione's, as Jarman's does David's, or as Jarman's cinematic approach to the past differs from that of more celebrated films of the so-called British Film Renaissance such as *Chariots of Fire* or *A Passage to India.*

Caravaggio's use of light to define fairly restricted, shallow spaces went against the prevailing artistic fashion, which was interested in fully illuminated, three-dimensional spaces that demonstrated a mastery of Albertian perspective. This is often read, rightly or wrongly, as a shortcoming of Caravaggio's technique. Hibbard notes that "His ability to paint figures in a believably receding space was deficient" and thus "He always worked within a relatively narrow foreground space."[53] Warwick argues instead that Caravaggio consciously rejected and challenged Albertian representation, "eschew[ing] that tradition in favor of bas-relief compositions, with the figures close to, even pressing through, the pictorial plane and a dark background immediately behind then closing off any illusion of deep spatial recession."[54] After *Caravaggio,* this treatment of space would also become an increasingly obvious visual feature of Jarman's narrative films: the later films show relatively little interest in composition in depth, often restricting the action to a single visual plane, and this restriction frequently results in *tableau vivant*-style compositions. In keeping with this lack of interest in visual perspective, outdoor scenes are not a prominent interest of either the painter or the director. *Caravaggio* is filmed entirely indoors, in sets that were spare owing to financial necessity, but that fortuitously evoke the spaces in Caravaggio's paintings. And, like Caravaggio's disinterest in Albertian perspective and receding background landscapes, Jarman's lack of long shots rules out the period film's dominant style of realism (and in particular the establishing shots of heritage properties and landscapes) in favor of a more self-consciously stylized approach to the past.

For Caravaggio, the restriction of space by light was crucial for creating a new relation between painting and viewer. Friedlaender notes that Caravaggio reverses the usual arrangement of the colors, so that the brightest are in the foreground, and they darken as they recede. The result is that "We no longer look into a fictitious world set apart by design, color, and light; the entire construction seems to come physically toward us as if entering step by step into the world. We are made recipients of the miracle."[55] Hibbard discusses a similar effect in the painting *Supper at Emmaus,* where an arm extends outward toward us:

The left arm of the gesticulating disciple unites the painted actors with us, the living viewers, in a manner that signals a new age of participatory art. The spectator is almost forced to take part in the painted religious drama. Mannerist artists had long been toying with the illusion of continuity between spectator and painted scene, but in general these were tours de force that called attention to themselves as illusions rather than to the subjects and their meaning.[56]

We get a similar and even more dramatic gesture in Jarman's film when, after Lena's death, Caravaggio turns, points directly at the camera, and shouts, "Curse you!" holding us somehow responsible for, or at least implicated in, her death.

As Hibbard's, Warwick's, and Friedlaender's comments suggest, the particular way of rendering pictorial space works along with Caravaggio's interest in the historical subject matter. The immediacy of the presentation works to impress on viewers the direct relevance of the historical material to their lives, implicating them in the lesson of the work. Other elements of the paintings support this particular relation — the naturalistic elements of dirty feet and fingernails, for example, or as Bersani and Dutoit note, the frequent thematization of the act of looking in the paintings:

> Not only are there all the looks, poses, and expressions that enigmatically solicit our attention, depriving us of the spectatorial luxury of a space outside the painting occupied only by an undisturbed, contemplative viewer; the engaged viewer . . . is also frequently incorporated into the work as a witness of its subject, thereby explicitly making the relation between the painting and the viewer that which the painting itself performs.[57]

Caravaggio's experiments with space, light, gestures, and color work to refashion the relation between the viewer and the imagined space of the painting: the world of the painting pushes outward the viewer, at the same time that it makes the spectatorial relation (and hence, the spectator) one of the subjects of the paintings themselves.

As we can see from the accusing finger that points out at us from the screen, Jarman learns from the painter and similarly makes the audience the subject of the film. This is partially realized by taking up the painter's approach to historical subjects and the historical vision it encourages. Along with the various formal techniques that push the composition outward, Caravaggio's use of contemporary models and his mixing of historical and contemporary costume insist upon the connection between the historical subject matter and the viewer. History, the paintings suggest, exists within the present, bodied forth by the models. Historically themed art offers us access not to the past but to the way the past is meaningful within the present. The anachronistic objects in *Caravaggio* can be seen to be working in this way, showing how the past inhabits the space of the present. As we have seen, these objects solicit the viewer in more and less complex ways, but always with the effect of preventing us from consuming the film as a coherently rendered spectacle of the past that allows itself simply to be passively observed. The golden calculator, upon which the banker and art collector Giustiniani taps, reminds us that commerce was just as much a factor in the production of art in the sixteenth and seventeenth centuries as it is now, whereas the Italian neorealist costumes make a slightly more complicated point by tying together the social impulse of Caravaggio's art, one of the more recognizably socially engaged filmmaking schools (Italian Neorealism), and the aims of this particular film.

As we saw in the discussions of the super-8 shorts, Jarman's interest in space went beyond reforming the relation between audience and screen (although this was clearly an important aim). Those films often acted as explorations of the experience of space, and in particular the social relations that different spaces fostered or allowed. I argued that this exploration was related to gay liberation discourse, which was concerned with colonizing public space and with challenging the meaning and the use of spaces—like the home—in order to facilitate new social relations and new ways of being in the world. Jarman's interest in these films was both documentary (attempts to record or convey the experience of these new spaces) and theoretical (looking at the possibilities of cinematic space for remaking affective relations or subjectivities). Both of these concerns find their way into *Caravaggio*, but, as with *Sebastiane*, locating the action in the past allows Jarman to portray a different spatial regime, which will allow for an exploration of different kinds of social and affective relations.

Caravaggio is clearly imagined by Jarman as an alter ego, the painter's studio as a film studio, and the canvas as an analogy for the cinema screen. The equation of canvas and screen is directly established in the title sequence, where the credits are superimposed on a canvas that is being prepared for painting. Jarman imagines the act of painting not so much as the creation of art, but rather as the analysis of a social field. Part of Jarman's method in the film is to pick up on Caravaggio's use of lowlife models and extend it, making the models all characters in an invented biography: del Monte, whose surname was Francesco, becomes the model for the Saint Francis paintings; Pipo, a young hustler, becomes Love in *Amor Vincit Omnia*. Whereas in the paintings there is a productive tension between the body of the model and the character portrayed (47), in the film the relations become even more complex because of the biographical dimension. Michele's struggle to paint Ranuccio as the executioner becomes a struggle to understand his own desire, which is bound up with a larger attempt to analyze and understand his world and all of its social relations.

Bersani and Dutoit argue in their study of the painter that, "Like all painting, Caravaggio's work is about forms of connectedness in space" (42). However, this investigation of spatial relations is particularly evident in the work of Caravaggio: "The ontological laboratory of Caravaggio's work includes many... models of relationality" (63). It is important to remember that the exploration of space and of spatial relations is more than simply a theoretical or formal concern: "Modes of relationality in human life are 'deduced from' our perceptions of spatial relations. More exactly, they are imitations of our body's experience of space" (ibid.). Moreover, as theorists of space from Benjamin to Jameson point out, spatial regimes are historically and culturally specific. Thus representations of space are at the same time representations of ways of being in the world, either actual or possible. The latter, suggest Bersani and Dutoit, is the main interest of Caravaggio's historical subjects: "Caravaggio's paint is the metaphysical X ray that compels us to see particular histories and particular myths as instituting relationalities" (42). Given that the canvas is in this film posited as an analogy for the screen, we can make a similar argument about Jarman's interest in historical subject matter, and particularly the Renaissance. Challenging the relationalities founded by "particular histories and particular myths" is central to his cinematic project.

The scenes of painting in the film show us a particular mode of thought in action, as Caravaggio oscillates between the models in front of him and their representation on the canvas. The occasional discrepancies between model and painting remind us of the work performed by art, something explored earlier in *Imagining October*. The film functions along parallel lines: the manifestly artificial space of the sets reminds us that this is not a pure reflection of the world, but rather a reflection on it. As James Tweedie notes, the film places much of the action in the artist's studio. Not only does this focus attention on the work and the process of art, it also shifts the locus of affective relations in the film into a semipublic, semiprivate space; the second sequence of the film makes this explicit, by taking the boy Jerusaleme out of his home and into Michele's studio. Later, Michele says to Jerusaleme: "You are my Saint John, and this is our wilderness." To abandon the home is also to abandon the modes of subjectivity and affective relations that it supports.

The studio is not a simple substitution for the space of the home, or, in Tweedie's account, "a refuge from and a microcosm of the social forces at work outside that seeming refuge,"[58] but a more neutral laboratory for explorations of spatial and affective relations that mirrors the explorations on the canvas. The studio becomes the locus for a whole range of options for being together, shown in the first instance through the relations between Michele and others: with his young assistant and companion Jerusaleme, his friend and sometime lover Davide, his older patron del Monte; his desire for the heterosexual Ranuccio, his nonsexual love of Lena, his camaraderie with the various hustlers who are his models and with whom he no doubt has affairs. Other kinds of relationships exist alongside this—Jerusaleme's competitive jealousy of Ranuccio, or his friendship with Lena, for example. In this alternative space of the studio exist many varieties of homosexual, heterosexual, and nonsexual relations, symmetrical, asymmetrical, and triangulated desires; this is perhaps most in evidence in the scene where Michele is painting Ranuccio as Saint John, while Pipo, Lena, and Jerusaleme exchange looks with the artist and his model.

The film offers not so much the exploration of a particular way of being in the world as the positing of a space of multiple, shifting, and
metamorphosing relations, a more complex and diverse sociality that
is not based on the values of the home. It departs from *Sebastiane*'s
rather narrower (and idealized) differentiation between two kinds of
homosexual desire (liberated and heterosexually identified) to consider
a whole spectrum of affective relations, a consideration that is bound up
with an exploration of alternative spaces. The film thus shares to a large
extent the project Foucault outlines in his essay "Friendship as a Way of
Life": "The problem is not to discover in oneself the truth of one's sex,
but, rather, to use one's sexuality henceforth to arrive at a multiplicity
of relationships."[59] The work of art and the work of homosexuality
merge in the studio, whether this is Caravaggio's or Jarman's.

Critics have tended to narrow the focus of the film's interest to
Michele's masochistic desire for Ranuccio, occasionally (and to my mind

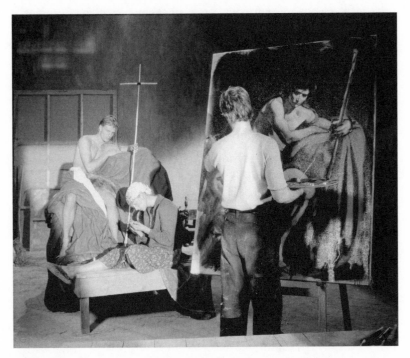

The world of the studio in *Caravaggio* (1986). Ranuccio (Sean Bean), Lena
(Tilda Swinton), and Caravaggio (Nigel Terry). Photograph by Mike Laye.

improbably) reading Ranuccio as homosexual. This is, of course, an understandable response to a filmmaker who puts sexuality at the center of his vision, but it downplays considerably the complexity of the film's representation of an alternative sociality. Such an approach to the film rules out the interpretation of Michele's killing of Ranuccio that emerged from the evolution of the script. For example, in one of the most perceptive discussions of the film, Murray argues that "Lena's gaze usually works in *Caravaggio* to enhance the homosexual passion of Ranuccio and Michele. This is especially true when she attends the painting sessions in which Ranuccio maintains manly erotic poses for Michele's epic canvases. Her presence seems to inflame the sadomasochistic intensity of the men's growing desire."[60] This leads Murray to the position that "Ranuccio's justification for the murder is that he drowned her to purify his 'hom(m)o-sexual' love for Caravaggio." There is, however, little evidence in the film that Ranuccio has any sexual desire for Michele, although he is happy to encourage Michele's desire if it means more money; he is, in essence, as Lena observes, a rent boy, with some friendly affection for his generous client.

A much more straightforward reading of Lena's murder is that Ranuccio kills her out of possessiveness and sexual jealousy because she has left him for another man. This jealousy is earlier on display in the studio, when he glowers at Lena and Michele after Michele has presented her with a sumptuous gown and the two kiss; Michele's economic power is clearly the cause of much envy and resentment. Ranuccio's jealousy is also prominent in his final exchange with Lena, when she announces that she is pregnant and that she is leaving him to become Scipione Borghese's mistress:

RANUCCIO: The child? Whose?
LENA: Mine and mine alone.
RANUCCIO: What about us?
LENA: You have Michele. I have Scipione. And the child shall be rich beyond avarice.

This announcement is accompanied by a quick montage of scenes of Ranuccio and Lena kissing, a montage that clearly acts as Ranuccio's memory. It is thus nonsensical to accept at face value, as many critics appear to do, Ranuccio's explanation to Michele that "I did it for you—for love!" Lena, having left, was already out of the way, and Ranuccio, having been saved by the now-powerful Michele, is simply continuing the flattery that brought him this far. Michele, on the other hand, now sees the relation clearly—or, more properly, the implications of that relation—for the first time. (Significantly, the voice-over at this point describes Pasqualone, the object of a boyhood crush, as Michele's "one true love.") Michele's realization is less about Ranuccio than it is about his own desire, a realization that the betrayal involved in desiring that which despises you is not simply a betrayal of the self, but also an acquiescence to the premises of that contempt. His murder of Ranuccio acts as a refusal of an entire system of murderous relations that extends far beyond Ranuccio, and of which Ranuccio is only in this instance the most visible manifestation and Lena the most immediate victim. It is at this point that we might see Michele as anachronistically taking up the heritage of Jean Genet, and willingly assuming the role of criminal, in order not to be implicated further in a corrupt and murderous sociality. It is in this restricted sense that Michele is a romantic figure in the film, when he embraces the motto on his knife: "No hope, no fear."

It is Pasqualone, not Ranuccio, who is identified as Michele's "one true love" in the voice-over that punctuates the film and that acts for the most part as deathbed reminiscences from Michele. These voice-overs are largely addressed to Pasqualone, and they tend to oscillate between the final moments of Michele's life and memories of his childhood idyll with his first love. The oscillation echoes the film's movement between the deathbed scene and the preceding events of his life, and induces the same kind of double vision that is called for in Caravaggio's paintings, seeing the past through the present and asking us to speculate on the connection. The voice-over works to create, as Dillon observes, an "auditory space" in the film that is largely separate from the images.[61] This particular kind of memorial or memorializing space will be most fully realized in Jarman's final film, *Blue,* where, coincidentally, Nigel Terry's voice is heard again. In both films, this auditory space divorced from visual representation allows for the most direct reflection on desire and, indeed, love.

We do see Pasqualone once, in a scene toward the end of the film that follows the killing of Ranuccio. A voice-over links the two scenes, although it describes events unrelated to the scene that we see. Pasqualone and the boy Michele are standing against a wall, watching a parade of Easter penitents carrying crosses who pass in front of them. Michele is dressed as an angel with golden wings, wearing a wreath in his hair that echoes both the wreath we have earlier seen worn by the sick Bacchus and a golden wreath seen in Cardinal del Monte's chambers.[62] Michele turns and enters a large doorway hung with a gauzy cloth, reminiscent of a proscenium arch. He calls to Pasqualone, who follows him in. They turn and look at a *tableau vivant* based on Caravaggio's *Entombment of Christ,* with the adult Caravaggio taking the place of Christ in the tableau. All of the other figures in the painting, two men and three women, will reappear almost immediately in different guises in the final scene of Michele's deathbed.

As we saw in the discussion of the development of the script, this replaces an earlier scene that had a gardener and the young Michele coming upon a cave, and entering to see a tableau of the *Resurrection of Lazarus,* with Ranuccio as Lazarus and Caravaggio as the gravedigger who is lifting him up. This would have worked with the romantic gay love story originally planned: Caravaggio accidentally murders his love, but can resurrect him through his art. This painting offers a rather more limited optimism, as the resurrection has not yet happened. Bersani and Dutoit argue that this scene and the deathbed scene that follows make visible an identification that the film makes between Jarman, Caravaggio, and Christ. If it is making such an equation, I would argue that the film is making it only in a very qualified way, or only as a way of making a claim about the potentially transumptive power of art.

The elements of this final tableau scene must be read in relation to the rest of the film and, indeed, to Jarman's earlier films. Angels and their classical equivalents show up most frequently as representatives of gay desire in his films: the character named Angel in *Jubilee,* the angel Ariel in the same film, the implied interlocutors of *The Angelic Conversation,* and of course, earlier in this film, the randy cupid figure in the tableau of *Amor Vincit Omnia,* modeled by the young hustler Pipo. That figure had rather tawdrier wings made of real feathers, as opposed to the young Michele's golden ones, but this difference clarifies rather than

The boy Caravaggio (Noam Almaz) as angelic desire.

denies the relation between the two figures. Further, the wreath in his hair suggests a relation between the young Michele and the young Bacchus he will later become. The boy Michele is the most innocent angel to show up in Jarman's work, and it shows up in the context of the purest and most idealized desire: the young boy's first awareness of love. The innocence works not to condemn as fallen the rather more earthly or sexual angels that will follow, but rather to insist on the purity of the desire that lies at the heart of that, and indeed all, sexuality. To quote the epigraph of *The Angelic Conversation:* "Love is too young to know what conscience is / Yet who knows not conscience is born of love."

The space of this encounter is also vital. The tableau is reminiscent of all of the other tableaux we have seen in the film, which connects this scene with the studio and the work of painting. We can expect, then, that, like the other studio scenes, this one will be concerned with relationality and with ways of being together. There is, however, no painter here, and the boy Michele enters through what appears to be a theater curtain or a primitive screen, framed by a proscenium arch. He and Pasqualone leave the world of the historical and enter into the space of art. There is no way of resolving this scene realistically, as we can do with the other tableaux in the film; the violation of temporality makes this what I have been calling a purely cinematic space. This is another version of the film's attempts to challenge the border between spectatorial space and aesthetic space, this time by having

Two versions of Cupid: Dawn Archibald as Pipo in *Caravaggio*.

some of the characters cross over into a space defined by, or at least associated with, Caravaggio's memory (although it cannot be real memory). It is also possible that this scene is Jersusaleme's imagining, combining the deathbed figures in front of him with the story of Michele's original desire. Some of the first flashbacks in the film belong to him, and certainly his relation with Caravaggio bears some similarities to Michele's with Pasqualone (although they are by no means equivalent). Having spent his life wordlessly observing Michele painting, this may be his final observation on the relation between art and life.

If so, it is a consoling vision. It is not Ranuccio that is resurrected by Caravaggio's art, but Caravaggio himself. The conferring of immortality is a familiar enough claim to make about the power of art, on offer as well in *The Angelic Conversation:* "Not marble, nor the gilded monuments / Of princes shall outlive this pow'rful rhyme" (55.1–2). Here it is also a testament to Jarman's art, and its power to resurrect his predecessor *as* a predecessor, as a part of a gay historical tradition. If it is read as an encounter of the boy with his destiny, it is important to link this to the situation of the viewing: the boy and his first love. This is not to suggest the gloomy reading that gay desire leads inevitably to martyrdom, but rather that in art lies the possible salvation of alternative desires, in its ability to figure forth new modes of being, and of being together through its negotiations with the past.

This does not, of course, remove the story of martyrdom altogether. The film does return to the deathbed and to Jerusaleme's mourning. The repetition of the figures in the painting and the figures at the deathbed enforces a connection between the two scenes and asks us to consider the relation between them. The painting is a final, optimistic comment about the power of art, coming at the end of what can be seen as an investigation into the possibilities of art for offering alternatives modes of sociality, in order to accommodate alternative modes of desire. This balances the rather more severe assessment about the possibilities of the artist in the world. The oppositional artist is faced with the choice of complicity or criminality, neither of which is a terribly attractive option. Only art, suggests the film, can accommodate idealism.

FIVE

Thatcherism, AIDS, and War

JARMAN WAS DIAGNOSED as HIV positive in December 1986. *Caravaggio* was his last work of art not to be marked in some way by the epidemic. Although they are by no means limited to the subject of AIDS, the films, books, garden, paintings, and installations that followed together offer a sustained and complex meditation on the effects of the disease on Jarman, his community, and the British nation.

The works discussed in this chapter constitute a first response to the combined trauma of HIV and Thatcherite homophobia, although *The Last of England* was filmed (but not finished) before Jarman knew of his positive status. Characteristically for Jarman, even the most autobiographical work of this period, the memoir *Kicking the Pricks,* is not terribly autobiographical in that it insists on going beyond a narrowly individual response to the epidemic, always seeing the self as a function of the social. Formally, the book and the films all employ montage as a structuring principle to create meaning. The films employ different recording media and employ shock cuts and shocking content. Neither uses sync sound, and both are heavily dependent on music to structure the emotional experience of the viewer. Neither film has much of a narrative or even fully realized characters: what they are aiming at instead is creating an emotional response. *The Last of England* surveys a savage and terrifying landscape of loss, attempting to reproduce in the viewer the shock of learning what the disease revealed about the nation. *War Requiem,* while occupying a similar terrain, formulates a more positive response to the crisis, articulating a gay ethics of care.

The Last of England and the Landscape of Loss

In *Kicking the Pricks,* Jarman writes: "I've always taken a great interest in form. It's part of a painter's training, form and content. Very few film makers do that here."[1] This comes in the middle of a book whose form at first glance seems entirely haphazard: it is comprised of five sections, each of which is made up of smaller sections addressing, among other things, events from daily life and postproduction work on *The Last of England,* personal history, family history, cultural history, observations about the making of his earlier films, observations about art in general, poetry, and finally a variety of fictional sequences: fantasies about a future England and about alternative personal histories (where he becomes Sir Michael Derek Elworthy Jarman, British cinema worthy, or Margaret Thatcher's minister of horticulture, on the hunt for a blue rose). If the book functions as autobiography or memoir, it would appear that a highly idiosyncratic or entirely new kind of subject is being thus composed or documented.

Early in the book we learn that it was written while Jarman was at work editing *The Last of England.* Questions of editing, it is clear, are central to both the book and the film, and to their innovations. The film, like the book, is on the surface a fairly confusing mix of heterogeneous materials that threatens to overwhelm the viewer with its speed and content. Michael O'Pray accounts for the new pace that Jarman constructs in the editing, which stands in stark contrast to the dreamy progress of *The Angelic Conversation,* by pointing to the music videos that Jarman had made prior to this film, in particular the brilliant short film for The Smiths titled *The Queen Is Dead:* "The jumpy, edgy, speeded-up pixilation technique bristled with anger and tension and was unlike anything he had done before."[2] In her *New York Times* review, Janet Maslin called it, with some justice, "the longest and gloomiest rock video ever made."[3] The sound track is more varied than this might suggest, and anticipates the aural collage created in *Blue.* It combines Terry's voice-over with occasional sound effects, clips from speeches by Hitler, found elements from television and radio, and music that ranges from Elgar's "Pomp and Circumstance" to Diamanda Galás's AIDS-inspired *Masque of the Red Death.* The various elements of the sound track productively interact with each other, and the collage similarly works with and against the images on the screen, creating meaning through juxtaposition, as well as coaching an emotional response.

Jarman's enthusiastic embrace and exploration of new technologies and forms is a hallmark of his career; he explains his use of music-video techniques in the film by observing that "Music video is the only extension of the cinematic language in this decade, but it has been used for quick effect, and it's often shadowy and shallow."[4] This shallowness, as he would be the first to recognize, is attributable to the commercial purpose of the promotional video: its function is to sell records, not to change minds (or to sell by records by changing minds). Given Jarman's sense that commerce (and in particular advertising) had infected political discourse and was poisoning the English soul, it is ironic that he employs one of the most commercially oriented of artistic genres for this highly political film. He would not, of course, be the first artist to deal with this dilemma: the revolutionary filmmakers of Soviet Russia similarly struggled with the question of whether one could use capitalist forms for communist purposes.

The theories and films of Eisenstein, in fact, provide an initial entrance into an understanding of the new forms Jarman is experimenting with. In a couple of early essays, Eisenstein argues for what he calls a "montage of attractions," a nonnarrative form of theater or cinema that, as David Bordwell observes, "did not present action as 'a consequentially motivated development of individual fate.'"[5] Eisenstein explains his terms as follows:

> An attraction . . . is in our understanding any demonstrable fact
> (an action, an object, a phenomenon, a conscious combination,
> and so on) that is known and proven to exercise a definite effect
> on the attention and emotions of the audience and that, com-
> bined with others, possesses the characteristics of concen-
> trating the audience's emotions in any direction dictated by
> the production's purpose. From this point of view a film
> cannot be a simple presentation or demonstration of events:
> rather it must be a tendentious selection of, and comparison
> between, events, free from narrowly plot-related plans and
> moulding the audience in accordance with its purpose.[6]

The cinema of attractions dispenses with plot and character in favor of montage, in the belief that "philosophical thought would 'emerge

solely through the shock-like montage of the material.'"[7] This is presumably the principle at work in the presentation of the heterogeneous material (which would qualify as what Eisenstein calls "attractions") in both *The Last of England* and *Kicking the Pricks*: that an
ideological awareness would emerge, on the part of the reader or the
spectator, through the juxtaposition of the material, and that this presentation was inherently more politically effective than the presentation
of the story of an individual consciousness. With that in mind, it might
be inappropriate to see *Kicking the Pricks* as autobiography: at most
we could say that it uses autobiographical elements to push the reader
toward a particular political awareness. These autobiographical elements are necessary not for documenting the progress of an individual life, but rather because one of the political projects of the book is
to understand subjectivity in a different way, or to understand the
changing dimensions of subjectivity in response to cultural shifts.

One thing that differentiates the book from the film is the experience connected to each. Reading a book, regardless of how experimental the form, is a fairly sedate affair, whereas watching a film can be a
physically and emotionally jarring experience. Jarman wondered about
the pace of one sequence in the film in particular that comes closest to
the style of the music video:

> The images in the disco are not arbitrary, although there is an
> element of chance in the way they rattle along. The cutting is
> staccato, and aggressive. It would not be possible to cut film in
> this way, although theoretically you might attempt it. 1600 cuts
> in six minutes. The sequence crashes into the film unexpectedly,
> the pace is relentless. It should wind the audience. Why do I
> want to do this?[8]

This is reminiscent of the audience response to Eisenstein's first film,
Strike. Anne Nesbit notes that "Even a positive review was likely to
contain expressions of puzzled amazement at the dizzying speed with
which images replaced each other on the screen."[9] In both cases, what
is at stake is both the shock of a new way of seeing (connected to and
meant to convey a new way of being in the world) and the way that
this mode is necessarily experienced (and in both cases intended) as

aggressive. Eisenstein in particular envisioned cinema as an assault on the audience, the most extreme articulation of this being his declaration that "It is not a 'Cine-Eye' that we need but a 'Cine-fist.'"[10] Elsewhere he observes, a bit more moderately, that cinema and theater are linked "by a common (identical) basic material—the audience—and by a common purpose—influencing this audience in the desired direction through a series of calculated pressures on the psyche" (39).

Within this definition is the fairly radical proposition that the audience, not celluloid, is the basic material of film. This is implied as well in Eisenstein's insistence that "the montage approach [is] the essential, meaningful and sole possible language of cinema, completely analogous to the role of the word in spoken material" (46). The film, in other words, takes place only in the viewer's head, where the effect of the juxtaposition of images is realized. Along the same line, Eisenstein says that "the socially useful emotional and psychological effect that excites the audience . . . [is] the content of the film" (65). This provides a useful way of thinking about *The Last of England*: we might, following Eisenstein, argue that the real content of the film is the emotional and psychological effect it excites in its audience. As with the early super-8s, it is the experience of the audience that Jarman is principally interested in, not the footage itself. Although the actual succession of sound and images recorded on celluloid or tape is clearly important, the film cannot be said to exist outside of the presence of an audience, who are experiencing it through time.

Bersani and Dutoit react negatively to this address to the audience in *The Last of England,* arguing that the film "complicitously repeats the violence it represents. There is no distance between what Jarman does with his camera and what he condemns our culture for doing to all of us."[11] This objection is similar to André Bazin's critique of montage, which he argued was more coercive than narrative cinema. John Hill, in turn, points to the a key difference between Jarman and Eisenstein: "In Jarman's cinema . . . montage is used not so much to close down meanings as to open them up to a process of play. This is particularly so given how a film such as *The Last of England* appeals primarily to the emotions and senses rather than critical faculties."[12] This is similar to Jarman's own take on the film:

> *The Last of England* is not as manipulative as a conventional
> feature; you know—jump here, be frightened here, laugh.
> Traditional features manipulate the audience. Apart from
> being stuck with my film for 85 minutes, my audience have
> much greater freedom to interpret what they are seeing, and
> because of the pace, to think about it. I have my own ideas but
> they are not the beginning or the end. The film is the fact—
> perhaps in the end the only fact—of my life.[13]

Even Eisenstein, who was unapologetic about his desire to manipulate, recognized that ultimately the meaning arising from montage cannot be completely controlled by the filmmaker, as images inevitably have both individual and collective associations.

Another aesthetic forerunner for the film, one closer both temporally and geographically, is Humphrey Jennings, whom Lindsay Anderson singled out in 1954 as "the only real poet the British cinema has yet produced."[14] The unnamed interviewer in *Kicking the Pricks* draws attention to the parallels between Jarman's work and Jennings's, "whose films merge landscapes and action in a very poetic evocation of England."[15] Jennings was part of the celebrated British Documentary Movement of the 1930s and 1940s that was centered on John Grierson. This group of filmmakers, who were influenced by the work of Eisenstein and other Russian directors, made films that appealed to a communal spirit in Britain, often celebrating the workingman and the possibilities of the industrial age. Jennings himself was looked upon with a bit of suspicion by the mainstream of the movement, for his general refusal to "type" the working class, his less didactic approach to his subject matter, his interest in surrealism, and for what they saw as his dilettantism.[16] Like Jarman, Jennings was also a painter and a writer.

Annette Kuhn spends considerable time comparing *The Last of England* and Jennings's *Listen to Britain* (1942), arguing that the films "share a constructionist aesthetic and a modernist sensibility."[17] Jennings's short film (made with Stewart McAllister for the Crown Film Unit) is a portrait of wartime Britain. It eschews narrative and voice-over in favor of a montage of sounds and images of urban and rural Britain, intended to showcase both the resolve of the British and what Britain is fighting for. Jennings frequently uses juxtaposition both between and within shots to move the viewer: in a pair of shots, a field of wheat is apparently swayed by a bomber passing over; in a single shot, tanks rumble down a village street past timber-and-plaster Elizabethan facades. Although there are a number of other formal similarities between Jarman's and Jennings's work, including editing sequences to music, the strongest parallel between the filmmakers is, as Kuhn observes, "the intensity of a sense of *place* in both of them."[18]

Although Kuhn focuses on *Listen to Britain*, one might also look at Jennings's slightly later film *A Diary for Timothy* (1945) as a precursor to *The Last of England*. The film is structured by a voice-over address to baby Timothy, born in September 1944, and it juxtaposes his early life with the final months of the war. As with *Listen to Britain*, we are offered a montage of British life, both urban and rural, showing how the war has and has not affected it, including along the way some astonishingly beautiful shots of landscape: a reverse image of trees in fog reflected in the water, or the banks of a river after a snowfall at Christmas. Anderson observes of it, in words that could also apply to Jarman's film, "National tragedies and personal tragedies, individual happinesses and particular beauties are woven together in a design of the utmost complexity. . . . Such an apparently haphazard selection of details could mean nothing or everything."[19]

Some of the juxtapositions of images in the film are more or less thematic or explanatory. For example, shots of a recovering soldier are intercut with scenes of coal being distributed, while on the sound track radio reports of Russian victories in Poland are heard, all suggesting that things are getting progressively better. Other edits are a bit more ambiguous and disturbing: most disturbing of all is a final sequence that intercuts shots of Timothy sucking on a missile-shaped bottle with scenes of a bombing raid in Germany. A shot of a burning forest dissolves into a victory celebration around a bonfire, and the shot of the bonfire then slowly dissolves into a shot of the baby in his crib, making it seem momentarily as if he is in flames. This is, at best, a highly equivocal rendering of victory.

What is most interesting about the film is its strange temporality. It is addressed to a future Timothy, and it wonders what Timothy will make of these events and this world, and what comes after: "What's going to happen in the years that follow, when you are here and we aren't?" It raises, somewhat ominously, the different problems of peacetime, when the imperative to cooperate will not be as strong, and one is once more free to complain and criticize and choose. These worries are contained to some degree by the structure of the film. Its address to a newborn infant means that everything in the film is assumed to be in need of explanation. Not just the events of the war, but also things like social inequality are potential enigmas to Timothy, and so have to be dispassionately explained. This fiction allows the film to address (if not directly acknowledge) an anxiety in its contemporary audience: with the war ending, all of the suspended questions about the nation, along with new ones raised by the war, will have to be addressed. Will the promised classless society, the reward for the people's support of the war, emerge, or will we be faced with some new version of the bad old days? The implication is clear that this is the last of one version of England, and no one is entirely sure what will take its place.

In that regard, *The Last of England* may be seen as offering something of a despairing answer to the anxious questions raised by *Diary for Timothy*, particularly those questions about social consensus. The narrator's question to Timothy—"Are you going to have greed for money or power ousting decency from the world as they have in the past, or are you going to make the world a different place, you and the other babies?"—is answered in the negative by the Thatcherite era. In one notorious sequence of *The Last of England*, a naked homeless man stands beside a fire in a vacant lot and crams raw cauliflower into his mouth, while a montage of clips from commercial radio and television is heard on the sound track ("Do you want to make money? Of course, we all do."). Coincidentally, Jarman's film includes home-movie footage of himself as a child playing in a garden during or just after the war, which strongly echoes the footage of Timothy in his middle-class house with his beatific young mother. In this Diary for Derek, however, the bombed-out buildings of the Blitz are replaced by the abandoned houses and factories of Britain's industrial decline, and a nervous optimism has given way to anger and despair: we go from the people's war to Thatcher's war on the people.

Steven Dillon draws attention to the opening image of Jarman writing in his studio, which is accompanied by a poetic voice-over spoken by Nigel Terry.[20] This opening evocation of poetry brings us back to the characterization of both Humphrey Jennings's and Jarman's compositional method as poetic, which helps to clarify the difference that John Hill draws between Jarman's method and Eisenstein's. Eisenstein's montage is in the service of demonstration, the early films illustrating political and to some degree philosophical theses. This kind of demonstration is foreign to poetry. Helen Vendler argues that the job of a poet is to create "aesthetically convincing representations of feelings felt and thoughts thought."[21] We might use this to think about the way that *The Last of England* proceeds. There are a couple of productive reminders in Vendler's description: the film is not, in the first instance, political or philosophical analysis, but rather an attempt to mimic or represent structures of thought or feeling, and the primary grounds on which to evaluate its effectiveness are aesthetic. It is inappropriate to look for either narrative or thesis. This answers to some degree the critiques of the film that charge that its political analysis is shallow and its political imagery is obvious. The immediate recognizability of the political imagery is in fact necessary, because the film is not trying to make an argument about Thatcherism but to use images of it as poetic topoi, starting places for the articulation of a particular structure of feeling or emotion.

Politically, the film was a part of a whole group that emerged in the mid-1980s that reacted against Thatcherite policies and ideologies.[22] These films were in turn attacked by the historian Norman Stone on the front page of the *Sunday Times* "Arts and Leisure" section on January 10, 1988. The article, titled "Through a Lens Darkly," discussed an aesthetically disparate group of films (*Business as Usual, Empire State, Eat the Rich, My Beautiful Laundrette, The Last of England,* and *Sammy and Rosie Get Laid*), arguing that "their visual world has been dominated by a left-wing ideology." The article holds up *A Passage to India* and *Room With a View* as positive models for the English cinema, before descending into insult, calling the group "worthless and insulting" and ultimately "tawdry, ragged, rancidly provincial films." There were responses the following week from Hanif Kureishi and Jarman, with Jarman charging that "Stone's attack is contradictory because it comes from a supporter of a government that professes freedom in the economist marketplace yet seems unable to accommodate freedom of ideas." He goes on to attack two of his favorite subjects: English nostalgia and mainstream directors whose ambition is to go to Hollywood.[23]

I wanted to spend some time on influences on and precedents for Jarman's methods in *The Last of England,* as well as mention some of the parallel works of his contemporaries, partly to avoid seeing the film as the outburst of a "troubled psyche," an approach that renders all formal aspects of the film largely accidental or unconscious and the content as "uncensored fantasmatic confessions."[24] Two particularly interesting and productive readings of the film compare its formal structure to the work of psychic processes: Annette Kuhn argues that the "'dizzying phantasmagoria' of memory fragments" is evidence of the work of mourning, while Daniel Humphrey argues that the film "enacts a 'dialectics of trauma.'"[25] The anger behind the outburst is generally identified as either Jarman's anger at the state of Thatcherite England or a more a personal response to his own diagnosis with HIV, or both. These are not illegitimate readings of the film, although some care must be taken in identifying the film purely with Jarman's anger. For one thing, films are collaborative affairs, and Jarman was an unusually collaborative director; the footage was shot by a team of four (including Jarman), and it was edited by Jarman and four others. Tilda Swinton later observed that in contrast to *The Garden,* which seemed to her an "intensely personal" film, "the preoccupations of *The Last of England* were shared."[26] Even if one assumes that the controlling vision is his (not an unreasonable assumption), there is still a problem with timing, if one wants to associate the film with Jarman's own HIV status. In *Kicking the Pricks,* Jarman writes about hearing his diagnosis a few days before Christmas (it was December 22, 1986, according to Peake);[27] filming of *The Last of England* had begun much earlier, in August. There are few mentions of AIDS in the publicity notes and interviews for the film. This is not to say that AIDS was not a conscious or unconscious subject of the film (it clearly is). Certainly, Jarman was well aware of the epidemic, and had stalled on getting himself tested. But it does mean, at the very least, that the origin of the film is not a personal response to Jarman's own diagnosis.

In *Kicking the Pricks*, Jarman himself offers two varying characterizations of the film. At one point he calls it a dream allegory. As with *The Tempest* the film opens with a dreaming magus, only this time the seer is Jarman himself, in his Soho flat:

> In dream allegory the poet wakes in a visionary landscape where he encounters personifications of psychic states. Through these encounters he is healed. *Jubilee* was such a healing fiction, it harked back to Pearl and Piers Plowman. Which was also a socio-political tract. In *Jubilee* the past dreamed the future present. *The Last of England* is in the same form, though this time I have put myself into the centre of the picture. Here the present dreams the past future.[28]

Elsewhere he says: "The film is a documentary. I've come back with a document from somewhere far away. Everything I pointed the camera at (my fellow cameramen pointed the camera at) had meaning, it didn't matter what we filmed. This film is our fiction, we are in the story. After all, all film is fiction, including the news, or, if you want to reverse it, all film is fact. My film is as factual as the news."[29]

Jarman's characterization of the time structure in the film, "the present dreams the past future," is reminiscent of the strange tense of *A Diary for Timothy*, and his identification of the film as documentary is reminiscent of Jennings's method in general. In both of Jarman's characterizations of the film there is an emphasis on the strangeness of the terrain: either as a "visionary landscape" or as "somewhere far away." All of Jarman's films, and much of his other work as well, show a strong interest in questions of place, and in the experience of social space. The early super-8s, to which this film is obviously related, document a new experience of social space and the new ways of being (and being together) that correspond with these spaces. *Caravaggio* is at least partially a theoretical examination of relationality. This film registers a seismic shift in the understanding or experience of space, one that is partially related to the appearance of AIDS. This is most poignantly realized in the film in a sequence where an archaeologist uncovers a home-movie projector and film, alongside an ossified corpse: the world documented in the early super-8s is as irretrievably gone as Pompeii.[30]

The archaeology of super-8: *The Last of England* (1987). Photograph by Mike Laye.

The opening scene of writing and the voice-over establish the tense of the film as retrospective: "Imprisoned memories prowl thro the dark. . . . They scatter like rats in the echo. . . . Ashes drift in the back of the skull." It is, however, a future retrospective: intervening between the present and the time of the narration is some event that has irrevocably altered the landscape, some kind of collapse of society extrapolated from the tendencies of 1980s Thatcherite England: "Citizens stand mute watching children devoured in their prams. Tomorrow the dinosaurs move on. . . . In the silence of an English suburb power and secrecy dwell in the same house; ancestral gods have fled the hearth. Strange forces are moving in."[31] This and subsequent voice-overs are addressed to a young man named "Johnny," which echoes the structure of *A Diary for Timothy.* This strange new world is in need of explanation.

The immediate result of this unnamed event or collapse is suggested in the first third of the film, which is dominated by images of ruined, unproductive landscapes. A thuggish youth in ripped jeans and a leather jacket (Spring)[32] wanders through heaps of rubble, shoots up in abandoned factories, and attempts to destroy a copy of Caravaggio's *Amor Vincit Omnia* (painted by Christopher Hobbs for *Caravaggio*). Later he rolls about on top of it, apparently masturbating. Intercut with this are shots of abandoned and boarded-up suburban row houses and ruined council estates. All of the spaces invoked—whether work, home, or outdoors—are similarly desolate and unproductive. These scenes are largely shot in black and white, and then tinted in yellow or orange hues, making the sky look jaundiced and diseased. Contrasted with these are a few brief segments from home movies of Jarman's childhood, often in brilliant color—in particular, a backyard garden where two children (Jarman and his sister Gaye) and their mother play on the grass among flowers. The home-movie shots do not function as a kind of generalized nostalgia for the middle-class nuclear family of the 1940s and 1950s; certainly, Jarman was scathing enough elsewhere about elements of his own childhood, and later segments of the family footage implicate that particular family with the work of empire. But here, as with similar sequences in *Imagining October* and *War Requiem,* the home-movie shots stand in for what might be called the human: they show landscapes that are not hostile to desire, and to life, the kind of space that for Jarman is most often to be found in a garden. To pick up terms from earlier discussions, we can see the space of the home movies, within the larger context of the dystopia, as heterotopic. At the same time, they evoke the people's war, along with all of the other references to World War II, drawing attention to the sacrifices of Jarman's parents' generation to found the welfare state and the reneged-upon promise of consensus governance.

This basic contrast between the present space of the film, which is hostile to life and desire, and a past that is not, is developed in further ways in the other two sections of the film. The second section introduces the motif of the refugees, herded up by either soldiers or terrorists on a wharf. We see a short sequence of soldiers dancing, and later an extended sequence of a drunken yuppie fumbling about with a soldier on top of a Union Jack, amid bottles and garbage. The squalor of the failed sex scene connects the unproductivity of these spaces with the action of the state and the ruling classes. Elsewhere in the film this collusion is visualized by scenes of society matrons bearing poppy wreaths for what might be a Falklands memorial. The third section develops this contrast by featuring a series of related scenes about a couple, played by Tilda Swinton and Spencer Leigh (we have seen him earlier in the film, wandering through ruins); the press kit calls this "imagined sections of a feature film." In the present of the film, we see him executed by a firing squad, and her participating in a travesty of a society wedding. This leads into what is the most celebrated sequence of the film, featuring Swinton on a dock, whirling about in a fury, tearing at her wedding dress. Her frantic, extravagant performance is matched on the sound track by Diamanda Galás's wailing performance from her "one-woman opera" about AIDS.[33] The dress, reminiscent of the poisoned dress Medea sends to Jason's bride in Pasolini's *Medea*, has, through the progress of images in the film, become a dense locus of associations, as John Hill suggests in his discussion of the film.[34] What might be a symbol of life, desire, productivity, or joy is a corrupted and killing straightjacket: the perverse embrace of the state-mandated sexual identity, desire conscripted for imperialist projects, the forces of death choking the impulse of life. Intercut with this are "home-movie" sequences of the Swinton and Leigh characters together. Earlier we have seen "home-movie" footage of her in a field of flowers, which seem to function as the memory of the Leigh character. As with the first section of the film, the home-movie sequences are memories of spaces conducive to life and desire.

The poisoned dress: Tilda Swinton in *The Last of England*. Photograph by Mike Laye.

As with *Kicking the Pricks*, these moments of personal history (whether Jarman's or the characters') are placed in conjunction with public history. Other sequences from the Jarman family archive show us the bomber flown by Jarman's father in the Second World War, military parades in India, and shots of the Jarman family at a tea party in British India. These work in combination with other images, including the Albert memorial and reminders of the Falklands/Malvinas war. The subject, clearly, is imperialism, and the squalid end of empire: how we got here, and how it all ended. *Kicking the Pricks* begins with a fictional fantasia on the aristocracy boarding the boats as they flee the ruin of England for safe havens, and another about a disconnected youth listlessly roaming through discos, having joyless sex in a washroom: "He spat onto the floor, dropped to his knees, and put Johnny's limp cock in his mouth. Johnny came as if fulfilling an obligation, evaporating like the last gaseous bead in the warm flat beer, he buttoned up."[35] In both the text and the film, the collapse of the state (its abandonment of the people) and the ruin of desire are parallel events, both symbolized by barren landscapes.

If *The Last of England* is a documentary as Jarman claimed, what it documents is a new psychic terrain. It is not so much about Jarman's own diagnosis with HIV, or with HIV in general, or even with Thatcherism, but about a new subjectivity born of the collision of these things. AIDS brings with it a new sense of time. In an interview before his diagnosis, Jarman mentions that he has to make his next film in a hurry, because "No metropolitan gay man can be sure he will be alive in six years' time."[36] Postdiagnosis, one lives in a weird state of suspended time: "The sword of Damocles had taken a sideways swipe, but I was still sitting in the chair."[37] The diagnosis occasions a kind of grim rebirth through the knowledge of death, and the experience of social space has changed entirely: "As I joined the crowds at Oxford Street, I thought—could my perception of all this change, could I fall in love with it again as I did when I left home early in the 1960s?"[38]

Along with a new sense of time comes, necessarily, a new sense of history. Simon Watney noted in *Policing Desire* that one of the clearest awarenesses that came with the disease was that "gay men are officially regarded, in our entirety, as a disposable constituency."[39] The collision of HIV and Thatcherism causes for those concerned a historical revisioning, a reevaluation of the past in light of this new knowledge of the world and of the self's place in it. "Those concerned" are, of course, not only those who contracted the virus, although they are perhaps most directly concerned, but also all those for whom the appearance of the virus revealed something new about the nation, and their place in it: most often, those in communities that were most affected by the disease—gays, blacks, and drug users—but of course they were not the only people who were horrified by what the virus revealed about the nation. In the film, this community is evoked by the refugees on the dock who will leave England at the end of the film, those for whom the appearance of the virus was the last of England as they knew it.

Although there is no narrative in the film, there is nonetheless a structure and a progression. As in poetry, images recur and are recombined to advance the structure of imagery, and we see similar motifs (most centrally, frustrated or unproductive desire) developed in different ways in order to expand or complicate our understanding. One particular motif, a figure wandering with a torch, runs through the whole film. The progress of the torch traces a path through this dystopian landscape, suggesting the progress of an explorer through a strange

Refugees on the dock: *The Last of England*. Photograph by Mike Laye.

and hostile land. This motif is connected with that of the refugees on the dock, so that in the final shot of the boat leaving England, the fleeing group bears torches as it sails away. The progress through the dystopian landscape is, as is established in the opening writing sequence, a metaphor for the progress of thought and emotion; it is the visual and aural realization of a mind reacting to the hostile terrain of Thatcherite England. To return to Eisenstein: the true content of the film is the experience of watching the film. *The Last of England* reproduces in the mind of the viewer what it felt like to come to grips with the appearance of HIV, and, equally difficult, with the knowledge of what the virus revealed about the nation.

War Requiem and the Army of Lovers

If *The Last of England* could be renamed "Diary for Derek," *War Requiem* might equally be called "Listen to Britten." Shortly after finishing *The Last of England*, Jarman began work on a film for the BBC to be based on Benjamin Britten's oratorio, which was written as a response to the horrors of the Second World War. Britten's *War Requiem*, dedicated to four young soldiers, three of whom died in the war, premiered in 1962. Written for three soloists, a mixed chorus, and a boys' choir, the piece incorporates traditional elements of the requiem mass with settings of the poems of Wilfred Owen, the soldier-poet killed in the final days of the First World War, whose modernist poems inject realist content into traditional lyrical forms, protesting the pity of war and the sacrifice of young men.

There were several constraints put on the film. The original Decca recording would have to be used complete and unaltered, with nothing added to the sound track. Some of the investors wanted a narrative, which would have to be achieved without dialogue, and the whole thing was to be made for £680,000. Budget constraints had had a fortuitous effect on the filming of *Caravaggio*, leading to a visual style that mimicked the spare sets of Caravaggio's paintings. The challenge of creating a narrative and fitting visuals to a preexisting, well-known piece of music seems to have had a similarly fortuitous effect here. While the film has elements in common both formally and especially thematically with *The Last of England*, the films are polar opposites in terms of the way they feel. *The Last of England* is a loosely structured, aggressive film that makes no accommodation to the viewer or any concessions to visual pleasure. If it has a beauty, it is what is generally identified as a terrible beauty, the grandeur of its unsparing portrait of destruction and despair. Although *War Requiem* similarly uses a mix of different media, employs montage and other Eisensteinian techniques, and has moments of anger and pessimism, the sound track largely keeps the emotions reined in, which allows for a quieter reflection on the themes of the earlier film and greater emotional impact when the emotions do inevitably burst forth.

The film was shot on location at Darenth Hospital, a decommissioned hospital that provided interiors similar to those used in *Caravaggio*. It opens in the present, with an old soldier (Laurence Olivier) being wheeled out of the hospital by a nurse (Tilda Swinton), while in a voice-over we hear Olivier reading from Wilfred Owen's "Strange Meeting." The poem is the dream vision of a soldier who travels to hell, where he encounters an enemy he killed. The enemy soldier addresses him as "my friend" and is clearly an alter ego; the poem establishes the dominant thematic of the film, which posits the space of no man's land as a meeting place beyond the borders of nations and the demands of national belonging. Starting the film with a dream vision connects *War Requiem* to its immediate predecessor, *The Last of England*, along with other dream visions such as *Jubilee*.

The reading of the poem triggers a montage of archival images of war, which appear to function as the old soldier's memory. He shows the nurse a picture of a nurse from the First World War, which is followed by more archival footage of nurses outside a house or hospital. There is no sync sound, which opens a gap between the image track and the sound track, and immediately pushes the film away from realism. Sound and image will be directly joined only occasionally in the film: we see choirs singing parts of the requiem, and once or twice characters in the film apparently react to the music. For the most part, however, it is through the editing that the music and images relate, as the film uses the requiem to structure the sequence of the images. And just as Britten mixes modernist settings of the poetry of Wilfred Owen with the classical elements of the requiem mass, Jarman uses a range of filmic media, including video, super-8, and 35mm.

From the images of the old soldier we move back to the space of a tomb. A memorial candle is burning at the foot of a soldier, whom we will later identify as Wilfred Owen, stretched out on an altar or plinth. At the head stands a nurse (once again Tilda Swinton). In the script Jarman notes that the arrangement consciously echoes Charles Sargeant Jagger's war memorial in Hyde Park Corner. The shot itself is very formally composed, lit from above in a manner reminiscent of Caravaggio's "cellar lighting." The film will repeatedly return to this space, finally ending when Swinton walks out of the tomb and closes a set of doors, leaving us inside. This has the effect of identifying the film itself with monumental or memorial sculpture or architecture, which we will see repeated to some degree in *Edward II*'s sets. Like Britten's oratorio, the film identifies itself at least initially with a form of public memorializing for communal or national loss, simultaneously working within and against the form. The film juxtaposes this kind of space with another, no man's land, which exists outside of national belonging. Ultimately, the film wishes to leave the space of the tomb and what it memorializes behind.

From the memorial tomb we go further back in time. The narrative that structures the film involves four figures: a nurse, Wilfred Owen, an Unknown Soldier, and a German soldier. We see Owen and the Unknown Soldier enlist in the army, dig trenches, and prepare for battle. The nurse, meanwhile, prepares bandages and cares for the wounded. Owen, an officer, is often seen in parallel sequences attending to and comforting his men. A central incident in this narrative involves the Unknown Soldier playing a piano in no man's land. The German soldier comes upon him, and rather than firing, he lays down his rifle and throws a snowball at him. The Unknown Soldier turns, reaches down to make a snowball, and runs toward him. Owen, meanwhile, has mistaken what was going on. He fires at the German soldier's hand, and the German in confusion stabs the Unknown Soldier, and then lays him on a tangle of barbed wire and fencing. Owen then bayonets the German soldier. Later we see the Unknown Soldier as a Christ figure, wearing a crown of thorns and bearing the dead Owen across a battlefield. (Owen frequently compared soldiers to Christ, and commented in a letter that "Christ is literally in 'no man's land.'")[40] Toward the end of the film, he reappears at the center of a tableau re-creation of Piero

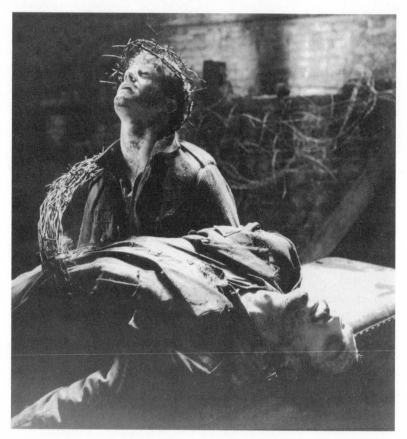

The soldier as Christ: The Unknown Soldier (Owen Teale) carries Wilfred Owen (Nathaniel Parker) in *War Requiem* (1989). Production still.

della Francesca's painting of the Resurrection, again as Christ. After Owen's death, we see Owen entering hell and encountering the German soldier, in an enactment of the poem "Strange Meeting."

With the exception of Owen, the characters in the film remain only loosely defined. We are never quite sure what the relation is between the nurse and Owen (they might be brother and sister), or whether in fact there is more than one nurse. The relation of the old soldier in the present-day frame to the characters in the World War I narrative is similarly undefined: clearly, he can't be any of the three main soldiers, because they all are killed. They remain, like the four main characters in *A Diary for Timothy* or the firemen in Jennings's *Fires Were Started,* or indeed, like most characters in an Eisenstein film, largely representative figures. The scenes in the narrative sequence are distinguished from other parts of the film by being shot in 35mm in warm colors, most often interiors in medium to close shots. The avoidance of exterior shots and long shots is, one assumes, attributable to budget limitations, as battles are expensive to stage. Nonetheless, it has the effect of creating an intimacy (if only by means of proximity) with these characters, who are not given any kind of psychological interiority. The rejection of filmic realism goes hand in hand with the rejection of psychological realism, which is part of the linkage Jarman's films make between spaces and subjectivities. We do see emotions, of course: in the film's tour-de-force sequence, we have a seven-minute, very tightly framed close-up of the nurse sitting on the tomb, rocking in time to the music and grieving. As we don't know what her relation is to the soldier for whom she is grieving, we cannot recuperate her grief into a psychological narrative; it remains, instead, the brute fact of grief, for the sufferings caused by war.

Although the characters aren't supplied with backstories and individual psychologies, they are given memories of home that are shot in super-8. Early in the film, Owen and the nurse reappear in civilian clothes with an older woman, attending to domestic duties like baking, hanging out washing, and planting seeds. The German soldier is given a memory of decorating a Christmas tree with his mother, and of diving under the bedcovers in a storm. Like the 35mm sequences, these scenes have an intimate feel; they often take place in pools of light with no visible sets, giving the impression of a floating, indistinct memory. What is notable about the sequences is that they are more or less the same domestic scene (with fathers conspicuously absent), making them a kind of no man's land of memory, existing outside of or anterior to national difference. The super-8 sequences function much like the home-movie segments of *The Last of England,* opposing the common humanity of the soldiers to the national differences to which they are sacrificed. This, of course, is one of the main preoccupations of Owen's poetry.

Owen's poetry is illustrated or referenced repeatedly throughout the film. The first time we see his corpse stretched out on the altar he is clutching a sheet of paper with "Anthem for Doomed Youth" written on it. We see him writing poetry at war, and reading from a book of poetry by Keats, his early poetic model. In one extended sequence we see him imagining the poem "The Parable of the Old Man and the Young," which retells the story of Abraham and Isaac with a significant shift at the end. As Abraham prepares to sacrifice his son according to God's command, an angel appears and tells him to sacrifice the "Ram of Pride" in Isaac's place. In spite of God's merciful intercession, Abraham "slew his son, / And half the seed of Europe, one by one."[41] As Owen sits with his eyes closed, we see the parable acted out. Abraham (Nigel Terry) looks like the priest in Eisenstein's *Ivan the Terrible,* with large gestures and exaggerated makeup, and looking on in approval as he sacrifices Owen are businessmen dressed like the caricatures of capitalists in Eisenstein's *Strike.* The use of the silent film conventions is appropriate because the sequence (like the rest of the film) works without dialogue, and it helps us to recognize that the parable is taking place in Owen's imagination. Moreover, the Eisensteinian conventions date from close to the same time as the action, and they signal a politically engaged art that parallels Owen's poetry. They fit in with the film's citation of a number of art forms that can be seen as responding to the horror of war.

The World War I narrative is interrupted by two other kinds of images. We are given images of the two different choirs singing parts of the requiem. These are shot on video against a blue screen, and imagery of war is matted in behind them. The film also integrates archival footage, most often from World War I. One longer sequence, however, includes footage from a number of twentieth-century wars, including footage from the Afghan resistance to the Soviet invasion. This sequence is dominated by shots of dead and dying soldiers, often being cared for by their comrades. In one, Afghani soldiers bind the face of a dead man, and then comb his hair in place. The inclusion of archival footage acts like the dirt on the feet of the pilgrims in a Caravaggio painting: it pushes the content of the painting out toward the viewer, insisting upon its connection to the other side of the screen. Moreover, by including footage from wars after Owen's death, it insists that the subject material cannot be comfortably located in the past. A similar argument can be made about the images of the choir singing,

Abraham (Nigel Terry) and Isaac/Wilfred Owen (Nathaniel Parker) in *War Requiem*.
Production still.

the members of which look directly into the camera. The film, in other words, draws attention to itself as film and as art.

The self-reflexive quality of the film is not an empty gesture toward the prevailing postmodernism of the time. A variety of elements in the film push the viewer toward a consideration of art's response to human suffering, and in particular to the sacrifice of youth in the name of national pride. In addition to the requiem itself, the film references, among other things, architectural monuments, poetry, the Francesca painting of the Resurrection, and film. Whereas *Caravaggio* looked at art's potential for reimaging relationalities, and the central question of *Imagining October* concerned the revolutionary potential of art, this film takes these inquiries in a different direction, in response to some of the same cultural developments that *The Last of England* reacted so strongly against: the appearance of AIDS, the Falklands/Malvinas war, and, a new cause for anger, the passage of the Local Government Act. The latter included the notorious Section 28, which forbade the promotion by local councils of homosexuality as a pretended family relationship.

In the published script of *War Requiem*, Jarman records a discussion that took place prior to the filming:

> At lunch today the conversation circled around Clause 28 and the homophobia that Benjamin Britten and Peter Pears were subjected to in the 1950s. Aldeburgh was sometimes referred to then—shamefully—as 'the two queers festival'. Perhaps, as my friend Duncan Campbell thought, the old consensus would seek its revenge. Donald [Mitchell] told me not to under-estimate the genuine anger that had fuelled the writing of this work. Benjamin Britten was a pacifist.[42]

Britten is often seen as an establishment figure, on the evidence of things like his opera *Gloriana,* his knighthood, and the condolence telegram sent by the Queen to Peter Pears on Britten's death. In spite of these, his position within society was precarious at best, as his interrogation by Scotland Yard at the height of the homosexual witch hunt of the 1950s would indicate.[43] Jarman's comments point to the connection between his era and Britten's: a Cold War Britain that linked homosexuality and communism, and which, as in the United States, pursued a terror campaign against suspected homosexuals, and 1980s Britain, when Thatcherite forces were fighting for family values and the Falklands Islands. The Local Government Act was passed into law on March 9, 1988, just as production was beginning on *War Requiem.* Jarman was not alone in seeing a connection between the two eras: "The Arts critic of *The Times,* on Feb. 4 [1988] argued that the resound-ing majority of the Clause proved that 'we have clearly returned to a pre-Wolfenden era of gay bashing . . . if not to Victorian values then at least to the long lamented witch-hunts and blackmail charters of the 1950s.'"[44] This return was reflected in the courts as well: "in England

and Wales in 1989, the police recorded 2,022 offenses of 'indecency
between males,' a figure which almost equals those caught up in the
first witch-hunt of the mid-1950s."[45] Just as he was caught up in the
earlier round of persecution, Britten in death came under official suspicion in the second: as a result of the new Section 28, schools in Kent
and Sussex canceled the performances of a touring production of Britten's *Death in Venice.*[46]

According to the composer Michael Tippet, Britten once remarked
that "I would be a court composer, but for my pacifism and homosexuality."[47] The qualifications that keep Britten from fully embracing the
nation—homosexuality and pacifism—are, of course, rather conse-
quential, and there seems to be a certain humor in the statement, even
if it is largely true. This resembles Jarman's own rather complicated
relation to national belonging, simultaneously conservative and radical.
In response to a question asking "why the Establishment is so upset
with [him]," he responds: "It's so simple. I am the Establishment."[48] He
goes on to deplore the current state of the nation, "a land in bondage to
the estate agent, PR, and runtish Tory MPs whose faces are deep in
the trough, selling off the Welfare State our fathers and grandfathers
died to create, to line their pockets. What patriots these?"[49] Britten's
operas are at least as pessimistic as Jarman's films about the dominant
culture. It has long been noted that in the operas, "the theme of innocence destroyed or betrayed, or evil triumphing over good, of purity
besmirched, or grace and virtue defiled or derided, frequently occurs."[50]
This story is most often centered on a conflict between a father figure
and a younger man. The older figure is often associated with patriarchal authority and mainstream masculinity, such as Captain Vere in
Billy Budd, erotically invested in the youth but fully prepared to sacrifice him to further his own interests. This is most obvious in Britten's
pacifist opera *Owen Wingrave,* where Owen refuses to follow in the
family line of soldiering and is subsequently killed. Jeremy Tambling
argues that

> It seems clear that Britten locates the war-spirit as linked to the
> oppression of the Father: 'But the old man would not so, but
> slew his son / And half the seed of Europe one by one' is

the end of the 'Parable of the old men and the young' in the
Offertory section of the War Requiem: the same happens in
Owen Wingrave, as it does too with Peter Quint and Miles in
The Turn of the Screw.[51]

It is also similar, we might note, to the dynamic between Severus and
Sebastian in Jarman's *Sebastiane*. The operas make an implicit connection that Britten made more explicitly in his remarks to Tippet, that
homosexuality and pacifism are logically consistent, and together they
are incompatible with the present form of the nation.

In the letter in which he asked the German baritone Dietrich Fischer-
Dieskau to sing in the premiere of the *War Requiem*, Britten says it is "a
full-scale Requiem Mass for chorus and orchestra (in memory of
those of all nations who died in the last war), and I am interspersing
the Latin text with many poems of a great English poet, Wilfred
Owen, who was killed in the First World War. These magnificent poems, full of the hate of destruction, are a kind of commentary on the
Mass."[52] Michael Kennedy argues that the Latin text and the poems
remain distinct, constituting "two planes of emotion, the ritualistic
Latin and the deeply personal English words."[53] As Britten's comments
suggest, the more private sentiments of the English words to some
degree work in opposition to or challenge the public sentiments of the
Latin. In Owen's intimate and subjective portrayal of the sufferings of
war, the causes of this suffering are continually signaled in the poetry.
"The Next War," for example, in the Dies Irae section of the requiem,
comments on the perversity of a war that kills men in the name of national ideologies. In "At a Calvary near the Ancre," included in the
Agnes Dei section, Owen points to the role that organized religion often
plays in the maintenance of national pride.

If, according to Kennedy's account, the Latin and the English remain
distinct, it is perhaps because they are ultimately irreconcilable, much
like Britten's own beliefs. Owen's poetry functions within the mass as
an inassimilable element that prevents any easy recuperation of the
losses the requiem memorializes, preventing us from seeing them as
necessary and worthwhile sacrifices in the interests of the nation.

It is not hard to see why Britten would have been attracted to the
poetry of Wilfred Owen, or how this poetry would fit into a work

that exploits structural oppositions to create productive dissonances. Owen's poetry itself incorporates stark realist elements into traditional lyrical forms, as a way of disrupting tradition. As an editor of Owen comments:

> Owen's major poems, drawing upon his searing experiences of the Great War, comprise a sustained subversion of poetic tradition. In his use of old and new techniques of parody, his ironic subversion of romantic forms and expression, and his innovative half-rhyme, he mocks the whole tradition of poetry. And in his content—the anti-romance, the anti-civilization of war in all its detail—he exposes the 'order' from which war emanated.[54]

These oppositional stances in Owen's work have been long been noted, and his relation to poetic tradition is partly visualized in the film by the book of Keats's poetry that the Owen character carries with him. Halfway through the film we see the book with grass growing from its cover, as if to suggest that this tradition of poetry has been rendered dead or obsolete by the horrors of the Great War (a gesture similar to the ossified corpse and the super-8 camera in *The Last of England*).

Douglas Kerr writes of Owen that following his meeting with the French modernist poet Laurent Tailhade, "The male body becomes established as the central theme of his work, a focus for his curiosity, desire and pity. And for him the question of writing modern poetry was henceforth never quite to be separated from the question of sexuality."[55] In his celebrated study of the literature of the Great War, Paul Fussell drew attention to the various homoerotic traditions of prewar poetry in England, and examined Owen's revisions of his poems. Of "Dulce et Decorum Est" Fussell observes that, "as in 'Disabled,' the effect of the revision is to efface indications of the poem's original Uranian leanings, to replace the pretty of 1913 with the nasty of 1917."[56] Fussell's remarks are astute, but we might want to see the revisions not as effacements of the poems' homoerotic elements (because they are still obvious), but rather as developments from them, an ethics that emerges in light of acquired knowledge. What the poems evince, to employ Shakespeare's terms, is a conscience that is born of (same-sex) love. As for Britten, for Owen homosexuality and an antiwar attitude are not just compatible, they are logically and necessarily related. For Owen as for Britten, the body of the youth was threatened by the Father, as is seen most immediately in the rewriting of the Abraham and Isaac parable. Britten's inclusion of Owen draws an explicit parallel between the impulses at work in the two world wars, and between their opposition to the sacrifice of youth in the name of national ideologies.

Jarman's film of Britten's work continues this forging of an oppositional tradition, based on a shared ethical understanding. Not only does the film connect the more recent wars in Cambodia, Afghanistan, and elsewhere to the two world wars, it implicitly connects, as we have seen, the Cold War witch hunts with Thatcher's moral crusade. This further solidifies the connection that both Owen and Britten make between twentieth-century nationalism and patriarchal masculinity. Stephen Jeffrey-Poulter notes that the appearance of AIDS fostered a resurgence of the 1950s figure of the dangerous queer in a new guise: "At the very time when the thawing of the cold war was making the old model of the homosexual as an automatic traitor outmoded, his role as a sexual fifth columnist was given a nasty new contemporary twist."[57] Leading the way in the promotion of this image of the queer-as-traitor were the British tabloids, who used the promotion of AIDS hysteria as a handy gambit in an ongoing circulation war. As Jarman documents in *Modern Nature* and *At Your Own Risk,* his public disclosure of his HIV status put him squarely in the tabloids' sights.

The spy scandal of the 1940s and 1950s involving the homosexual Guy Burgess was in fact the lightly fictionalized subject of *Another Country* (1984), one of the decade's more successful heritage films. As Richard Dyer and a number of critics have observed, the heritage film as a genre was unusually interested in the topic of homosexuality, and a number of other films or serials where homosexuality did not emerge as an explicit subject, such as *Chariots of Fire, The Jewel in the Crown, Brideshead Revisited,* and *A Passage to India,* were nonetheless marked by intense, highly eroticized relations between men.[58] This led some critics to defend the politics of the genre as liberal and progressive,[59] which many (including Jarman) saw as nostalgic and conservative, marked, argues Andrew Higson, by a "sense of timelessness rather than historicity in relation to a national past which is 'purged of political tension.'"[60] In those films where homosexuality is explicitly thematized, such as *Another Country* or *Maurice,* it is often pictured as antithetical to membership in the nation; in those films where it is not, an intense homosocial desire is often a key component of the affective pull of national belonging. As *War Requiem* would suggest, this is not a contradiction.

One example of the latter sort of heritage film, which places homosociality at the center of national belonging, is Kenneth Branagh's *Henry V,* released in the same year as *War Requiem.* This was the first of the Shakespearean adaptations produced by Branagh's Renaissance Films, released on Saint Crispin's Day, 1989 (the anniversary of the victory that acts as the climax of the film). Both directors claimed that their film carried an antiwar message, and both attempted to establish this critique through the juxtaposition of traditional music forms with scenes of battlefield realism. Both also came with complex cultural filiations: Branagh's film was closely related to an explicitly anti-Falklands production of the play by Adrian Noble (it features many of the same actors but little of the political commentary), but it is more obviously indebted to Laurence Olivier's patriotic 1944 version of the Shakespeare play.[61] Coincidentally, then, both *War Requiem* and *Henry V* invoke Olivier as the specter of a past war, and a past version of the English nation. It is worth noting, however, the differing ways in which Olivier is invoked by the films: in *Henry V* it is the youthful, vigorous Olivier of memory, reincarnated by Branagh as he delivers his Saint Crispin's Day speech from the same cart on which Olivier's Henry spoke. This is a doubled moment of nostalgia, both for the people's war (via Olivier) and glories of the Elizabethan stage, the latter of which was itself invoking an earlier moment of national triumph (Henry's fifteenth-century victory over the French). By contrast, in *War Requiem* Olivier appears as a very frail veteran, hands shaking too much to pin his medals on his chest, his voice still recognizable but quavering with age as he reads "Strange Meeting" in the voice-over.

The professed antiwar impulse of *Henry V* has to be balanced with Branagh's stated desire to popularize Shakespeare and to present Henry as an action hero. Henry's Saint Crispin's Day speech that summons his men to fight against the odds—"We few, we happy few, we band of brothers"—exhorts his men to invest in a central homosocial cliché of the action film, the band of brothers that acts as a metonymy for the nation. The antiwar message of the film is largely conveyed through a conventionally realistic presentation of battlefield carnage, backed by swelling religious music. Branagh describes the climactic scene in his autobiography: "To the accompaniment of a single voice starting the Non Nobis hymn, the exhausted monarch [bearing a dead youth] and his men would march the entire length of the battlefield to clear the place of the dead. As they marched, the music . . . swelled to produce a tremendous climax. There would be no question about the statement this movie was making about war."[62]

Indeed, even for the most sympathetic and approving viewers there was little question: "Embodied in this massive musical interlude is the quintessence of four centuries of popular British patriotism. Its incredible build-up in volume and intensity is like nothing so much as the old Promenade Concerts at Royal Albert Hall, where a thousand voices finally joined as one in singing 'Rule Brittania.' It creates a dream that is difficult to want to awaken from."[63] Although the battlefield scenes are not meant to trivialize the sufferings of war, the music encourages a particular attitude toward the spectacle. The crossover from a single voice attached to an on-screen body, to a huge, disembodied choir on the sound track singing a traditional hymn of victory removes the spectator from any implication in the scene, encouraging instead a pious attitude of acceptance and gratitude: this was a necessary loss, a worthwhile struggle. Worth remarking on is the figure of the dead youth that Henry bears across the battlefield, which unconsciously exemplifies Owen's critique of a nationalism that piously, and indeed joyously, sacrifices its young men on the altar of national pride, a nationalism that is seen in Britten's operas to be erotically invested in the youth thus sacrificed.

The film, like other heritage films, does not invite any explicit comparison between the past and the present day, in spite of its origins in an anti-Falklands theater production. This is the most important point of contrast between *Henry V* and *War Requiem*. Although period costumes and some props are used for the central Great War narrative, the possibility of creating the sustained illusion of the period film is impossible given the use of suggestive rather than realistic sets, the disruption of the 35mm sequences by super-8 and video, the direct address of the choir to the audience, and the incorporation of archival footage. Chris Lippard and Guy Johnson argue that the set itself constitutes a concrete political statement: "That the AIDS virus has created war conditions in Britain is materially expressed by Jarman's filming *War Requiem* in the newly abandoned hospital at Darenth Park in Kent. . . . Its setting, resonant of a decline in public health facilities, continues the demand for attention to physical suffering that pervades the earlier films."[64] The abandoned hospital is used to forge a direct link between the past and the present, between the attack on "the Welfare State our fathers and grandfathers died to create"[65] and the actual sacrifices they made. As with many of Jarman's films, a complexly layered temporal space results: the soldiers proleptically occupy a space that will act first as compensation for their sacrifice and later as the betrayal of it. They anachronistically haunt the ruins of the Welfare State.

Although the set is the most visible reminder of Thatcher's war on the people, and implicitly, her government's willful neglect of persons with AIDS and her homophobic legislation, the film responds not with the anger of *The Last of England* but rather with what might be seen as an ethics of care. It is vital that the climax of the Great War narrative, the snowball fight, takes place in no man's land. The film posits various versions of this no man's land that are not entirely divorced from the nation but can act as a refuge, and implicitly a site of resistance, within it. The film continually juxtaposes the realm of the human with the mechanized and dehumanized world of war, which is also the world of the nation and of the Father. We see this not just in the similar memories of the domestic that the soldiers are given, but also in the way that they care for each other in the trenches. The film parallels the actions of the nurse in the field hospital with the actions of Owen as he goes through the trenches, looking after his men. Rather than seeing the men fighting, we more often see them sharing food and cigarettes, shaving or comforting each other. Santanu Das argues that "the world's first industrial war, which brutalized the male body on such an unprecedented scale, also nurtured the most intensely intimate of male bonds. . . . A very different order of male experience, one that accommodated fear, vulnerability, support, succor, and physical tenderness sprang up."[66] These new modes of relation can be observed in the novels and particularly the poetry of the war, with which

Jarman was very familiar. This emphasis on caring for the male body, which stems most immediately from the Owen poetry, is indicative of a larger tendency in the film: the male body becomes, quite unusually, the recipient of tenderness rather than violence at the hands of other men. We see this in the archival footage as well, as soldiers care for the dying or rescue the bodies of their dead comrades. This further connects outside the film to the gay community's response to AIDS, and the responsibility it took on in the face of government inaction.

One departure that the film makes from Owen is its inclusion of women. Owen, C. Day Lewis observed, "had no pity to spare for the suffering of bereaved women."[67] Following the lead of Britten's work, which features prominently a female soprano, the film repeatedly turns to two female-defined spaces: the domestic sphere and the hospital ward. And, notably, it contains three substantial sequences of Swinton mourning: early on we see her grieving Owen, dressed as a nurse; we see her in braids and a loose white garment in the seven-minute sequence at the foot of the memorial, and later we see her in the same dress, digging into the mud of the battlefield with her hands. She, like the two central soldier figures, is also given a memory of home. The film is careful to underscore the parallels and the connections between the world of women and this other space of men, existing beyond the Father. Again, as with the AIDS crisis, women are shown to be bearing a substantial burden of the care and the grief.

Juxtaposed with the world of the bodily or the human or the domestic in the film is the world of the nation, most often represented by politicians and businessmen. Early in the film we see a boy wandering up to watch a recruitment pageant, as four men in clumsy drag dance around a grotesque Britannia figure, "while behind them four fat businessmen, in top hats and tails, carry scythes."[68] This echoes the society wedding of *The Last of England,* which similarly highlighted the lethal and perverse desires of the nation. The same visual style and message continues in the Abraham and Isaac section, where the caricatures of businessmen applaud Abraham's sacrifice of his son. The biblical parable is intercut with footage of George V and his staff, military victory parades, and fields of white memorial crosses. The message is relatively clear: while the pageant of nationalism might be grotesque and inhuman, its effects are nonetheless real and lethal.

There are no real authority figures in the "realist" sequences; Owen is the only officer we see for much of the film. Banishing the father figure from the trenches allows Jarman to concentrate on what might be called a Foucauldian ascesis, an art of the self that can lead to a different ethics of relations. This is where we see most clearly how the film develops the investigation into the oppositional possibilities of art that were explored most centrally in *Caravaggio. War Requiem* extends what was an almost hypothetical discussion—what are the possibilities for being together?—into the ethical dimension: how are we to relate to each other, in the face of this political and medical crisis?

By situating its action in various versions of no man's land, the film rejects the borders of the nation, and along with that those versions of selfhood that comfortably coexist with it. The film reminds us that along with nations go subjectivities and that subjectivities respond to national allegories, a point that Britten also makes in *Owen Wingrave,* and which was amply demonstrated by the response to Branagh's *Henry V.* The film instead returns to an ongoing project in Jarman's films, the Foucauldian project of forging new kinds of relations,[69] which here depends on a new relation to the male body. This brings us back to the timeliness of the film's political intervention. Foucault argues that "what most bothers those who are not gay about gayness is the gay lifestyle, not sex acts themselves . . . the common fear that gays will develop relationships which are intense and satisfying even though they do not conform to the idea of relationship held by others."[70] Foucault's words are directly applicable to the language of Section 28, which is not about homosexuality per se, but rather about the promotion of homosexuality as a "pretended family relation." The fear is not that homosexuals will have families, but rather that the meaning of the family and hence of the social may thereby be radically reconfigured. This is not an unreasonable supposition. It was, as we have seen, one of the central ideas of the Gay Liberation Front. But the Section 28 controversy also highlights the state's (and the press's) unseemly interest in homosexuality, and its willingness (indeed, eagerness) to sacrifice certain of its citizens.

The force of *War Requiem* is to reconfigure the lines of the nation by portraying modes of relationality and sociality that are at odds with the ones currently structuring the nation, modes that are the consequence

The grotesque pageant of nationalism: Claire Davenport as Brittania, with Spencer Leigh, Milo Bell, Richard Stirling, and Kim Kindersley. *War Requiem*. Production still.

of his homosexuality and pacifism. At the same time, the film works to consolidate a tradition of protest and dissent in twentieth-century British culture, by linking three artists—antiwar, homosexual patriots all—who protested against three successive British wars and, more specifically, against the sacrifice of youth in the name of the nation, without at the same time foreclosing entirely on the idea of the nation. Their oblique relation to the nation is characterized by a similar aesthetic move in all three artists: the interruption of "classical" forms (whether romantic poetry, the mass, or 35mm narrative film) with other more "personal" forms (realism, song, and super-8). The dominant is not thereby rejected, but rather interrupted. This inclusion of inassimilable "foreign" elements is not to suggest that the artists are interested in a liberal accommodation in the nation, but rather that they wish to commandeer the present version of the nation in order to redraw its boundaries.

Filmed at a time when the heritage film was flourishing, *War Requiem* both suggests and enacts a countertradition that consists of a series of countermoves, a history of interruption that is peculiarly appropriate for the construction of a gay history. In an interview regarding his relation to homosexual relations in history, Jarman states that "an orgasm joins you to the past. Its timelessness becomes the brotherhood; the brethren are lovers; they extend the 'family.' It was then, is now and will be in the future. I like the idea that we are linked in orgasm with Alcuin, St. Anselm or St. Aeldred, all of whom loved men physically."[71] *War Requiem* constructs a tradition of opposition that embraces the work of both Britten and Owen, a tradition based on a brotherhood of lovers rather than a murderous pact between father and son. In so doing it challenges the foundations of the nation through a contestation both of the meaning of history of Britain in the twentieth century and of the way that history was being filmed.

War Requiem's interest in the space of no man's land acts as a possible way forward from the ruined landscapes of *The Last of England*. Previous films had explored alternative or oppositional spaces like the studio, or the space of art itself; here, given the subject matter, the alternative space is one specifically defined in relation to the space of nationhood, the latter of which is materialized most ominously in the memorial tomb, which venerates the body of the sacrificial young man. No man's land allows for relations between men that do not correspond to the normative spaces of nationhood, which, while premised on homosocial attachment, nonetheless require the sacrifice of the male body in the name of national pride. The formal choices the film makes harmonize with this spatial construction: the rejection of interiorized, psychologically real characters is part of an almost Brechtian refusal to allow an easy recuperation of the traumas of war, as is the rejection of a coherent narrative that might engage our emotions rather than our intellects. The film refuses to allow the past to remain in the past, insisting instead on how it both shapes and haunts the present, while simultaneously constructing via the past an alternative space supportive of alternative kinds of community and communion.

SIX

Time and the Garden

IN 1986, Jarman purchased an old fisherman's house, called Prospect Cottage, in Dungeness. Located in the southeast corner of England, "Dungeness is set apart, at 'the fifth quarter', the end of the globe; it is the largest shingle formation, with Cape Canaveral, in the world," according to Jarman.[1] A protected environmental site, the ness is rather desolate in appearance and constantly buffeted by strong winds. It is, according to an article in the *New Scientist* magazine, an "extremely harsh" habitat, and "only specialist plants can survive such rigorous conditions."[2] Dungeness features some unusual freshwater pits, and is host to a number of plant, bird, and insect species that are only to be found there. The man-made elements of the landscape consist, for the most part, of small fisherman's houses, huts, and fishing boats, a lighthouse and a rescue station, a narrow-gauge railway that winds through the center and a couple of other notable human intrusions. One is a vast nuclear generating station, and the other is a military installation, the Lydd Ranges, which is near enough to hear the sounds of the shelling practice that takes place there.

On January 1, 1989, Jarman started keeping a diary (always intended for publication) of the progress of the garden he was making at Prospect Cottage. The diary comes to incorporate other details of his life, including the generally lukewarm reception of *War Requiem*, ideas for future films like *Edward II* and *Glitterbug*, and, more centrally, an account of the origins and the makings of the film *The Garden*. Three major works by Jarman are thus intimately connected: the memoir *Modern Nature*, the film *The Garden*, and the garden itself. The space of the cottage and the land around it is the literal and figurative ground of all three works.[3] One of the questions to be directed at the three is the nature of the connections between them: To what extent are they parallel works and to what extent are they complementary? How do they inhabit or qualify the terrain that all three occupy? What kinds of strategies do they have in common, and how do they work with the particular resources of their own artistic or cultural medium?

Time is a basic concern of all three, although it works in different ways in each: film is a time-based medium, a garden exists through time, and the book, by taking a diary structure, foregrounds sequential and calendrical time as its organizing principle. The experience of time in each is a central part of the way each work structures its relation to its audience. Watching *The Garden*, for example, is not an easy experience. For one thing, the film does not offer a narrative, which often serves to comfortably anchor the viewing experience. As with every film, the audience is at the film's mercy for the allotted time span: we do not control the time of the film or the pace of the experience. We are more aware of this subjection with *The Garden* for a number of reasons: the film thematizes different experiences of time, it plays with the literal speed of the images, and at points the film's direct address to the audience returns us to the space of the cinema, and hence to our own time. At other points we give in to its dreamy progress and simply drift with the images. The lack of a narrative means that we are left without a story's recognizable temporal markers, which frequently alert us to how far along in a film we are.

A book, on the other hand, is read at the pace of the reader. In the case of this book, the diaristic structure as organizing principle breaks the momentum of narrative. The progress or passage of time in the book is not determined by aesthetic demands (equivalent to the constructed time of a narrative film) but rather by an unrelated, abstract structuring principle: the sequential progress of the days. The fact that this kind of time is not responsive or even related to human concerns is something that the book exploits, given that one of its themes is mortality, and the amoral nature of disease.

The temporal experience of the garden is another matter still. One inhabits a garden in real time: what we might call the experiential time exactly coincides with spectatorial time, and duration is controlled by the visitor. However, as Jarman repeatedly insists in *Modern Nature*, time in the garden is not the same as the time of the clock:

The gardener digs in another time, without past or future, beginning or end. A time that does not cleave the day with rush hours, lunch breaks, the last bus home. As you walk in the garden you pass into this time—the moment of entering can never be remembered. Around you the landscape lies transfigured. Here is the Amen beyond the prayer.[4]

Time, and in particular the passage of time, is at the very heart of the experience of a garden, paradoxically, perhaps, because the story of time in the Western imagination starts with the exit from a garden. A garden solicits the attention of its visitors, but it does not structure the encounter in quite the same way that a film or book does. It is, in a sense, indifferent to the viewer, in spite of its solicitation: a garden exists through time and so we cannot comprehend it in a single visit, nor in the case of this particular garden resolve it into a particular perspective. A garden is forever a work in progress or process; we cannot step into the same garden twice. This brings us to one formal similarity between the book, the garden, and the film: all work against what might be seen as a comforting narrative coherence, directed toward a unified, spectatorial subject. As the opening voice-over in the film warns: "I offer you a journey without direction, uncertainty, and no sweet conclusions." The payoff is a certain freedom within the work for the addressee to wander. The experience of the actual garden becomes paradigmatic for the engagement of the reader or the viewer with the other two texts. We enter into the space of the work, which solicits our collaboration in the creation or elaboration of its meaning.

The Garden at Prospect Cottage

Martin Postle places Jarman's garden in the tradition of the English cottage garden, which became in the late nineteenth and early twentieth century both a key signifier of Englishness and a largely suburban, middle-class phenomenon.[5] A more recent classic of English gardening, a grass lawn surrounded by a privet hedge, is wildly out of place in a terrain like Dungeness, although there are examples of it there. In the harsh shingle, these gardens appear like almost defiant statements of suburban Englishness in the face of a hostile nature, much like the garden in *Jubilee* that is filled with plastic plants. By contrast, Jarman's garden, lacking fences and hedges and composed in large part of native species, appears rather to emerge out of the shingle, and then disappear back into it, harmonizing the cottage with the terrain rather than making it appear as a refuge from it. Jarman's embrace and reclamation of this middle-class art form is thus analogous to his interest in the home movie (and both, it could be argued, are strategic reclamations that have autobiographical dimensions).

Although the cottage garden emerged as a style in the nineteenth century, the cottage garden itself has a much longer history, and of which Jarman was well aware.[6] In *Modern Nature,* he makes frequent reference to Renaissance texts like *The Country Housewife's Garden* that instructed one on the construction, layout and maintenance of modest cottage gardens, and he makes occasional reference to the much grander and more famous pleasure gardens of the English and Italian Renaissance. The title *Modern Nature* is reminiscent of the Renaissance thinking about the nature of pleasure gardens. In *The Afterlife of Gardens,* John Dixon Hunt writes that the Renaissance saw the space of the garden as qualitatively different from other terrains, noting that "The sixteenth century even invented a term—third nature—for this garden world to distinguish it from both the second nature of the cultural landscape (fields, urban developments and infrastructure) and the first world of unmediated nature or wilderness."[7] The pleasure garden differs from these other spaces in being simultaneously meaningful, artificial, and specifically nonutilitarian: an aesthetic space, in other words. The concept of third nature is useful for reminding us that garden spaces inevitably offer a commentary on the relation between art and nature (something of an obsession with the Renaissance), and their respective valuations within a particular culture.

Jarman's garden is divided into two contrasting spaces, front and back, which are mediated by the two side gardens. In the east-facing front of the house is a more formally arranged garden consisting of symmetrically arranged geometric groupings. These forms consist of borders made using large flints from the beach, enclosing concentric rings of colored stones, shells, and plants. The technique is similar to that used in the construction of Renaissance knot gardens[8] (although the arrangements are far less elaborate here) and bears a resemblance as well to Japanese gardens, as Roger Wollen observes.[9] As in a typical late-Renaissance garden, statuary is interspersed throughout, although here the statuary is for the most part assemblages of found objects.[10] Disrupting the ordered formality of the arrangement is a large rowboat that appears stranded in a corner of the garden near the road. Interestingly, there is no path that allows one a direct access from the road to the front door, so that one submits to the formal arrangement, rather than being flattered by it.

On the north side of the house is a traditional kitchen garden. Here three raised beds with vegetable and herb gardens at one point enclosed and sheltered a four-story beehive. On the south side of the house is a large rectangular bed made with old railway sleepers or ties. There are fewer plant groupings here and larger, looser sculptural arrangements. On the black tar–varnished wall, which is punctuated by the yellow frames of two windows downstairs and a smaller window on the upstairs loft, there is a lengthy excerpt from John Donne's poem "The Sun Rising" in raised, black wooden script: "Busie old foole, unruly Sunne, / Why does thou thus / Through windowes and through curtaines call on us? / Must to thy motions lovers' seasons run?"[11] Text, notes John Dixon Hunt, has been a part of gardens at least since the younger Pliny's Tuscan villa; in England, Ian Hamilton Finlay's textual insertions into the landscape are the most prominent recent examples of the art. Hunt argues that "Texts in gardens, like buildings, have perhaps always been dialectical, confrontational, simply because they do not partake of the botanical materials that otherwise make up that site and are what people now expect gardens or landscapes to be."[12]

The poem, as with all text in gardens, is a surprising intervention into the space, which serves to orient the visitor's response to the terrain. This works in more and less specific ways. The intervention of text alerts the visitor to the constructedness of the space, and by extension, implies that the whole space is to some degree meaningful and readable. The poem itself is a lover's fanciful protest to the sun entering the lovers' bedroom, which turns into a metaphysical boast that since all that is valuable in the world is contained within the room, the sun, by warming them, warms the world. The contracted space of the lovers' bedroom evokes the microcosmic space of the garden, because

Prospect Cottage, Dungeness (side shot). Photograph by Malcolm Tute.

both are alternative spaces of desire with complex relations to the rest of the world. In both the bedroom and the garden, time and space work differently than they do in the outside world. At the same time, here as elsewhere one cannot but be struck by the openness, literal and figurative, of this garden to the world. If it is an alternative space, it is not an exclusive one.

The back garden offers a more informal arrangement than the front, with groupings of plants and found objects; the compositional principles on display provide a link with the collage aesthetic in Jarman's experimental films and in his writings. Here we see groupings of similar objects (a pyramid of metal floats, for example), unlikely pairings, and witty juxtapositions: a battered metal pot planted with sempervivum looks on first glance like a bowl of raspberries; a rotting red rubber glove holds a stone in its hand. Sticks are topped with lobster claws and garlands of stones. Rusty corkscrews of metal that were used to anchor World War II antitank fencing curl together, plants climbing up and through them. A rectangular metal box filled with pebbles contains two smaller rectangular boxes, one filled with white stones and shells and one filled with black. Although there is clearly a certain basic structure and logic of arrangement, there is no one perspective that

Jarman's garden at Dungeness (back). Photograph by Malcolm Tute.

the back garden orients itself toward; it reveals itself as one wanders through it. There is no fence around it, and no obvious point where the garden ends; it simply trails off, gradually blending into the shingle.

The plants are a mix of native species, either grown from seed gathered on walks or by transplantation, and a few foreign species. Jarman notes that his garden is "ecologically sound" in its use of local flora, and "In any case, so many weeds are spectacular flowers: the white campion, mallow, rest-harrow and scabious look wonderful. Introducing these local flowers into the garden makes a little wilderness at the heart of paradise."[13] Included in his herb garden are a number of plants cited in Renaissance herbals for their medicinal properties (among them thyme, lavender, rue, hyssop, and rosemary), which will be discussed at greater length later; in *Derek Jarman's Garden* he notes that the garden was originally planned as "a therapy and a pharmacopoeia."[14] The exuberant growth of the plants stands in opposition to the generally harsh terrain and severe weather conditions, which Keith Collins observes in the book's preface took on an obviously metaphorical quality: "the plants struggling against biting winds and Death Valley sun merged with Derek's struggle with illness, then contrasted with it, as the flowers blossomed while Derek faded."[15]

Here in this garden, one cannot fully inhabit the fantasy of a pre-lapsarian, natural space because the entire garden is qualified by the enormous nuclear reactor that looms like a massive ocean liner in the background. The reactor functions much like the constructed ruins inserted into an eighteenth-century picturesque garden, prompting the visitor toward a certain reading of the landscape. It acts in an analogous manner to the images of the radar towers in *The Angelic Conversation,* an unavoidable reminder of potential violence that serves as a contrast to the pastoral scenes of desire in the Elizabethan gardens. The garden at Dungeness is nonetheless an essentially optimistic work: a link between the past and the future, and an attempt to create an Edenic space in what is to some degree a ruined landscape. In that regard, it can be seen as a movement forward from *The Last of England*'s despair.

The garden's geographic situation partially explains the connections Jarman sees with "the most amusing and surprising garden I ever saw, the sister of Prospect Cottage, . . . in Baku, Azerbaijan. The landscape there is pretty much like Dungeness but it is black with oil from the polluting oilfields; in the middle of the grim housing blocks is a little circular walled garden that an old power worker, avuncular, smiling, looking much like Picasso, built as a memorial for his daughter who had died in a swimming accident."[16] This was the garden that Jarman had filmed on his trip to Russia, and which figures prominently in *Imagining October* as a contrast to the antihuman Stalinist architecture that dominates the first half of the film. Here the memorial dimensions of the garden are equally important in conjuring up the parallel: the creation of a garden as a productive act of mourning, one that asserts a commitment to life in the face of death and a landscape of destruction.

The garden at Dungeness is in many ways the culmination of a related series of interests in Jarman's career: most obviously his childhood interest in gardens (sites of resistance and refuge, which were very much bound up with an early awareness of his ill fit with heteronormativity), which was sporadically continued through a series of unrealized garden designs he produced over the years;[17] his interest in landscape painting;[18] the early set designs; and the continual interest in his films in the relation between the space of the artwork and the spectator. Here, finally, is a work of art that the spectator fully inhabits, an accommodating space that is dedicated to pleasure and community. As with so many of his works, the garden is a reclamation of both literal and figurative sites, an assertion of historical continuity that is forward-looking. The planting of the garden, moreover, foregrounds to a large degree process over final result, which reflects Jarman's attitude toward filmmaking in general: a work in progress, extending through time, never finished, only fully realized through its encounter with a visitor. The garden at Dungeness becomes in turn both the literal and the figurative ground of the other two works. The book and the film overlay the actual garden, building on its particular engagement with space, time, and history, and qualifying it in different ways.

Gardening History in *Modern Nature*

The book *Modern Nature* is, in the first instance, a diary of the making of Jarman's garden at Prospect Cottage. He offers details, day by day, of what is coming into bloom, what has perished in the latest storm or drought, and what has made it through the winter. We hear of trips to various nurseries, of walks across the shingle that yield seeds, cuttings, and whole plants, of beachcombing expeditions and the various bits of flotsam and jetsam dragged back. Often the mention of a plant will lead into some discussion of the history and lore of that plant, its mythical origins and pharmacological properties. Ancient, medieval, and early-modern authorities are quoted regarding appropriate times to transplant particular species, along with their mystical powers and practical uses. The planting of the garden thus becomes an act of continuity with the past and the plants act as a living embodiment of marginal knowledges.

In the entry for Saturday, March 25, 1989, for example, he records a gift of purple sage from a neighbor. This is followed by the citation of a proverb about sage and a quotation from John Gerard's *Herball* (1597) regarding the medicinal properties of the herb. He notes that "Sage attracts toads. Boccaccio's toad that lived under the sage bush was one of a long line." This is followed by a passage from Thomas Hill's *The Gardener's Labyrinth* (1577) which observes that just as toads like sage, serpents like rocket, but that they dislike garlic and ash trees.[19] Finally, he recounts a walk later in the evening, during which an ash tree is spotted with no serpents about. He does, however, find some periwinkle to bring home.[20]

While a wide range of texts are quoted in *Modern Nature,* the most consistent reference is to English Renaissance herbals. The first herbal to appear in English was Hill's *Gardener's Labyrinth,* and the most famous, even in the period, is Gerard's *Herball.* Other herbals referred to by Jarman include the medieval *Herbarium* by Apuleius Platonicus (also known as the Pseudo Apuleius); an English translation of *The boke of Secrets of Albartus Magnus, of the virtues of Herbes* (c. 1560); William Lawson's *The Country Housewife's Garden* (1617); Nicholas Culpeper's *The English Physician* (1652); William Coles's *The Art of Simpling* (1656); and John Evelyn's *Kalendarium Hortense* (1666). These books aimed to counsel the reader in the growth and use of medicinal plants, or what were called "simples," which might be assembled into a "physick garden" or combined with the house's kitchen garden.

A typical entry in Gerard's *Herball* details the different varieties of a particular plant, offers a description of it and the times of its growth, where it is found, its names in different languages, and its "virtues": its various uses, whether culinary, medicinal, or cosmetic. The herbals were a central component of Galenic medicine, which saw health as a balance in the body of the four qualities of hot, cold, moist, and dry. Different plants had different temperatures and degrees, and could thus be used to cure imbalances in the body. According to *The Art of Simpling,* for example, marigolds are moist in the first degree, lettuce is cold in the second degree, and sage is hot in the second degree. Some plants were better for different parts of the body than others, according to certain correspondences between them (sometimes signaled by the appearance of the plant). Figs and fennel seeds were useful for heating and drying the breast and lungs, whereas violets and French barley would cool and moisten them. The herbals, and Galenic medicine in general, are premised on sympathetic connections between the body and its environment. Many of the herbals assert that the diseases of a particular country can always be cured by the particular plants that grow there, and English writers use this as a justification for publishing new English herbals devoted to the description and the uses of local plants (counseling their readers, at the same time, against unnecessary and expensive imported medicines).

The herbals almost invariably have a preface that notes that Eden was the first garden, and Adam, who named the plants, the first herbarist and botanist. Gerard, for example, tells the reader that "the world can brag of no more antient Monument than Paradise and the garden of Eden; and the Fruits of the earth may contend for seniority, seeing their Mother was the first Creature that conceived, and they themselves the first fruit she brought forth. Talke of perfect happinesse or pleasure, and what place was so fit for that as the garden place wherein Adam was set to be the Herbarist?"[21] William Coles's *Adam in Eden, or the Paradise of Plants* (1657) makes the argument that "To make thee truly sensible of that happinesse which Mankind lost by the Fall of Adam, is to render thee an exact Botanick, by the knowledge of so incomparable a Science as the Art of Simpling, to re-instate thee into another Eden, or, A Garden of Paradise." The writing of an herbal, in other words, is an attempt to reassemble the knowledge that Adam had in Eden, and which was subsequently lost; the seventeenth-century botanic garden had a similar aim.[22] The herbal itself is imagined as a kind of garden, as titles such as the medieval *A Garden of Health* would suggest. The Renaissance herbal is thus an act of historical recovery. Jarman's book (and garden) offer a parallel project of historical translation, meditating on a lost Eden and its potential recovery. This links up with all of the other lost Edens in the book, and all of the other consequences of the Fall.

During the early-modern period, the medical knowledge contained in the herbals was challenged by the chemical theories of the Paracelsians, which eventually led to the development of modern pharmaceuticals.[23] This happens at the same time that medicine is establishing itself as a profession, and defining its knowledge in sharp contrast to the folk wisdom of the amateur practitioner, the herbarists and apothecaries, the cunning women and the country housewives at work in their stillrooms. Although they were dislodged from their place in medicine, the herbals did become the foundation of modern botany, and much of the more practical information about planting and maintaining gardens they contained was used for centuries.

There are a few things to note about Jarman's interest in this genre. It can be seen as a continuation or development of his interest in marginal or forgotten Renaissance knowledges. Early in his career, he made frequent reference to the writings of the early-modern alchemists and hermeticists (John Dee figured in *Jubilee*, *The Tempest*, and *The Angelic Conversation*, whereas Giordano Bruno is referred to in *Caravaggio*), comparing these fringe groups to sexual minorities. The arcane knowledge and dubious reputations of these writers gave him an opportunity to think through the particular situation of gay artists and intellectuals in the post-Stonewall era. Early in *Modern Nature* he notes his longstanding interest in historical arcana and the reasons for it, saying that "A personal mythology recurs in my writing, much the same way poppy wreaths have crept into my films. For me this archeology has become obsessive, for the 'experts' my sexuality is a confusion. All received information should make us inverts sad. Before I finish I intend to celebrate our corner of Paradise, the part of the garden the Lord forgot to mention."[24] The herbals answer to a different situation than the earlier alchemical writings, namely, his HIV status, by reaching back to an alternative medical tradition. This is not to suggest that he entertained a naive belief in an herbal cure for his condition:

> I water the roses and wonder whether I will see them bloom.
> I plant my herbal garden as a panacea, read up on all the aches
> and pains the plants will cure — and know they are not going
> to help. The garden as pharmacopoeia has failed. Yet there is a
> thrill in watching the plants spring up that gives me hope.[25]

It is not the plants themselves that offer any salvation, but rather what the planting of the garden represents. The citation of the herbals signals a different understanding of the relation between the self, the body, and the world, which stands in stark contrast to the alienating experience of modern medicine ("my chemical life," he calls it elsewhere)[26] and "received information." In a similar vein, Jarman's use of the herbals links up as well with the perceived need in the gay community at that time to challenge the medical establishment's monopoly on health care, and aggressively seek out scientific and medical information, including unorthodox or non-Western traditions (although Jarman remained firmly on the side of taking the available pharmaceuticals).[27] The planting of a garden is an act of optimism, and in this particular case, a statement of faith in the possibility of alternative knowledges and practices.

As the book progresses, the daily entries encompass a wider range of subjects. The mention of various plants spurs not just plant lore, but also personal reminiscences. We learn of Jarman's early involvement with plants and gardens, and with the various gardeners, mostly women, who encouraged this interest. This is intertwined with his sexual development: boyhood loves (often associated with gardens), the harsh regime of the public school, his first experiences with sex, the sexual revolution of the 1960s, and the various spaces of gay sexuality. This is terrain previously discussed in his earlier books, but which gets reframed here within the larger gardening context, as the act of constructing the garden becomes in every way a multifaceted engagement with history, and a parallel activity to the construction of life and a community in a generally hostile terrain. The garden and the book are parallel heterotopias constructed in opposition to the generally unforgiving landscape of English culture.

This hostile terrain is reflected in the text's interest in the history of sexual minorities, and the contemporary political climate that included Section 28 of the Local Government Act, the government's inactivity in the face of the AIDS epidemic, and the tabloid press's homophobic campaign of terror. The entry for May 11, 1989, for example, responds to a piece about him: "The *People* has a lurid article: '*Movie Boss With AIDS—Glad to die in a shack!*' What people do to sell newspapers!"[28] This climate of hostility was addressed in a gallery installation at the Third Eye in Glasgow, the making of which is documented in the book. Among the features of the exhibition were a collage of tabloid pages with homophobic headlines, various tarred-and-feathered objects, and in the center a four-poster bed surrounded by barbed wire, on which a male couple embraced.[29] The installation as a whole evokes many of the same themes that surface in *The Garden.*

AIDS is a recurrent topic in the book, both for the way that it appears in the public realm and for the way it continually surfaces in his private life. Throughout the book are entries about the sickness and

death of friends and colleagues, along with his own, typically icono-
clastic, reflections on the experience of being HIV positive: "The perception that knowing you're dying makes you feel more alive is an error.
I'm less alive. There's less life to lead. I can't give 100% attention to
anything—part of me is always thinking about my health."[30] Later in
the book, we begin to get the progress of his illness, as the symptoms
of AIDS begin to emerge, and he goes in and out of clinics and hospitals. The book ends, quite abruptly, after another bout of illness and
an appendectomy: "Ten days later I pick up a pen, my appetite lost for
recording and writing. It's six months since I became ill. I've lost a stone
and a half and the razor bumps across my face again."[31] There is no attempt to sum up, to offer assurance or consolation, or to find meaning
from the events. Ultimately, the book, like *The Garden,* offers "a journey without direction, uncertainty, and no sweet conclusion."

The title of the book, *Modern Nature,* offers some guide to its interpretation. The oxymoron invites us to consider in what ways nature,
which we generally think of as existing outside of history, is in fact historical. This involves a consideration of various figurative and literal
terrains, and various meanings of "nature." A clear referent of the title
is the English landscape, for which Jarman had a deep and abiding
love, and against whose continuing degradation he continually protested
in his work. Over the course of the diary we get observations about
how we have changed nature, both in terms of how we interact with
the landscape (the disappearance of cottage gardens, for example) and
how climate change is affecting the length of the seasons and the appearance and disappearance of certain species (sightings of butterflies,
in particular, are continually being recorded).

Another obvious referent in the title is gay subjectivity and the new
world that came into being with the sexual revolution, along with the
various historical turns that have taken place in that world. Documenting this historical, social, and psychological terrain—"the part of the
garden the Lord forgot to mention"—occupies a central place in Jarman's career. In the book he comments on "The terrible dearth of
information, the fictionalization of our experience, there is hardly any
gay autobiography, just novels, but why novelise it when the best of it is
in our lives?"[32] Within this context, the daily record of his circle and

the mundane details of the various kinds of lives and relations assumes both a political and a historical importance. Like the Renaissance herbal, the book is itself a garden, an assemblage of useful and salutary knowledge.

The meaning of modern nature shifted considerably with the appearance of HIV, which presented a severe challenge to the most basic understandings of the nature of the gay self: "it's not much use warning that each cigarette knocks three minutes off your life when a fuck can stop it in its tracks."[33] For a community that came into being with the sexual revolution, a sexually transmitted fatal disease was the cruelest irony. For a gay subjectivity that placed sexual expression at the core of selfhood and community, HIV arguably presented a far greater trauma to the experience of selfhood than would an equally fatal disease such as cancer. The challenge to identity that HIV occasions is reflected in the richly allusive title of Eric Michaels's AIDS diary, *Unbecoming,* which also hints at the pariah status of the ill. Jarman's entries continually reflect on this challenge to his sense of self that his seropositivity causes, as well as how it changes his experience of the world: "Dearest Alasdair on the phone for nearly an hour, he's in the same state, says the world is a foreign country. He goes through the motions with friends, whose fears and preoccupations he can no longer share. We are refugees here."[34]

The oxymoronic title also indicates an interest in time, history, and experiences of temporality, just as the diary structure heightens our awareness of the passage of time. Two time schemes dominate the book: the progressive, linear time of the calendar and the cyclical rhythms of the natural world, which is most present in the discussions of the progress of the seasons and the life cycles of the plants. These two experiences of time are related to different relations to the world; they might be summed up in the most central contrast in the book, which is time inside the garden and time outside of it, prelapsarian and post. This contrast is related to his experience of the passage of time in Dungeness, which is related to the ebbs and flows of the natural world, and the hectic life of London and the film business. Another frequent, related contrast is the child's experience of time and the adult's; the child's experience of time is often characterized as Edenic in its cyclical, seemingly unprogressive dimensions. There is also a contrast between time in the mundane, daylight world and a sexualized time at night, especially in gay clubs or cruising on Hampstead Heath. Less happily, there is the hallucinatory time of illness. Finally, and perhaps most crucially, we get the experience of time when one is HIV positive: what it means to live in accelerated, foreshortened, or borrowed time, a time that is associated with the garden of Gethsemane and the acute awareness of mortality.

These contrasting temporalities are presented along with different pasts. As with some of his earlier texts, we get a blend of different kinds of histories: his family history, his personal history, his artistic career, the history of sexual minorities in general, and the history of gay artists in particular. The history of the garden at Dungeness, which is the ostensible subject of the book, is interspersed with the histories of plants and plant lore, the history of gardening, garden design, and accounts of particular gardens and their histories. A number of complementary historical projects are at work here: one is to construct an alternative history of the present, of "modern nature." To do so is to challenge, as Jarman does throughout his career, the mythologies used to make sense of the present: "Surely we were the angels denied hospitality by the Sodomites. Was not Sodom a tight little suburban dormitory mortgaged out to the hardhearted, somewhere beyond Epsom?"[35] Many of the histories in this book are directed toward specific kinds of spaces, all of which have Eden as their prototype. These heterotopias are characterized by different experiences of time, as well as by a dedication to life and to desire.

Connected to this is a certain impulse in history or for history, one that might be partly responsible for Jarman's only half-ironic self-identification as conservative. This is the function of the plant lore in the book. The plants begin to function as material, living connections to history, to gardens of the past, and to past gardens, analogous to the way that an orgasm connects you to homosexuals of the past. Jarman is connected to Pliny and Gerard by planting the same plants. Some of this is a meditation on connectedness, continuity, a good kind of conservatism: an emphasis on a shared cherishing of life. The garden at Dungeness is connected to a tradition of other gardens, generally spaces of sexual freedom, whether mythical—Eden—or historical:

the Borghese Gardens and Sissinghurst.[36] The book, in turn, becomes
one of those spaces. Like the Renaissance herbal, it is a historical project
that attempts to reconstruct Eden within its pages. The recourse to the
herbals clarifies that this book-as-garden is also a pharmacopoeia: an assemblage of lore directed toward healing all those things that currently
beset modern nature (most immediately, homophobia and Thatcherism). Although, as Jarman sadly observes, the garden as pharmacopoeia
has failed in relation to his own disease, the book aims not so much at
the epidemic but at the grounds of its flourishing.[37]

Histories of the Fall in *The Garden*

The film opens with a title sequence incorporating moving and blurry
shots of a film shoot being organized at night; we hear voices asking
for quiet, someone calling for the camera, one of the actors questioning
someone about something. In a voice-over by Michael Gough, we hear:

> I want to share this emptiness with you; not fill the silence
> with false notes, or put tracks through the void. I want to
> share this wilderness of failure. The others have built you a
> highway, fast lanes in both directions. I offer you a journey
> without direction, uncertainty and no sweet conclusion. When
> the light faded, I went in search of myself. There were many
> paths and many destinations.

When this ends, we hear Jarman on the set, congratulating people on
a good rehearsal and announcing there will be a thirty-minute break.
Then someone yells "Quiet." At this point, a cello starts playing on the
sound track, and we get a series of images in black and white: water
dripping on a stone, water dripping on a crucifix with a reproduction
of a painting of the crucifixion hanging on the wall behind, and a shot
of Jarman asleep in the cottage with his head on his desk, with water
dripping on it from above. This is intercut with color images from the
filming outside: an actress being made up, a male figure in S&M gear,
and a couple (one of whom is the actress just pictured) embracing, the
two weeping. Juxtaposed with the images from the outdoor set are
documentary images of the landscape around Dungeness: waves rolling
into the shore, plants blowing in the breeze.

These two opening sequences establish the frame for what will follow. They establish, first of all, two of the principal references of the title (beyond the location of the film in Jarman's garden at Dungeness). The couple outside, it becomes clear, are acting out the expulsion from the garden of Eden, and through metaphoric associations we connect the crucifixes and the dozing Jarman with the garden of Gethsemane, where Christ meditated most fully on his bodily condition and on the necessity of his martyrdom. In both cases, the film signals that it is interested in both the myth and the way the myth has been remade, by showing us various technologies of representation, old and new, and by including modern reinterpretations of the myth. These gestures will be repeated throughout the film, showing us a variety of representations of biblical stories and their contemporary incarnations. There are two familiar strategies at work here. One is to draw attention to the ways in which these myths are perversely deployed in the service of hate, and the other, related strategy is to challenge the ownership of these narratives by rewriting them, most centrally by putting a gay couple at the center of the Passion narrative.

Opening the film with the sounds of filming establishes the nonnarrative, antirealist conventions the film will follow, while the voice-over and the shot of the sleeping Jarman (which echoes the opening of *The Last of England*) suggest that the particular genre with which the film identifies is the trance film, in the tradition, argues Tony Rayns, of Cocteau's *The Blood of a Poet,* as well as the work of Maya Deren, Kenneth Anger, Gregory J. Markopoulos, and others.[38] The film positions itself as autobiographical, or at least as the personal vision of its maker; Jarman himself compared it to a medieval dream allegory.[39] Structurally, it resembles the movements of a classical score, sequences of sounds and images developing a thought or mood, punctuated by blackouts and silences.

Given its autobiographical or subjective stance, it is clear that one of the film's subjects is AIDS, and in particular Jarman's experience with it. This has become the dominant way of reading the film, and it does make a good deal of sense: one of the recurrent motifs of the film is a band of photographers who always act as a harassing mob, which clearly mirrors Jarman's experience with the tabloid press, particularly after his public disclosure of his HIV status. And in other parts of the film we get visual suggestions of AIDS. The film's most famous image is of Jarman in a troubled sleep on a bed that sits in water just off the beach. Circling him are five male and female figures wearing only flowing white skirts and holding torches overhead, all shot in a hallucinatory slow motion. The image is strikingly evocative, suggesting perhaps the man with night sweats, circled by angels who watch over him. Elsewhere in the film the stigmata on various Christ figures become suggestive of the lesions caused by Kaposi's sarcoma, which were at that point the most iconic signifiers of AIDS.

It is too restrictive, however, to see the film as only about AIDS or even as principally about AIDS. Jarman himself later said that "*The Garden* was made into an AIDS-related film but AIDS was too vast a subject to 'film'. All the art failed. It was well-intentioned but decorative—the graffiti artist Keith Haring raised consciousness and did much good but failed to turn the tragedy beyond the domestic."[40] While AIDS came to occupy a central part in Jarman's life and his thinking, his experience with the disease existed on a continuum with his experience with homophobia, and with political conservatism; these things were inextricably related, which expands the range of the work beyond the simply autobiographical, however subjective it might seem. This emphasis on the larger contexts is not unusual to Jarman. As Chambers notes in his discussion of AIDS memoirs, "the affliction of AIDS [entails] the proverbial double whammy: it is a serious disease with a fatal prognosis, and the patient simultaneously lives a social and political nightmare."[41] Addressing the social and political ramifications of the disease, and in particular homophobia, is thus an unavoidable part of the genre. For example, the American documentary *Silverlake Life: The View from Here* (1993), which is principally a video diary of Tom Joslin's experience with AIDS, nonetheless incorporates parts of an earlier documentary about homophobia and the process of coming out. If anything, Jarman's film is more oriented toward the political and social situation than his experience with the disease; further, the film is less directed toward the immediate political context (which he discusses in *Modern Nature* and which will be more centrally addressed in *Edward II*) and more about exploring the underlying mythologies that are the foundations of that situation.

The most obvious of these founding mythologies is of course the Passion of Christ. The opening juxtaposition of the images of the crucifix with images of Jarman has led some critics to talk about what they see as Jarman's martyr complex, an investment in passivity and suffering that starts with *Sebastiane* and encompasses any number of the subsequent gay characters in his films, many of whom do end up dead. (*Modern Nature* records a conversation with Jon Savage: "Of *The Garden* he said, 'Oh Derek, more of your martyr complex.'")[42] Here, the meditation on and identification with the suffering of Christ, a tradition ultimately associated with Augustine, is used in the first instance to evoke the dilemma facing a person who is HIV positive (particularly before the advent of drug cocktails): can I face the horrible physical suffering that is very likely coming?

For Jarman, this was accompanied by another imperative, given his very public status, of not backing away from the principles that he had always proudly espoused: "How could I celebrate my sexuality filled with so much sadness, and frustration for what has been lost?"[43] In a passage unconsciously echoing Christ in Gethsemane, Jarman writes:

> As I sweat it out in the early hours, a 'guilty victim' of the scourge, I want to bear witness to how happy I am, and will be until the day I die, that I was part of the hated sexual revolution; and that I don't regret a single step or encounter I made in that time; and if I write in future with regret, it will be a reflection of a temporary indisposition.[44]

The very politicized nature of the general cultural response to AIDS (reflected in the widespread "guilty victim" and "innocent victim" distinction that Jarman alludes to) provides another parallel to the state persecution of Christ. At the same time, it is worth noting that although there are various Christ figures and representations of Christ in the film, Jarman never directly figures himself as Christ: it is less an identification with him than it is a meditation on his life or a thinking through it. Whereas Michael O'Pray objects to this identification, Gerard Loughlin argues that it "saves the film from being simply anti-Christian polemic; indeed, it allows the film to perform the story of Christ now, seeing contemporary lives in the life of Christ, and Christ in those lives."[45]

In the film, the opening expulsion from Eden sets in motion a number of narrative threads. Eden stands in for a number of things: the first is the sexual revolution, and in particular gay liberation. In his writings, Jarman persistently associates gardens with sexual freedom: the cruising on Hampstead Heath after dark is the most notable of these comparisons in *Modern Nature,* which he implicitly places in a lineage with historical sites like the Borghese gardens in Rome, and Vita Sackville-West's garden at Sissinghurst, which he claims were marked by sexual freedom. Another fall from Eden in the film is the destruction of nature, symbolized in the film by the nuclear reactor, which is, as Chris Perriam notes, "much iconised in the film and which in Britain is the ultimate stigma of geopolitical abandonment for a place and its community."[46] These two Edens—nature and sexual freedom—are firmly linked in Jarman's mind: the central parallel in *The Last of England's* critique of the state is of a ruined landscape with unproductive or frustrated desire. There is, however, a tonal difference between the two films in response to what *The Garden's* opening voice-over calls "this wilderness of failure." Here, the wilderness of failure is simultaneously the compromised landscape of Dungeness, the political climate in England, Jarman's compromised immune system, and his frustrated artistic ambitions. Whereas *The Last of England* alternately rages against and despairs over this landscape of failure, *The Garden* accepts it as a terrible given, while working toward some necessary accommodation with it.

Another Eden in the film is the garden of childhood. In sequences reminiscent of the home movies in *War Requiem,* we see a boy playing in the garden at Dungeness, helping to wash a young man's hair, splashing about in water, and playing with snails. The boy is at times readable as Christ, and the older man, who acts as his protector, might be seen as a figure of John the Baptist. Subsequent scenes portray the fall that comes with growing older: we see him on top of a table circled by schoolmasters who beat out a rhythm with canes while he writes on the blackboard. One master slams a huge tome open and shut, while another obsessively turns an hourglass. On the blue screen behind him are matted in images of a chain-link fence and the nuclear reactor. The expulsion from the garden of childhood is thus linked to the regimentation of time and orthodox knowledge.

Later still in a representation of a Latin lesson, we see him marching about on the table with a Roman helmet and sword, as if he has incorporated the violent lessons of the educational system. Matted in behind this scene are pages from books, including numerical tables and Leviticus, the best-known source of biblical prohibitions against sodomy. In *Modern Nature,* Jarman talks about his own experience with the nuns at St. Juliana's convent day school: "God's iron maidens, armed with clamps and shackles of Catholicism, invaded my innocent garden with sugary promises—icy orange juice lollipops; but for the recalcitrant, a ruler on the back of the hand. . . . These intimidating automata, brides of a celibate God, hacked my paradise to pieces like the despoilers of the Amazon."[47] These representations of school-day persecutions are balanced by other scenes of a flamenco dancer on the same table. Later we see the boy joining her in the dance and falling asleep beside her, wrapped in her shawl. These scenes evoke two other terrains of refuge that recur in Jarman's films and writings: the world of women and the world of art.

The most central narrative that follows from the film's expulsion from the garden is the biblical narrative of the life of Christ. This encompasses a number of different scenes in the film, which are loosely related to each other. A man dressed in the flowing robes of a Christmas pageant apostle reads the Nativity narrative from a large book, while blue-screened behind him are images of Christmas lights in an urban setting, presumably meant to evoke the commercialization of religion. In a different register, we see a figure identified in *Modern Nature* as the Madonna of the Photo Op: Tilda Swinton, wearing an elegant green and gold sari and looking like a cross between a fashion model and a Russian icon (and perhaps Princess Diana). Carrying a child, she is harassed by journalists. Later, in a similar vein, we see a drag queen, Mary Magdalene, being chased by a mob of debutantes and photographers.

There is a figure of Christ, dressed in the usual robe and sandals, who is most often seen on a boardwalk that weaves through the shingle, with power lines and towers from the nuclear station looming above him; "a visitor," writes Loughlin, "from earlier, more straightforward Christ films."[48] He is clearly baffled by what he sees, and a jogger whom we often see in the same space doesn't recognize him either. In one scene we see him with a good-looking young man who might be Judas (on the sound track, we hear a rooster crow). They appear to embrace, and the young man kisses him when they are set upon by a horde of photojournalists. Elsewhere we see him tormented by naked demons, who attempt to scramble out of a pit holding flares.

The most prominent references to the biblical narrative come with a gay couple who go through various scenes evocative of the life of Christ. When we first see them they are on a beach, sitting back to back wearing similar clothes, chucking stones in the water. They are next seen as part of a group of men attempting to move a boulder. One of them stoops down and picks up the Madonna of the Photo Op's abandoned crown. A subsequent sequence crosscuts between scenes of one of them washing the other in a tub on the beach, and scenes of the boy playing with a young man in the garden. Toward the end of the sequence the boy appears with the two lovers who are now both in the tub, and they all playfully splash each other. Putting the boy and the two lovers in the same space connects the two idylls: the garden of desire and the garden of childhood, a connection that was made differently in the penultimate, enigmatic sequence in *Caravaggio.*

The doomed garden of desire inhabited by the lovers is connected with the sexual revolution, which gives the expulsion a more pointedly political and historical resonance: Thatcherism and the appearance of HIV. In one of the more incongruous moments of the film, a cabaret singer (Jessica Martin) performs "Think Pink" from the musical *Funny Face,* while matted in behind her are images from a gay pride march. She is joined by the two lovers, who are dressed in identical pink suits, and who hold a baby. The gold rings they wear suggest that they are married. The combination of all of these elements reflects some of the cherished goals of the gay liberation movement, including the transformation of the nuclear family and the claiming of public space. Midway through the film, however, the tone shifts considerably. We return to a sleeping Jarman, followed by a quick montage of shots of the expulsion, of the S&M serpent in the garden of Eden, Jarman on the bed in the water, now clearly anguished or in pain, the tormenting demons with torches, and a screaming Madonna. The rest of the film will be dominated by images of persecution and torment.

Christ (Roger Cook) amid the Pylons in *The Garden* (1990). Production still.

This starts with the assault on the drag queen/Mary Magdalene by the harassing mob. As the lovers sleep, they are set upon by three camera- and cell-phone-wielding Santas, who sing an angry and sarcastic version of "God rest ye merry gentlemen." This leads into a scene of the lovers together in some kind of spa filled with lecherous old men, suggestive of the temple elders or Pilate. These and other scenes work to signal the prurient and hypocritical interest of the mainstream in the spectacle of homosexual depravity, that it both deplores and anxiously pores over. The film presents in satirical fashion a variety of authority figures in order to draw a connection between the media, the establishment, and contemporary Christian institutions. The combined activity and inactivity of these modern Pharisees both stalled an effective response to the AIDS crisis and demonized those caught in it.

A pillow fight between the boy and two young friends, which results in clouds of feathers, is echoed by an extended torture sequence of the two lovers, in which they are tarred and feathered by policemen in a café (actually using treacle and the synthetic lining of a jacket). The scene is, in many ways, as difficult to watch as comparable torture scenes in Pasolini's *Salo*. The juxtaposition of the torture scene and the pillow fight solidifies a series of connections about the essential innocence of both childhood and adult sexuality, and society's persecution of both. The torment of the lovers is later followed by a scene of them tied by the hands to a post and whipped by men who could be judges or members of the House of Lords. We see them bearing a cross, and then lying on a beach, apparently dead, with stigmata on their hands and feet, as a woman mourns them and covers them with a shroud. Late in the film we see the lovers approaching a table of old men. We hear a final voice-over about the toll AIDS has taken upon Jarman's generation:

> I walk in this garden, holding the hands of dead friends
> Old age came quickly for my frosted generation
> Cold, cold, cold, they died so silently
>
> Did the forgotten generation scream,
> Or go full of resignation,
> Cold, cold, cold, they died so silently

A final scene offers some consolation, and brings together some of the main repeated threads: around a table we have the boy, a woman (Tilda Swinton), the two lovers, and an old man. They eat sweets wrapped in paper that the woman gives them, and then roll the amaretto wrappers into tubes and set them upright on the table. The boy lights them, and as they burn down, the fragile remnants of the burned paper lift up into the air and float away. It is an old conjurer's trick, and one that provides a fittingly beautiful image for death, transcendence, and the consoling power of art.

These are only some of the main threads of the film: there are other repeated figures and images interspersed among them. Although the film does not use different media in the same way that *War Requiem* does, there are a number of different types and qualities of images, which correspond to the different elements of the film. The film's hallucinatory time, anchored in the opening image of a sleeping Jarman, incorporates a number of other schemes of temporality, some of which are indicated by alterations of the filmic speed through slow-motion or time-lapse photography, or through the music on the sound track. We have, for example, different experiences of what might be called human time, most obviously seen in the maturation of the boy, as he moves from the limitless time of the garden to the measured regime of the clock. There is historical time, reflected in the political references to the media, the courts, gay pride, and so on. The various representations of biblical figures partake in mythical time. And finally, we have various schemes of natural or cyclical time, reflected in the many images of nature and the time-lapse photography of the skies that generally suggest a longer, more impersonal scheme of time: the time of the universe.

Connected to these different schemes of temporality are different spatial regimes, including different experiences of the same space, most obviously the space of the garden and the surrounding area. We get many shots of nature that appear documentary, in which humans sometimes appear, reminiscent of the Baku shots in *Imagining October*. These do not always work to suggest a "pure" experience of nature that is sharply differentiated from the human world; we see figures gardening or otherwise working in this space, and other shots place less benign human intrusions such as radar towers, chain fences, and the ubiquitous power station. Other shots of staged scenes in these natural spaces change the experience of the space quite dramatically, as they become sets. In the opening of the film and elsewhere, nature becomes both set and "set," as we see the lights and cameramen and the actors acting. The juxtaposition of these markedly different spatial regimes that all occur in the same place points not just to the fact that the experience of space is always a function of subjectivity, but also to the differing kinds of spectatorial relations that a film can construct or suggest: from the apparently unmediated access to space of the documentary, to the highly mediated spaces of the narrative film, to those moments when the film makes visible the purely imaginary space of the filmic spectacle.

These spatial juxtapositions are formally matched by other contrasts: the estranging effect of the Madonna of the Photo Op seated in front of a shed in the harsh natural terrain of the shingle, or the drag queen in the sequined gown, feather boa, and heels being hounded against the decaying hulk of a World War II listening wall, create productive dissonances that echo other dissonances in the film. The most obvious of these are the two cabaret-style scenes that resemble other such moments in films like *War Requiem* and *Edward II*. The "Think Pink" sequence is matched by another scene with the tone of a television commercial, in which Satan and Judas (hanging from a noose, with a grotesquely swollen, blackened tongue) extol the virtues of credit cards.

This direct acknowledgment of (and address to) the audience exists on a continuum with another type of scene, most often played at a long table in front of a blue screen. This echoes the fellowship sequence in *Imagining October*, the choir scenes in *War Requiem*, and, more generally, the various tableau setups in films like *Caravaggio* and *Edward II*. These manifestly artificial spaces combine staged actions, which generally face the camera directly, with images matted in behind. In this tableau arrangement we get a table of women making music with the rims of wine glasses, the flamenco dancer, the school scenes, and the table of old men near the end of the film. Abandoning composition in depth and using only one visual plane is a trick that Jarman learned from Caravaggio's paintings: for both artists it is a way of pushing the space of representation outward toward the space of the viewer.

Whereas *Caravaggio*'s theoretical interest in space was mostly linked to an investigation of relationality and the possibilities for different ways of being together that are implied by different spatial regimes, *The Garden*'s interest in space extends into an investigation of the relation between the experience of space and the experience of time. Every film is to some degree about the experience of time, given that film is a time-based medium. Film works, to no small degree, by exploiting the differences between the constructed time scheme of the film and the regularly linear time of the viewing. The interest in time in this film has a political resonance, directly related to Jarman's sense of living in borrowed time owing to his HIV status. By extension, the film suggests that time is always politically inflected: just as there is no nature outside of time or history, as the title of the book *Modern Nature* suggests, there is no experience of time that is neutral. And as with spatial regimes, temporal regimes imply forms of subjectivity.

The spatial disjunctions in the film are often matched by temporal disjunctions. The most persistent is the meeting on the boardwalk of Christ and the jogger. This jarring encounter of the biblical and the contemporary has a number of different effects, but one of the more notable is the clash of two different ways of being in the same space, that are characterized by two different temporalities: the wandering of the Christ figure, and the purposeful, regulated leisure of the jogger, who is seen glancing at his watch. The forced encounter brings into focus certain aspects of the other encounters of biblical and contemporary in the film, such as the lovers going through events of the Passion, and the film crew filming the expulsion from the garden.

The film's interest in reading the present in relation to the past is related to its interest in temporalities, and the way that different historical narratives structure our understanding and experience of time. The story of the expulsion from the garden is about the origin of human time, understanding time in direct relation to death and in opposition to happiness. "Time itself must have started in earnest after the Fall, because the seven days in which the world was created we now know was an eternity."[49] Measured time is understood or experienced as a falling away from bliss, which in the film is aligned with the expulsion of the child from timelessness into the regulated time of the classroom. The other, related biblical temporality in the film is even more closely associated with death and the fact of corporeality: the reference to the Gethsemane, which is time experienced in the shadow of one's own death.

We might remember here the Renaissance concept of three natures: wilderness, human, and garden spaces. All three kinds of nature are represented and investigated in *The Garden,* as well as the relation between them. The term "third nature" is reminiscent of Jarman's "modern nature," as well as, of course, Foucault's concept of the heterotopia, a constructed space whose spatial and temporal relations are different from those that govern the rest of a society's spaces. What all three concepts stress is the ability of a garden to act as an interrogatory space, where new modes of being can be posited and explored. Hunt compares this "third nature" of the garden to the more familiar concept of virtual reality, drawing attention to "this combination of a felt experience of both organic and inorganic materials with a deliberate creation of fictive worlds into whose inventions, systems and mythological or metaphorical languages we allow ourselves to be drawn."[50]

It is useful to think about the garden as "a deliberate creation of fictive worlds" in relation both to the actual garden at Dungeness (the poem on the wall drawing attention to the space as a created, meaningful world) and to the film *The Garden,* with its more explicit attention to mythological spaces, and the way these spaces colonize or make meaningful actual spaces. We might remember Bersani and Dutoit's argument that "Caravaggio's paint is the metaphysical X ray that compels us to see particular histories and particular myths as instituting relationalities."[51] *The Garden* undertakes a similar historical project by using two key biblical gardens as the starting point for an investigation of how certain Christian myths and narrative patterns have structured our understanding and experience of the social, and its temporal and spatial regimes. This was an especially timely project in the 1980s, when the appearance of HIV allowed for the most virulent forms of homophobia to sound reasonable in certain quarters. Issues of relationality were at stake in very direct ways, as various kinds of quarantine were discussed, and less directly, as Susan Sontag notes, in the peculiarly archaic way in which the disease was understood: "In contrast to cancer, understood in a modern way as a disease incurred by (and revealing of) individuals, AIDS is understood in a premodern way, as a disease incurred by people both as individuals and as members of a 'risk group'—that neutral-sounding, bureaucratic category which also revives the archaic idea of a tainted community that illness has judged."[52]

Jarman's garden, *Modern Nature,* and *The Garden* all engage with history in complex ways: challenging, rewriting, and even resurrecting forgotten or discredited modes of thought. In complementary ways, they explore the possibilities for alternative ways of being. Interestingly enough, the garden itself emerges as perhaps the purest embodiment of Jarman's cinematic theory: a nonnarrative work of art that is nonetheless an erudite conversation with history; a space that opens itself to the audience, inviting the fullest collaboration; a space dedicated to the beauties of life and desire.

SEVEN

Blindness and Insight

THE FINAL WORKS I WILL CONSIDER are again a disparate group: another memoir, a book on color, published scripts, and three films, including an adaptation of an early-modern play, a biopic about a twentieth-century philosopher, and an experimental feature whose image track consists of an unwavering field of deep blue. In spite of the fact that the first two originated in scripts written by others, the three films pose a related set of questions, principally concerning an ethics of being. What constitutes an ethical life? What is one's responsibility to others? Whether explicitly or implicitly, the questions are framed within the context of the AIDS epidemic, which gives them both an urgency and a particular focus. How does one live within disaster?

The films also raise the issue of art's responsibility to life, and the potential of art to effect change. *Blue,* which is inspired by the work of the French conceptual artist Yves Klein, addresses these questions most explicitly, although the other two films offer a series of considerations of art and artists. Characteristically for Jarman, the films' most direct engagements with these questions are at the level of form. Drawing on lessons learned from earlier films and from his engagements with other artists, these films constitute a final exploration of the possibilities for time and space in the cinema. Both *Edward II* and *Wittgenstein* play with narrative time, scrambling the events of a life to foreground the questions of that life's meaning. Both also make productive use of the disjuncture between the past and the present, and the relation between them. *Blue,* which does not have a narrative as such, nonetheless engages with these questions to some degree, while playing on a more elemental disjuncture, spectatorial time and aesthetic time, attempting to make them collide or coincide in productive ways. Predictably, space is similarly complex in these films, as Jarman experiments in *Edward II* with the psychologically inflected space of the gothic to prompt the audience toward an apprehension of the minority experience of space in post-Thatcherite England. In *Wittgenstein,* Jarman uses the lessons learned from Caravaggio about light and color to define the on-screen space in ways that push it outward toward the viewer. *Blue* is a culmination of these experiments. By eschewing the image, *Blue* becomes all space, spilling out into the audience, erasing the line between the spectacle and the spectator, inviting the audience to become the film.

Edward II: Queer Gothic

In 1992, when *Edward II* appeared in North America, it was seen to be part of a new cinematic movement, identified as the "New Queer Cinema." Gay filmmaking had finally caught up with Jarman. B. Ruby Rich, who first documented the trend and gave it its name, identified Jarman as "the grand old man" of the group.[1] Among the films most frequently discussed under this rubric were *Poison* (Todd Haynes, 1991) *Swoon* (Tom Kalin, 1992), *The Living End* (Gregg Araki, 1992), *Paris Is Burning* (Jennie Livingston, 1990), and *My Own Private Idaho* (Gus Van Sant, 1991). Although on the face of it a fairly disparate group of films, they did share certain characteristics, most obviously an affinity with the new queer activist movement that was identified in the United States with Queer Nation and in Britain with OutRage! Both of these were highly media-savvy groups, performing stunts that were reminiscent of the zaps of the Gay Liberation Front and, more recently, of ACT UP (the AIDS Coalition to Unleash Power). OutRage! emerged specifically out of a response to an increasing number of gay-bashing incidents, an escalation of police harassment, and the more general climate of political hostility, most obviously in relation to Section 28 of the Local Government Act.[2] While OutRage! had much in common with ACT UP, it was more specifically directed, like the GLF, to combating homophobia. Like the GLF, it defined itself at least partly in opposition to the more conservative gay advocacy group of its day, in this case Stonewall, a lobby group known more for behind-the-scenes advocacy with powerful politicians. Unlike Stonewall, OutRage! practiced grassroots democracy, eventually suffering from some of the same problems as the GLF. Whereas the GLF had preached the affirmative message that "Gay is good," OutRage! was seen to be more confrontational ("We're here, we're queer, get used to it!"), although the differences between the groups should not be overstated: they both infiltrated and disrupted conservative conferences, confronted clergy, practiced radical drag in public, protested against their ill-treatment by gay establishments, and proselytized in gay cruising grounds. Jarman was loosely associated with both groups, although more clearly identified with OutRage!, holding benefits for it, showing up at media events, and including a group of OutRage! activists in *Edward II*.[3]

In spite of the genre's apparent newness, the politics that found their expression in the New Queer Cinema had been characteristic of Jarman's cinema for some time. Rich identified some of the formal similarities in terms that could equally describe Jarman's oeuvre: "there are traces in all of them of appropriation and pastiche, irony, as well as a reworking of history with social constructionism very much in mind. Definitely breaking with older humanist approaches and the films and tapes that accompanied identity politics, these works are irreverent, energetic, alternately minimalist and excessive."[4] One of the common features of a number of the films was their willingness to abandon positive images and embrace or reclaim negative stereotypes. *Swoon*, for example, is a stylish, black-and-white revisiting of the 1920s amoral lovers and murderers Nathan Leopold and Richard Loeb (previously the subject of *Compulsion* [1959] and the ultimate inspiration for Alfred Hitchcock's *Rope* [1948]). According to the publicity, the filmmakers aimed to put "the Homo back in Homicide."[5] *The Living End* is a dystopic, AIDS-inflected road movie, and *My Own Private Idaho* appropriates via Orson Welles's *Chimes at Midnight* (1967) scraps of *Henry IV, Part I* in its story of scruffy gay hustlers.

The film that is aesthetically closest to Jarman, however, is Todd Haynes's *Poison*, which features three intertwined narratives titled "Hero," "Homo," and "Horror." "Hero" tells the story of a boy who murders his abusive father and then flies away from a second-story window; "Homo" is an homage to Jean Genet, using dialogue from his novels to tell a prison love story; "Horror" is a pastiche of a 1950s sci-fi/horror movie with clear references to AIDS. In this segment, a scientist accidentally ingests a human sex-drive serum, and becomes, in the words of a newspaper headline, a "leper sex killer." The film begins with the title "The whole world is dying of panicky fright," which belongs most directly to this narrative, but is clearly an epigraph to the entire film. José Arroyo argues that AIDS is a subtext of many examples of the New Queer Cinema, whether they directly address it or not. In particular, he argues of *My Own Private Idaho* and *Edward II* that "both films depict the context of the pandemic through their use of style, their romanticism, their representation of sexuality and time, and their dystopic viewpoint."[6] The dystopic viewpoint and the related rejection of positive images is linked to the politics of OutRage! as well as ACT UP, both of which were premised on the understanding that asking politely for one's rights was not effective in the political climate of the 1980s and 1990s.

Jarman addressed the issue of positive representation in a roundup of interviews connected with the New Queer Cinema published in *Sight and Sound:* "One of the problems was that with the word 'gay' came a drive for positive images, but all the artists I knew and respected were involved with negative images because that was the intelligent thing to do in a culture which promoted all that false positivity through advertising and so on."[7] In making *Edward II,* Jarman was well aware that the film would not please everyone. In the published script he addresses the issue of possible charges of misogyny in the portrayal of Isabella, and observes that "Andrew is not playing Gaveston in a way that will endear me to 'Gay Times,' only Edward comes out of this well and even he has bloody hands."[8] Edward and Gaveston are both seen committing quite brutal acts, with Gaveston in particular looking like "a vicious, Kray-like gangster in the beating up of the archbishop,"[9] according to Jarman (the film does at times resemble the look of Peter Medak's biopic *The Krays* [1990], part of a resurgence of British gangster films). Whereas mainstream and academic critics did for the most part respond in the predicted way to the figure of Isabella,[10] Rich wrote that "For women, *Edward II* is a bit complicated. Since the heroes are men and the main villain is a woman, some critics have condemned it as misogynist. Indeed, Tilda Swinton's brilliance as an actor—and full co-creator of her role—invests her character with more weight, and thus more evil, than anyone else on screen. But the film is also a critique of heterosexuality and of a world ruled by royals and Tories, and Isabella seems more inspired by Thatcher than woman-hating."[11]

Edward II (1991). Isabella (Tilda Swinton) and Edward (Steven Waddington). Production still.

The film makes it clear that if Isabella and Gaveston are monsters, they are the products of a monstrous society.

One of the key moments in the film that inspired the charges of misogyny is also one that brings it closest to the heart of the New Queer Cinema. Late in the film, after Isabella has been rejected by Edward and has joined Mortimer's opposition forces, she murders Edward's vacillating brother Kent by biting him on the neck and drinking his blood.[12] This picks up on an earlier moment in the film where Mortimer and Isabella first seal their alliance, by sharing a kiss under Isabella's veil. Of this scene Jarman notes: "There is an element of a real horror film (Corman's 'The Tomb of Ligeia' perhaps?)—after all, we were making this in Hammer's old Bray studios."[13] The vampiric Isabella parallels an earlier moment in the film when Gaveston, after being banished from the kingdom, crouches in the rain, howling like a werewolf in a raging thunderstorm. As Jarman's comments indicate, these gothic echoes are partly an homage to the studio where some of the best-known examples of British horror films were created. From the 1950s to the 1970s, Hammer Films produced a distinctive series of genre pictures that blended horror and sexuality, from the classic

Frankenstein and Dracula adaptations of the 1950s featuring Christopher Lee and Peter Cushing, to the soft-core lesbian vampire films of the late 1960s and early 1970s.[14] As Harry Benshoff argues, there has always been a sexual component in horror films (and more generally the gothic genre), which frequently equate aberrant sexuality with monstrosity. Rather than reject this heritage, the practitioners of the New Queer Cinema largely embraced it, much as queer politics in general embraced the formerly disparaging term "queer."

This reclaiming phenomenon was seen in audience responses as well. While some gay and lesbian groups protested the figure of the killer lesbian in *Fatal Attraction* as yet another in a long line of offensive characterizations, other queer activists reveled in the image of the dangerous and sexy outsider. Benshoff argues that "the rise of queer social practice and theory... have led within the last ten years to an opposing trend in cinematic horror, one that in some cases actively overturns the genre's conventions in order to argue that the monster queers are actually closer to desirable human 'normality' than those patriarchal forces (religion, law, medicine) that had traditionally sought to demonize them."[15] Part of this embrace of the monstrous can also be seen (as in *Poison,* for example) as a more specific response to mainstream images of gay men in the context of the AIDS epidemic, who, as Ellis Hanson observes, were often implicitly or explicitly figured as vampiric: "while vampire films and novels may have lost their original capacity to excite homosexual panic, this collapse arrived just in time for a replacement genre: the AIDS documentary."[16] In *Edward II*, significantly, it is the representative of the state rather than the person associated with HIV who is figured as vampiric, although the entire film occupies the territory of the gothic.

There is a further appropriateness for *Edward II* in invoking the horror genre, which is the way that horror employs architecture and landscape as concretizations of psychological space. In that regard, the film follows in the tradition of German Expressionism, which was similarly invested in the gothic. The stark, monumental sets in the film work as something of a negative of the bright, white sets Jarman designed for *The Devils*, although both are meant to be expressive of the psychology of a political terrain. The clean, open, modernist lines of the city of Loudun in *The Devils* proclaim its political difference from the rest of France, and its refusal to bow down to the terror of the Inquisition. The sets in *Edward II*, on the other hand, with their oppressive, dusty, barren rooms, are to some degree an externalization of the psychological experience of living in Thatcherite England. Insofar as it is impossible to resolve the relation between its various spaces, the geography of *Edward II* is reminiscent of Prospero's decaying manor house in *The Tempest*, which similarly worked to suggest a parallel between a disordered state and a disordered state of mind. The stark lighting of the sets evokes both the studio scenes in *Caravaggio* and the monumental spaces of *War Requiem*, but whereas in *War Requiem* these monumental spaces found a contrast in the more human spaces of the trenches or the soldier's memories, in *Edward II* there is no refuge to be found outside the exposed, dusty rooms. The towering stone walls dwarf the characters, who often occupy only the lower half of the frame in a full shot. The sets work to suggest that in the moral climate of Thatcherism there is no meaningful notion of private space beyond the intrusive reach of the law, particularly where sexual minorities are concerned, and the entire country has become something of a prison.

Edward II is thus in many ways a continuation and culmination of earlier developments in Jarman's career. The film, as with *The Tempest* and *The Angelic Conversation*, draws upon an English Renaissance text, revisiting this key period of English history to comment on current political matters. As in *The Tempest* and *Caravaggio*, it employs an episodic structure that moves backwards and forwards in time—arguably, as with *Caravaggio*, starting with the title character's death and ranging over the events of the life. As in the historical films, anachronism is used to signal a different approach to historicism, and as in films like *The Garden* and *War Requiem*, moments of camp and cabaret significantly break the frame of the film to disrupt the realism often associated with narrative cinema. And, like *The Last of England* and *War Requiem*, this is to some degree a war film; as in the former, civil war serves as an allegory for the violence Thatcher's social policies visited upon her own people.

This last point is made abundantly clear in the published script, titled *Queer Edward II*, which is "dedicated to the repeal of all anti-gay laws, particularly Section 28." It resembles the book Jarman published to accompany *Caravaggio,* each page presenting a heterogeneous collage of information. Whereas *Derek Jarman's Caravaggio* combined quotations from historical sources, the shooting script, and observations by Jarman, *Queer Edward II* brings together OutRage! slogans, dialogue, and comments on the process of making the film by Jarman, Stephen McBride (who cowrote the screenplay), Ken Butler (Jarman's "Ghost Director"), and Tilda Swinton (whose comments are identified by "I. R.," Isabella Regina). On facing pages are photographs, some of which are promotional stills, but most of which are photos that show the filming process. As with so much of Jarman's work, the book is more interested in the process than the product, and it views that process as a collaborative one. The function of the "insider information" is different than in a "making of" book: the details about Jarman's illness, the visit of the activists, and the OutRage! slogans work not to take us behind the scenes, but rather to show us the continuity between what is happening in front of the camera and what is happening all around it. By insisting on this continuity, the book works in tandem with other of the film's strategies for challenging commonly accepted notions of what the borders of a film or a work of art are, and the ways in which this particular film both emerges from and participates in its own historical moment, in spite of its distant historical setting.

On the dedicatory page of the published script, Jarman claims that he adapted Christopher Marlowe's play for purely practical reasons: "How to make a film of a gay love affair and get it commissioned. Find a dusty old play and violate it." Clearly, however, the play held far more intrinsic interest than this, and while Jarman does rearrange and reduce the text considerably (as he did with *The Tempest*) there is a faithfulness to the spirit of the play, if not necessarily to the plot. The script artfully and radically restructures the drama, breaking up and reassigning speeches, reducing both the number of characters and the political intrigue, in order to focus the drama more squarely on the love affair of Edward and Gaveston and its disastrous consequences.

The film opens with Edward already overthrown and imprisoned in the dungeon, asleep and clutching a ragged piece of paper, which the script identifies as a postcard of the Eros statue in Picadilly, the site of one of OutRage!'s more famous demonstrations. His jailor Lightborn reaches down to examine the postcard, which turns out to be the

letter that Edward originally sent to summon his boyhood lover out of
exile in France: "My father is deceased; come Gaveston, / And share the
Kingdom with thy dearest friend."[17] After the titles we see Gaveston in
a nightshirt entering a room with a couple of mugs of coffee. He
reads the postcard to his friend Spencer while on the bed behind them
a pair of male hustlers grind away. Aside from the hustlers, who are
naked, the other characters in these two scenes wear historically unlocatable costumes reminiscent of the vaguely Victorian pastiche of the
Hammer films. Oddly, it is the hustlers who seem most anachronistic,
both because of their butch 1990s buzz cuts, which contrast with the
longer, looser hairstyles of the other men, but also because of the
forthright presentation of their bodies in a sexual embrace, which can
only impress the viewer as emphatically and shockingly contemporary, however absurd that might seem on reflection. This scene is different from the more romanticized presentation of the nude gay
lovers in Jarman's first film, *Sebastiane*, a difference that registers some
of the distance between gay liberation and queer politics. Here, for example, there is no suggestion that this is anything more than sex, and
the men's recreation acts as a backdrop for the seemingly cynical rumi-
nations of Gaveston. Whatever relation they might have had with him,
Gaveston dismisses them abruptly upon learning of his change in fortunes, after mocking their rough, working-class accents and telling
them "there are hospitals for men like you."

Whereas these first two sequences could possibly have worked
within a spare if not terribly accurate costume film, some of the line
readings give Marlowe's words contemporary and ironic echoes. (Gus
Van Sant would later achieve a similar effect in his updated but shot-
for-shot remake of Hitchcock's *Psycho* [1998].) Upon reading the letter,
for example, Gaveston says, "What greater bliss can hap to Gaveston /
Than to live and be the favourite of a king? / Sweet prince I come." The
pause before saying "Sweet prince I come," and the little laugh that
follows, give the line an obvious double reading. In a similar fashion,
the "hospitals" line quoted above brings the AIDS epidemic immediately into the picture, especially since Jarman has substituted the two
hustlers for what the play designates as "three poor men" who have
come to Gaveston to ask for his patronage. With these two sequences
the film establishes a layered temporality that involves both shuttling

back in forth in the plot and reading events in relation to their outcome, but also moving between two historical periods, invoking the same kind of double vision called for in *Caravaggio*. This temporal structure is further complicated when the dungeon set is used for scenes other than flash-forwards, as when, for example, Edward awaits Gaveston's second return from exile. Edward, these scenes suggest, has always been in this prison.

But whereas *Caravaggio* maintained a reasonable consistency with both sets and costumes, breaking this only occasionally with clearly anachronistic props, *Edward II* begins to depart almost immediately from even the loose vision of pastness that the two opening sequences establish. The next brief sequence offers us one of the "pleasing shows" with which Gaveston proposes to delight the king upon his return to the court. We see a well-muscled performer wearing a crown of golden leaves and a jockstrap, doing his act with a large snake. He is lit from above, so that no sets are visible, and he faces the camera directly, as if he is performing for us. This is followed by a long shot of the king on his throne, lit from above and behind. The shot is devoid of props, with the throne sitting on a platform at the top of a ramp, backed by a high central wall panel. This central panel (which anchors the brighter, central area of the frame) is flanked by two side walls that are parallel but slightly forward, giving wide, dark borders to the composition. Almost everything in the shot is gray, and covered with a layer of sand or dust. The only exceptions are the glittering throne and the sparkling gold robe that Edward wears. Although the robe is certainly kingly, the costume works to dispel any notion of periodicity rather than to conjure up a particular historical period. This is the case as well with the simple black suit and white shirt that Gaveston wears when he enters. The absence of props and historical markers, along with the Caravaggio-esque cellar lighting that isolates the figures from their surroundings, locates this scene in an unreal or unlocatable space that in earlier films has been associated with aesthetic space: those moments in *Caravaggio* or *Imagining October* when we cross over into the space of the painting. Remembering that in those films painting was an activity directed at the analysis of a social field, we might surmise that the space in this film will be used for a similar purpose. It is, very clearly, an "elsewhere" that is meant to be read as a meditation on the experience of "here."

In the sequences that follow, the mix of costumes grows increasingly dense. In the next scene, the archbishop is dressed in the timeless (if originally medieval) robes of his office, whereas Edward and Gaveston resemble Krays-era gangsters in their business suits as they confront him. Most of the other principal characters in the film dress in 1980s clothing. Mortimer, the principal figure in the opposition, appears at times in a military uniform that conjures up the British occupation of Ireland. The peers around him dress as contemporary politicians (the notice of exile they sign has the House of Commons logo on it and is dated 1991), and Isabella dresses in haute couture, looking like a cross between Eva Peron, Princess Diana, and Margaret Thatcher. Bette Talvacchia observes that "Isabella is lavishly turned out in a self-conscious parody of Hollywood glamour; her costumes never recede into being mere clothing." The result, she argues, is that "the progression of elaborate outfits forms its own narrative discourse."[18] To use Stella Bruzzi's distinction, we look *at* the costumes rather than *through* them,[19] another instance of the film's nonrealist approach, and one that works well with its general emphasis on understanding the formation of character and subjectivity in relation to social forces.

In fact, in contrast to *Caravaggio* or *The Tempest,* few if any of the costumes or props conjure up the past, whether medieval or Renaissance, although we continually have that expectation. We expect, for example, when we hear in one scene the sounds of horses' hooves coming from outside the frame that we are getting a reference to the past, but it turns out to herald a contemporary foxhunting group that enters with Mortimer to challenge Edward. What the sound editing here suggests is that the truly anachronistic elements of the film are the values associated with the peers, and hence with Thatcherite moral conservatism. Although the sets seem vaguely medieval in their stony austerity, they are too open and too formalist to clearly signal actual rooms or buildings, and it is really only the language that belongs to another era. But if the costumes are largely present-day, the effect is not the same as a contemporary-dress version of Shakespeare, perhaps because the lighting and sets place the action in an unreal "elsewhere," even if this is a contemporary elsewhere. The inset performances by the snake handler, the dancers from DV8 Physical Theatre,[20] or the string quartet, which in Jarman's other films would function as breaks of frame, are less disruptive here because of the unreality of the mise-en-scène. The result, as I have suggested, is that the action of the film presents itself as an exploration and analysis, from a queer perspective, of particular dimensions of the contemporary political landscape. In that regard, the film acts as something of an update on *The Last of England*, only this time within the context of a narrative film.

It is important to bear in mind that from the perspective of the late 1980s and early 1990s, and the particular set of circumstances that spawned OutRage!, that the political climate of Britain was experienced as an almost overwhelmingly hostile and dangerous place by many queer people. This helps to explain some of Edward's actions in the film, including his extravagant and apparent overvaluing of Gaveston, his frantic defense of him against all odds, and the brutal vengeance he enacts on one of the agents of the state. To the peers' question "Why should you love him who the world hates so?" Edward responds, "Because he loves me more than all the world." The peers find it incomprehensible that Edward would choose someone rejected by the rest of the world, forgetting that from their perspective, both Edward and Gaveston are members of the same despised minority, and that no amount of good behavior will win them anything more than polite and conditional tolerance. Arroyo argues that "Edward and Gaveston overestimate the powers of class to shield their sexual orientation. They are unable to imagine the reverse—that socially transgressive sexual practices can be the excuse for stripping away class privileges."[21] Although this is certainly an insight that the film offers, it is doubtful that Edward and Gaveston are unaware of the transgressiveness of their desire: the film starts, after all, with Gaveston being recalled from his exile in France, where he had been sent by Edward's father. The film seems instead to be insisting on the difference between rights and privileges, and, in particular, the unpopular but timely notion that political rights are not only for the nice.

Gaveston in particular seems continually aware of the dangerous, provocative game he is playing. In his discussion of the relation between the play and the film, Lawrence Normand notes that in the play, the principal objection to Gaveston is not sexual but political: "for the barons Gaveston is objectionable because his access to favour means their exclusion, and their anger is expressed in political terms."[22]

Jarman says that in the film, "Gaveston is sexuality and class combined,"[23] which would appear to agree with Normand's identification
of the Foucauldian thesis underlying the film: "In these incidents and
imagery sex is entwined with power, and power is realized through
sex. And there is no ground which defines the natural or the authentic: power is realized as the satisfaction of sexual desire, sexual desire
as the effect of the play of power, and sex as the means to power."[24]
What has to be appended to this, however, is the film's further insight
that it is the state's obsessive and oppressive interest in deviant sexuality that produces the various subjects who operate within its terrain.

This helps to explain the necessity of what some critics have identified as "a hackneyed image of heterosexual perversity"[25] in the scenes
featuring Mortimer engaging in kinky sex with prostitutes, scenes that
operate on a continuum with the obvious sexual pleasure of Mortimer
and Isabella as they occupy the throne. This is not evidence, as some
critics have suggested, of Jarman's heterophobia, or evidence of gay liberationist as opposed to queer politics.[26] The queers in the film are not
posited as the "natural" or the "authentic" either, as the central example of Gaveston continually shows. The first scene of Mortimer with
the prostitutes is immediately followed by a shot of a naked Gaveston
crouching on the throne like an animated gargoyle or incubus. The
point is that the same system has produced both monsters or, more
accurately, has produced both as monsters. This is also the function of
the provocative overstatements and reversals in the queer slogans that
punctuate the published script, such as "Heterosexuality is cruel &
kinky" or "Heterosexuality isn't normal, it's just common," which really
work to suggest that all sexual choices are equally natural or unnatural,
that they are all, in effect, modern nature.[27]

One of the most pertinent slogans in the published script is "Intercourse has never occurred in private," which might be taken as the
central point of the film's mise-en-scène. As I have argued above, the
sets conjure up a world where there is no refuge from the intrusions of
the state. Even the characters' beds seem to be adrift in the vast, open
spaces that are harshly lit from above. Any clandestine activity must
be conducted quickly, in corridors and shadows, in whispers. Whereas
those subjects operating under the sanction of the law might not have
occasion to notice or object to it, those whose sexual practices are

proscribed quickly learn that there is no meaningful notion of privacy that is operative. Such an awareness cannot but do violence to the Western sense of selfhood, which is to some degree premised on the sanctity of the private, interior self. In the characters of Gaveston and Isabella, the film shows us the effects of such violence on those subjects who are outside the law, or who cannot become "full" subjects.

Indeed, one of the most chilling and difficult scenes in the film is the central confrontation between Gaveston and Isabella. A tightly framed close shot brings us into an uncomfortable intimacy with the two. Gaveston begins a seduction of Isabella, and when she appears to respond to his attentions, he pulls away and cruelly laughs at her. The humiliated Isabella protests, saying, "Villain, 'tis thou that robs me of my lord." At this point Gaveston stops his mocking laughter and responds in a serious voice: "No madam, 'tis you who rob me of my lord." (Elsewhere in the script Jarman notes that "Gaveston had lived with Edward ten years before the marriage to Isabella.")[28] Gaveston exits and the camera stays on Isabella's face, while in a voice-over we hear her saying, "Fair blows the wind for France, blow gentle gale." In the sequence that follows, we see the peers at a council table preparing the order to banish Gaveston to France. The camera occupies a position at the head of the table, and although we never see whose point of view the camera is assuming, the implication is that it is Isabella's. In a later, parallel scene, after Isabella has realized that she will never win this particular battle and therefore begins plotting Gaveston's death, the camera turns to show her there, while the peers applaud her scheme.

The film here is making the familiar point about the way that less powerful groups are put into competition with each other—here, women and gay men—as a way of keeping them apart, parallel to the dynamic between Caliban and Miranda in The Tempest. This film goes further to show the consequences of that competition. Gaveston, as a result of his exile, has already been warped by his experiences of oppression, and we have already seen the effects in his violent and thuggish treatment of the archbishop, and the cruel humiliation of Isabella. Isabella will, after this point, begin to solidify into the vampiric Thatcherite figure we see at the end of the film. The film refuses to idealize the effects of suffering, oppression, or victimization, avoiding what Dominick LaCapra identifies as the "unearned confidence about the ability of the human spirit to endure any adversity with dignity and nobility."[29] Such experiences do not necessarily ennoble those who live through them; they are at least equally likely to transform them for the worse, and to make this observation is neither homophobic nor misogynist. The film shows, as Thomas Cartelli observes, "why resistance may come to resemble what it opposes."[30] (This, we might note, is also a dominant theme of the films of Fassbinder.)[31] The film does not ask us to admire Gaveston or Isabella, but rather to understand that they did not become evil on their own. They are playing a game the terms of which they did not dictate, using the limited resources available to them.

This power game becomes increasingly violent as the film progresses. The function of the political story is to move the film out of the realm of private, romantic intrigue, and to insist on the larger political context of the regulation of sexualities. In the past, the sexual lives of monarchs could have effects in the political sphere, as the case of Henry VIII amply shows, and thus there was something of a state interest in these sexual affairs. The principal change in emphasis that results from moving the story from the Renaissance version of the Middle Ages to the present has to do with the way that the play moves from being a history of a bad king to being an allegory of a deviant citizen. In the play, Edward's liaison with Gaveston is only a problem because of the way it violates class lines, and thus the sex is almost inadvertently caught up in the politics; in the contemporary setting, the sexual problem *is* the political problem, and now not only for kings and queens. The film is not exploring a situation that is constrained only to the realm of the private, because of the way the state has made the regulation of the sexuality of all its citizens a public matter.

The consequences of sexual and political deviance escalate in the film from the humiliating exile of Gaveston, where he must run a gauntlet of priests who spit on him as he leaves, to his violent, bloody beating and murder at the hands of Mortimer's forces. The contemporary dress in these scenes, particularly Gaveston's queer outfit (T-shirt, leather jacket, and jeans), makes the parallels between the fate of the historical figure and the contemporary fact of gay bashings clear. In this context,

Spencer's urgings to Edward to remember his dignity and nobility in the face of these outrages, and to fight back, are also a call to arms to contemporary queers, who face similar affronts to their dignity:

> Were I King Edward, England's sovereign,
> Son to the lovely Eleanor of Spain,
> Great Edward Longshank's issue, would I bear
> These braves, this rage, and suffer uncontrolled
> These Barons to beard me thus in my land,
> In mine own realm?[32]

Just as Spencer claims for Edward ownership of England, the film itself by taking up this story claims for its own community a similar ownership of the realm. Spencer's citation of Edward's lineage echoes an earlier moment in the film where Kent cites famous male couples in history:

> The mightiest Kings have had their minions;
> Great Alexander loved Hephaestion,
> The conquering Hercules for Hylas wept,
> And for Patroclus stern Achilles drooped:
> And not Kings only, but the wisest men. . . .[33]

Spencer's outraged call to arms is followed closely by the entrance in the film of the OutRage! protesters, which cements these histories together. The resulting statement is not a plea for tolerance, but rather an assertion of rights. This claim on a past is, as we have seen, a recurrent feature of Jarman's career, from his reimagining of Shakespeare's *Sonnets* in *The Angelic Conversation* to his various autobiographical projects, all of which work to assert a place within English history, and thus within the English nation. The historical example of Edward acts both as claim on history and a call not to repeat it.

The violence in the film continues as Edward and Spencer butcher a member of the security forces who is chained to a huge, splayed carcass hanging from the ceiling, while on the sound track we hear the squeals of hogs being slaughtered. The arrangement evokes Francis Bacon's *Painting* (1946), a grotesque portrait of power that places a leering politician of some kind in a butcher-shop setting, in front of a similar crucifix-like animal carcass. The scene is followed by the sum-mary execution of three of the protesters, the capture of Edward, and Mortimer's beating of Spencer, where Mortimer whispers a contemptuous "girlboy" in his ear after he snaps Spencer's neck. Kent is then murdered by Isabella, and finally, Edward is killed by Lightborn in the famous poker scene, although this latter death is suspended by the film's doubled ending. In the following scene, Edward appears to awake from a nightmare, and thus perhaps from history, and he and Lightborn embrace.[34] A series of scenes that follow combine to make a somber but essentially optimistic conclusion to the story: a queer young Edward dances on top of a cage imprisoning Mortimer and Isabella, and then the camera tracks through a room full of OutRage! activists, suggesting that the future lies with this particular community, if only they can seize hold of history.

Operating alongside this more general story about queer political activism amid the violence of Thatcherite social conservatism is another story about the experience of living with AIDS. The two are obviously related, particularly in light of the government's neglect and mismanagement of the AIDS epidemic, and its utter disregard for its victims: "This dungeon where they keep me is the sink / Wherein the filth of all the castle falls. / And there in mire and puddle have I stood."[35] In this reading of the film, the sets can be seen not so much as a prison but, as Steven Dillon suggests, as a crypt.[36] Restructuring the narrative by beginning and ending with Edward in the dungeon waiting for death has the effect of making the film reflect one dimension of the psychological landscape of a person with AIDS: How does one live in the face of a death that is uncertain but likely imminent? What new horrors lie in wait before the end?

Aside from the various contemporary echoes of Marlowe's lines that summon up the epidemic ("there are hospitals for men like you"), the film's most direct citation is the appearance of Annie Lennox. After the order for Gaveston's exile has been signed, he and Edward meet before parting. On the sound track we hear Lennox singing, "Ev'ry time we say good-bye," the song she recorded for the Red Hot & Blue AIDS benefit album. She had asked Jarman to direct the video for the song, but he was too ill. The video that was made instead became something of a tribute to Jarman. Home movies from Jarman's childhood such as those that appeared in The Last of England are projected onto a screen, in front of which stands Lennox, so that the images play across her body. The song thus imports into the film two significant contexts: one is the world of AIDS activism, and the other, via the video, is the autobiographical dimension of Jarman's own experience with AIDS.

We first hear the song on the sound track as Gaveston and Edward talk in a close shot, while a spotlight plays on them. Then, somewhat surprisingly, we have close-up of Lennox singing, her head leaning against a stone wall that resembles those of the sets. The nondiegetic sound has crossed over to become diegetic in some way, as the sound track spills over into the world of the film. The film then alternates between shots of the two lovers wearing pajamas, dancing in the middle of a large, empty room with a spotlight on them, and shots of Lennox, in a similar space, also with a spotlight. At the conclusion of the song a long shot puts them both in the same space, and the lovers watch as Lennox exits the room, disappearing into the strong backlighting. The inclusion of Lennox in the space of the film is similar to the appearance of Elisabeth Welch singing "Stormy Weather" in *The Tempest,* although here it is a little less jarring, in spite of the fact that Lennox is only very loosely incorporable into the narrative. Her performance could perhaps be seen as one of the "idle triumphs, masques, [and] lascivious shows" that the barons have complained about, examples of which we have already seen with the snake handler and the dancers from DV8. Because of the general unreality of the mise-en-scène, which has been established as something of a psychological terrain, Lennox's appearance is less of a break in the frame than it might be in a more naturalistic film. Moreover, it clarifies what the audience already suspects, that this is a film at least partly about AIDS. This is apparent not just through the contexts that Lennox's inclusion imports into the film, but also through the way the lyrics of the song register the cumulative effects of AIDS deaths on the community ("ev'ry time we say good-bye, I die a little") and through the pajamas that the two lovers wear, which make their parting the equivalent of a deathbed scene.

Lennox's appearance does not so much disrupt the film as expand its boundaries. The two lovers watching slightly starstruck as the singer exits the room echo the audience's frisson at seeing a well-known personality, with whom they likely have a phantasmatic relation, enter the fictional frame. It feels, oddly, as if something that belongs to us has crossed over into the space of the film. The film has, however, continually gestured outward, both in the performances that seem to directly acknowledge the audience and in the style of the film's address, including its forgoing of realism in the expressionist sets, its direct citation of filmic genres (gangster and horror films), and its frequent tableau setups. Thus the casting of the OutRage! activists as Edward's forces is fully prepared for, as is their appearance in the final shot of the film. Jarman says in the published script that "in our film all the OutRage boys and girls are inheritors of Edward's story."[37] Their appearance, like that of Lennox, helps to clarify the subject of the film as well as its politics, and in the case of the activists, its first audience.

To this audience, the combination of the various components of the film's ending offers a particular message. In showing us the famous version of Edward's murder, with its grotesque visualization of a homophobic poetic justice, it acknowledges that history cannot simply be wished away. As the rest of the film has argued, the state is involved in the clandestine murder of many queers, either through police harassment or government inaction on AIDS. This desire for violence is echoed in society at large either literally through gay bashing or, more psychologically, in the pronouncements of the media and the pulpit. Edward's murder, the most famous if historically unlikely element of the story,[38] is the logical conclusion of the narrative, which has been emphasized throughout the film by shots of the phallic poker. By staging it as a dream sequence, Jarman does not erase it, and certainly does not diminish its force. Indeed, in some ways the other ending might equally be seen as the dream narrative, the unlikely, if wished-for, salvation. Although it comes as a relief, we have no way of knowing that the other ending isn't still going to happen.

The final series of images is decidedly unreal. We see Edward's son sitting on the throne, wearing the crown and gold robes, holding an orb. Four flames burn across the bottom of the frame, giving the scene a hellish glow. On the sound track we hear the slightly creepy music of a xylophone and cello playing the "Dance of the Sugar Plum Fairies," which continues into the next shot. There we see the young Edward dancing on top of a cage holding Mortimer and Isabella, who are covered with a chalky white dust. In his speech, Mortimer reflects on the medieval concept of fortune's wheel, which stresses the inevitability of change in worldly affairs. Of this scene Jarman observes that "The little boy is always there. He's a witness and a survivor."[39] Edward is wearing a suit like Gaveston's, combined with Isabella's earrings and shoes. He is clearly something of a queer figure, and acts as a promise of continuity and future survival. This is a character that frequently shows up in Jarman's films, and one that almost always lends an optimistic note in what are often pessimistic scenarios.

In spite of this promise of survival in the figure of young Edward, the final tracking shot does not make a triumphalist statement. The camera moves slowly through the group of protesters, who stand silent and unsmiling. On the sound track we hear the music for the hymn that accompanied the execution scene ("Resurrexit": "He is risen"), a motif that subtly brings the murder back to mind. In a voice-over, Edward says:

> But what are kings when regiment is gone,
> But perfect shadows in a sunshine day?
> I know not, but of this I am assured,
> That death ends all, and I can die but once.

The Boy (Jody Graber) as witness and survivor in *Edward II*. Production still.

> Come death, and with thy fingers close my eyes,
> Or if I live let me forget myself.

On the line "Come death" the screen fades to black, the familiar cinematic representation of death. Interestingly, given its prominence, the speech as a whole does not appear in the play, and is assembled from three different sections of Edward's dialogue.[40] The speech is a call to bravery, suggesting that although suffering is an unwelcome part of our past and our present, the point is to work toward the future. Because of the presence of the protesters, the words have an unmistakably autobiographical ring to them. Just as the inverted narrative structure turns the entire film into something of an AIDS allegory, Jarman here speaks to his own coming death and to a determination to live and die well.

The ending provokes us, as audience, to reflect on what we have seen, and our relation to it. The protesters in contemporary dress both stand in for us as our on-screen representatives and also confront us with their silent presence. This resembles the moment in a masque when the line between audience and spectacle is crossed or broken down, and the actors reach out to include the audience members in the dance, so that the moral vision of the masque expands to encompass everyone present. By pulling back to reveal a figure of its audience, and thus stressing its own fictional nature, the film invites us to read its narrative as something of a morality play or parable. The trappings of the past are used to establish the "once upon a time" space that allows us to ignore temporarily our implication in the events while we absorb the lessons of the story, before being reminded once again that the story is about us. But the film reminds us as well that the past isn't just an elsewhere, where diverting stories can be played out for our amusement, but rather that the past inhabits the present in complex ways and that we ignore it at our peril.

Wittgenstein and the Queer Life

Unlike most of his films, Jarman's involvement with the Wittgenstein project started after the first version of the script was completed. Producer Tariq Ali had originally commissioned Terry Eagleton to write a script for a fifty-minute telefilm on the life of the twentieth-century Austrian-born, Cambridge-educated philosopher, and then asked Jarman to direct. Once the two were involved, there was more interest in the project and hence more money, and Jarman was asked to expand the script into a feature-length film. He and his collaborator, Ken Butler, apparently sent Eagleton versions of the revised script, and invited him to watch the filming, but received no replies.[41] When the film was finished, however, Eagleton was extremely unhappy with the results, and he vented his dissatisfaction in a number of prominent venues. In an essay published in the *Guardian,* for example, he wrote:

> Jarman, for all his admirable radicalism, has a very English
> middle-class sensibility, which is light years removed from the
> austerity and intellectual passion of his subject. The film, then,
> is not uniformly brilliant. Hunky young men for whom Spinoza
> is probably a kind of pasta shamble around ineptly disguised
> as philosophers. A camp Martian crops up for no particular
> reason, uttering wads of embarrassing whimsy. . . . If you're
> filming the story of a philosopher, you need a director with
> some respect for the mind.[42]

Eagleton's very public disavowal of the film (his name, however, remained in the credits) is revealing in a number of ways, not least for how, this far along in his career, Jarman could still attract the same kind of sneering condescension that was directed at his first films, even from left-wing intellectuals. The familiar complaints about camp and frivolity were answered by Wittgenstein's biographer, Ray Monk, in a laudatory review of the film in the *Times Literary Supplement.* Without directly referring to Eagleton's comments, Monk observed that "If one were not aware of its roots in Wittgenstein's own work, the figure of the Martian might appear as the sort of camp excess for which Jarman is known."[43] In the film, the Martian answers in advance Eagleton's thinly veiled homophobic jibe about the "hunky young men" whose good looks apparently disqualify them from a life of the mind, by asking the young Ludwig: "How many toes do philosophers have?"[44]

In the introduction to his script, Eagleton writes: "My own script strikes me as reasonably strong on ideas but short on dramatic action;

Jarman's, minus my own interpolations, seems to me just the other way around."[45] We might think about this in relation to an earlier comment Eagleton makes about Wittgenstein's style: "Like all good artists, Wittgenstein is selling us less a set of doctrines than a style of seeing; and that style cannot be abstracted from the feints and ruses of his language, the rhetorical questioning and homely exemplifying, the sense of a mind in ceaseless ironic dialogue with itself."[46] Hans-Johann Glock concurs with this, noting that Wittgenstein "had self-professed aesthetic ambitions, and regarded 'correct' style as integral to good philosophizing."[47] What both of these statements emphasize is that ideas are inseparable from the style through which they are conveyed, and therefore that style has philosophical implications. In assessing a film, then, we cannot so easily separate ideas and dramatic action, or the various elements of filmic style from the content of the film.

If one is to attempt to film a philosopher's life, or, more particularly, Wittgenstein's life and ideas, what is the appropriate style? It could be argued that the realist style employed by Eagleton in his script is antithetical to Wittgenstein's thought. Realism in the English tradition is most often associated with the rise of the novel and the "middle-class sensibility" that Eagleton locates in Jarman's treatment, and in particular with an exploration of the private, interiorized self. In his later writings, as Eagleton observes, Wittgenstein directly opposes such an understanding of the self: "What the *Investigations* try to therapise us out of is just that Western bourgeois notion of 'inwardness'—of an inner life so deep, subtle and evanescent that it eludes the reach-me-down categories of our social existence."[48] Arguably, the strategies of filmic realism, with its emphasis on the effacement of the mechanisms of production and the visually accurate reproduction of a surface reality, function precisely to suggest the presence of such an evanescent, unreachable depth beneath the surfaces portrayed. This is not to say that Wittgenstein did not believe in the existence of interiority, but his emphasis on the essentially social nature of language argues for an understanding of a more socially constructed version of subjectivity. Thus, if one is going to have a Wittgensteinian film, as opposed to a film about Wittgenstein, a different kind of cinematic form than realism will have to be employed.

I have argued of Jarman's writings that the form they employ or invent is part of an attempt to document a new version of subjectivity: the new understandings of selfhood that came into being as a result of the sexual revolution, in tandem with new forms of relation and new experiences of space. *Dancing Ledge, Kicking the Pricks,* and *Modern Nature* all eschew more familiar narratives of selfhood, employing a fragmentary, collage aesthetic that mixes different kinds of histories to tell, in different ways, the emergence of these new forms of being and new ways of being in the world. We see a similar formal experiment in *At Your Own Risk,* a memoir published in the year prior to *Wittgenstein's* release, and subtitled "A Saint's Testament." The subtitle most immediately refers to Jarman's canonization as Saint Derek of Dungeness by the Sisters of Perpetual Indulgence, the radical drag activist group founded in San Francisco in 1979. But the title also signals a particular genre of writing, one that acts as a testament to faith and often a record of suffering. As he says in the benediction that concludes the book, "I had to write of a sad time as a witness—not to cloud your smiles."[49] The book is broken into decades, each section charting the progress of gay rights while testifying to Jarman's own experience as a gay man, and including the testimony of others as well. He introduces evidence, reproducing documents such as the GLF Manifesto, and juxtaposes articles from the mainstream and the gay press documenting the AIDS epidemic.

As befits the genre, this testament is the documentation of a public self, a self that has emerged or come into being in relation to larger historical currents; indeed, as with *Edward II,* it suggests that in these latter and perilous days, the notion of a private self is an illusion available only to the privileged. As with all saints, private passions become, for better or (more usually) worse, the catalyst for public dramas. One of the most prominent effects of this mix of history is to highlight the social nature of the self, and how stories of the self are inevitably bound up with larger histories, and that the truth of the self is not buried deep within the individual, but rather must always be understood in relation to the larger social contexts in which the self participates and from which it draws its meaning.

This is the case as well in the films. We might recall that Jarman got his start in feature films working with Ken Russell, who reinvented the artist biopic, introducing startling fantasy sequences and ostentatious camera movements that broke with conventional realist representation of historical individuals. In the films of Jarman that we might label biographical, there is no real interest in character as conventionally understood. *Edward II*, for example, is not particularly interested in giving us a new insight into the title character's interior life. What the film explores instead is what happens when individual lives and desires get caught up in larger historical processes. In what might be seen as the most conventional of his portraits, *Caravaggio*, the visual style, the fractured temporality, and the fragments of the life story of the artist prevent us from imagining that we are seeing into the historical figure's soul. In both cases, we are offered not an authentic portrait of a historical individual, but rather a meditation on contemporary concerns that self-consciously exploits historical difference.

Similarly, Jarman's title for his introduction to the script of *Wittgenstein* is "This is Not a Film of Ludwig Wittgenstein," stressing that we will not be offered a conventional portrait of the philosopher's life. Accordingly, we are directly addressed in the film by the child Ludwig (Clancy Chassay). In the first scene we see him writing in a notebook and then reading to us the sentence, "If people did not sometimes do silly things, nothing intelligent would ever get done."[50] These lines suggest the seriousness underlying the apparent lightness and frivolity of some of the following scenes, making an implicit claim for the philosophical and ethical importance of art and cinema. In the next scene he pops up into the foreground of the frame, dressed in costume-party Imperial Roman clothes, and introduces his rich and cultured Viennese family to us. They are gathered around a grand piano on which his brother Paul, wearing a tuxedo, plays Brahms. The piano is the only piece of set in the scene, which, like much of the film, is played against a black backdrop. Other members of the family appear out of the dark as they are introduced, including ones that Ludwig tells us are dead, and all except the pianist wear classical Roman garb. The costumes are obviously metaphoric rather than realist, evoking a lost world of imperial luxury that is about to disappear in the tumult of the twentieth century. The combination of these various elements announces that we are not to expect a conventional realist treatment of the subject.

To render a queer life, it is necessary to employ a queer aesthetic. The film's mode of address, much like the film's style, pushes outward into the space of the audience as it violates all rules of temporality. The figure of the young Wittgenstein speaks to the camera directly as he narrates, in the past tense, his future life. At one point the Martian further breaks the frame by asking Ludwig, "I know this film studio is in Waterloo, but how do I know that you are Ludwig Wittgenstein?" The story itself is highly fragmentary, and occasionally punctuated by enigmatic images: Wittgenstein sitting in a large bird cage, contemplating a bird in a smaller cage, or the philosophy student Johnny playing dominoes beside the blue flame of a welding torch. These visual emblems are reminiscent both of Wittgenstein's epigrammatic style, which requires of the reader some imagination and patience to fully unfold their implications ("II.79. There is gold paint, but Rembrandt didn't use it to paint a golden helmet")[51] and of Sergei Eisenstein's theory of the attraction. Occasionally, these images are more immediately readable but nonetheless extremely evocative. The most striking example is an early scene where we hear about Wittgenstein's initial studies in engineering and aeronautics at Manchester University. Staring directly into the camera, he wears kite wings on his back and holds lawn sprinklers in his hands. The sprinklers send out swirling jets of water that resemble the spinning propellers of a plane. The artifice is effective, visually stunning and rich, evoking visual precedents as diverse as da Vinci's engineering drawings and Kenneth Anger's filming of water fountains in *Eaux d'Artifice*.

Except for one sequence toward the end, the scenes of the film are played against black backdrops, in pools of light. Revolving scenes, slow pans, raked angles, and tight shots are all used to define the space and give it depth. Simple and obvious effects are used in lieu of realism. The movement of a boat being rowed through the water, for example, is suggested by dappled blue light. Similarly, the spare, isolated elements of the sound track work as a kind of aural shorthand. Both the color and the use of light to define and restrict space can be linked to the style that Jarman initially explored in *Caravaggio*. As in Caravaggio's paintings, backdrops are minimal or absent, scenes are reduced to their essential elements, figures gesture outward, and bright colors pop to push the composition forward, toward the viewer. This works in tandem

The adult Wittgenstein (Karl Johnson) in *Wittgenstein* (1993).

with the film's direct address to the audience. Space here is aesthetic space; there is no pretense toward a fourth wall.

The style Jarman employs, as with the autobiographical writings, is meant to convey a different understanding of selfhood or subjectivity than is conveyed by a realist treatment, which generally uses a familiar narrative to marshal the events of a life into a recognizable form (the tragic artist, the triumphant outsider, etc.). Although realism, and its attendant interest in a particular kind of psychology, has been jettisoned, this is not to say that the film has no interest in the interior life or character of the title subject. There is a suggestion that, like *The Tempest* or *Edward II,* the film might be taking place in the central character's mind, so that the whole film could be seen as a portrait of that mind, and all of the other characters exist within the character's memory or fantasy. There is, for example, a noticeable difference between the acting style of Karl Johnson and the rest of the cast. Whereas Johnson performs the character more or less naturalistically, the others present their characters in largely two-dimensional form, reminiscent of Brechtian styles of acting. As Michael O'Pray notes, this difference between characters is further underscored by the costume design.[52] Johnson wears the same drab outfit throughout much of the film, a gray tweed jacket, white shirt, blue trousers, and suspenders, while the other characters, particularly Lady Ottoline Morrell (Tilda Swinton), wear flamboyant, brilliantly colored outfits that change hue from scene to scene. If the film is understood as the fantasy or memory of Wittgenstein, the presence of the other characters reminds us of what both Jarman and Wittgenstein would see as the intersubjective or essentially social nature of selfhood.

Wittgenstein's sexuality is not the central and singular dilemma in the film, but neither is it an incidental aspect of his personality that is acknowledged and relegated to the sidelines. We hear from the young Ludwig about his "bent" brother Rudolf, who moved to Berlin and later killed himself, and through the film we see the adult Wittgenstein struggling with what he saw as the libertine world of Cambridge and the Bloomsbury set, and with his sexual desire for men. The objects of this desire are condensed into the single figure of a student named Johnny (Kevin Collins), with whom he has an affair: "I have known Johnny three times. And each time I began with a feeling that there was nothing wrong. But after, I felt shame."[53] In spite of this feeling of shame, he doesn't seem any more tormented by this desire than by the more general questions of existence that plague him, and it appears by the end of the film that he has serenely accepted it. Characteristically with Jarman, the relation with Johnny is not simply a sexual one; as *Edward II* shows, it is no more possible to have a private sexuality than it is to have a private language. At various points, Wittgenstein attempts to counsel Johnny away from a life of the mind, and at other points worries about the influence he might have on his students. All of this is part of the larger question of how one is to best live with others, and the responsibility one bears to oneself and to others. In that regard, the film is exploring some of the same terrain as *War Requiem* and *Edward II*, tracing out an ethics that has its ultimate origin in same-sex desire, but which is further shaped by a particular set of experiences. In all three cases, this ethical position has to do with an estrangement from the nation, whether from conscious refusal of the price of belonging, as in *War Requiem*, or through disenfranchisement, as in *Edward II*. In *Wittgenstein*, the struggle with sexuality is part of a more general estrangement from the world, and thus coming to terms with sexuality means at the same time coming to terms with living in the world.

Wittgenstein's sexuality is thus a part of the portrait of Wittgenstein's larger problem of sorting out how to live an ethical life. As Ray Monk notes in his review of the film, the figure of the alien in the film, Mr. Green, is a useful metaphor for Wittgenstein himself, for whom the rest of the world is for the most part painfully foreign. The film details his flight from his family, his various educational experiments, and his flight from Cambridge after he had become Russell's favorite pupil. He volunteers to fight in the trenches in the First World War, teaches in a rural school in Austria, builds a house in Norway with his own hands, volunteers to do manual labor in Russia, and late in life moves to a remote cottage on the coast of Ireland. The film suggests the connections between the geographic restlessness, the quest for an ethical life, and finally an acceptance of desire and the human condition.

The use of brilliant color in the film is related both to the implications of Wittgenstein's work and to aesthetic concerns in Jarman's work. In the film, the contrast between Wittgenstein's drab clothing and the flamboyant outfits of the Bloomsbury set is related to the central dilemma that the script constructs for Wittgenstein between the purity of logic and the messiness of life and desire, between ice and earth. The former vision corresponds to Wittgenstein's early work, the *Tractatus Logico-Philosophicus,* which sought to solve all problems of philosophy through logic, and the latter to the *Philosophical Investigations,* in which Wittgenstein rejects his earlier ideas and expounds his new theory of language. As he says in the film, "Philosophy hunts for the essence of meaning. There's no such thing! There's no such thing—just the way we do things in everyday life" (114). In the film, the acceptance of the world of earth is an acceptance of desire, including Wittgenstein's own desire for men.

In his writings, Wittgenstein uses the example of color to some degree as a demonstration of his larger theories about language. One of the implications of the argument that there is no private language is that language can only be understood by looking at how it is used. As the script says, "We learn to use words because we belong to a culture. A form of life. A practical way of doing things. In the end we speak as we do, because of what we do" (136). Or, as the script says elsewhere, "To imagine a language is to imagine a form of life" (104).

Color, like language in general, is part of a shared system of usage and understanding, and thus scientific investigations into the nature of color can only be secondary to an understanding of how color words are used in a particular culture. Or, as William H. Brenner explains, "Understanding a meaning is catching on to a use, not catching hold of an object."[54] We might think about this in relation to the project in *Chroma,* which works to historicize the apparently ahistorical colors in much the same way that *Modern Nature* challenges ahistorical understandings of both the natural world and human life. Color is not a stable thing that exists outside of time, but is rather a product of human interactions.

Two comments in Jarman's introduction to the script are worth quoting here: "The forward exploration of Colour is Queer" and "What is a picture of Queer? There is no one picture."[55] Color in the film is associated with an acceptance of the diversity of the world, reminiscent of the command of the angel Ariel in *Jubilee:* "Consider the world's diversity and celebrate it." The second statement about a picture of queer is reminiscent of comments in Wittgenstein's *Remarks on Colour* about the contextual nature of color perception: "Imagine someone pointing to a place in the iris of a Rembrandt eye and saying: 'The walls of my room should be painted this colour.'"[56] Arguing that there is no one picture of queer anticipates the antiessentialist statement in *Blue,* "I am a Not Gay." Queerness, like color, is a matter of definition and usage; queer doesn't designate a stable thing or identity but rather a way of being in the world, an ethics of existence.

One of the implications of this connection between queerness and color returns us to an earlier point—that there is an ethics of style and aesthetics, and that aesthetic choices may have ethical dimensions. This belief is a feature of Jarman's work from the beginning, particularly with respect to his interest in understanding and reforming the relation between the audience and the screen. Implicit in all of his films is the belief that the remaking of aesthetic space can have an effect on the occupants of the spectatorial space, that political art can offer more than simply argument and demonstration, and that the affective and sensual experience of the work can be transformative. Whereas different films employ a variety of means to explore and exploit the possible dimensions of filmic space, in this film, it is prin-

cipally color that is used, which has the beneficial side effect of making
Wittgenstein among his most joyful and visually pleasing.

The high artifice of the film's style goes hand in hand with its continual citation of art, including music, dancing, and most often, not
surprisingly, painting and cinema. Wittgenstein's sister Hermine is seen
painting a very queer Odalisque who sports tattoos, piercings, and a
butch haircut; elsewhere in the film Lady Ottoline paints a portrait of
Bertrand Russell that is a monochromatic red painting. Both of these
acts of painting offer some challenges to the audience. The queer
woman's body being posed by Hermine offers the by now familiar jolt
of anachronism, and the painting by Ottoline prompts us to wonder
in what sense a monochrome can be a portrait of Russell: what theory
of color, and what idea of selfhood, is in play?

The other art form frequently cited in the film, cinema, is credited
by Jarman with changing Wittgenstein's view of the world: "Ludwig
believed language was a series of pictures. Later, when he had watched
too many films, he abandoned this notion."[57] In the film, we see Wittgenstein at the cinema a couple of times with Johnny. In the first of
these, we see Johnny taking notes on the philosophy seminar they
have just come from, as Wittgenstein is engrossed by the screen:

WITTGENSTEIN: Are you mad? You'll ruin the plot.
JOHNNY: Shh. There is no plot.
WITTGENSTEIN: There might be.[58]

The exchange offers a witty comment on Jarman's own nonnarrative
films, and this largely plotless one in particular, but it can also act as a
commentary on Wittgenstein's and Jarman's interest in seeing the
world differently. Cinema can be just as potent an education in vision
as philosophy, which is suggested in the following scene as well. Here
we see the young Ludwig wearing 3-D glasses, playing shadow pup-
pets in the beam of the projector. Given the content of the scene
before it (the philosophy seminar), this can be read as an allusion to
the Parable of the Cave from Plato's *Republic*, which discusses the
education of the philosopher. Ordinary people, writes Plato, are like
slaves chained in a cave, mistaking the shadows on the wall in front of
them for reality. Only when we are taken up out of the cave, and
acquire a philosophical vision, can we see things the way they truly

are. The 3-D glasses that Ludwig wears sport one red lens and one green one, alluding to this film and the next's contention that through color we can apprehend a fuller, more dimensional reality.

In a voice-over Wittgenstein says that "There was no competition between the cinema and seminar. I loved films. Especially Westerns and Musicals. . . . I hated the newsreels—far too patriotic. I felt the makers must have been 'master pupils of Goebbels'. As for playing the national anthem at the end—I'd sneak out."[59] The vision of the world offered by art is preferable to the normative construction of the world presented in the documentary reels, but neither is to be mistaken for reality. It is, however, in the space of the cinema, in the second scene set there, that we see Wittgenstein reaching out and taking Johnny's hand for the first time. Jarman observes in the introduction that "The cinema was Ludwig's escape. Mine, a garden."[60] We have, of course, seen this paralleling of alternative spaces before. Here, the cinema works for Ludwig as the kind of antinationalist, no-man's-land gestured toward in *War Requiem,* where bonds between men are privileged over national belonging. There are in fact a number of parallels between these two films to be observed. They are set in the same time period, and both include representations of the First World War. In filming the soldier's similar memories of childhood, *War Requiem* uses light to define the space, rather than sets. The most important parallel, however, which we have already noted, is that both films connect homosexuality with an ethics, and associate it in turn with an alternative experience of space, which grows out of an estrangement from the dominant.

To some degree, the possibility of such spaces is signaled by the presence of the boy in the film. The young Ludwig who narrates the film is part of series of similar figures in Jarman's films, the boy who stands to the side and observes the unfolding action, often without making any direct comment on it. In a couple of instances, this character is the unfortunate recipient of a harsh education, as in *The Garden* or *Wittgenstein,* scenes that are suggestive of the violence of a more general pressure to conform to society's norms. In *Wittgenstein,* the adult character is horrified to find himself repeating this pedagogical violence in the rural school where he briefly and disastrously teaches, and at a later moment with Johnny where the memory of this violence resurfaces. The young Ludwig notes that "I was to spend a lifetime disentangling myself from my education,"[61] which echoes statements Jarman made about his own childhood. Even in the most pessimistic of the films, however, the boy typically lends a note of optimism, either as a signifier of innocence *(Caravaggio)* or the hope for a better future *(The Garden, Edward II).*

This is especially the case toward the end of the films, where the boy often appears in the penultimate or final scene, often juxtaposed with the death scene of the central figure. Implicit in this juxtaposition is the promise of survival. We first see the figure at the end of *Caravaggio,* where the boy Caravaggio looks at a tableau of the crucified Christ, which may be seen as an optimistic statement about the potentially transcendental power of art. At the end of *The Garden,* the two crucified lovers and the boy-Christ are reunited, where the boy lights a paper tube that again offers a vision of spiritual transcendence. The boy Edward at the end of *Edward II* performs a dance in partial drag on the top of a cage holding Isabella and Mortimer, the chief persecutors of his father, which suggests that the future might hold more promise for sexual dissidents.

Given that *Wittgenstein* is a more playful, intimate, and optimistic film than any of his others, it is fitting that this film offers us one of the most beautiful images yet of the transcendental power of cinema. Intercut with the older Wittgenstein's death scene we see the young Ludwig dressed in the kite wings we earlier saw the adult Wittgenstein wearing, in the aeronautics scene. Now, however, instead of sprinklers, Ludwig holds in each hand bunches of white balloons, which lift him into the air. This is the only scene in the film that is not shot against a black backdrop. Here, the curtain is pulled away to reveal a backdrop of clouds and sky. This is as artificial as all of the other sets in the film, because it is obvious we are still in the studio, but the effect is nonetheless exhilarating. As with the final scene of the burning paper in *The Garden,* the knowledge that something is an illusion does not necessarily lessen the pleasure one takes in its effects, or even necessarily its effectivity. This is perhaps the most optimistic statement that Jarman would make about the power of the cinema.

The boy Wittgenstein (Clancy Chassay) in *Wittgenstein.*

Queer Vision in *Blue*

Jarman's final film, *Blue,* is a without a doubt his most conceptually challenging and formally severe, and is in many ways the logical extension of number of key concerns in his work. Like *Wittgenstein,* it started its life as a biopic and turned into a film about color, being, and the ethics of representation. And while more somber, *Blue* shares with the previous film an optimism about art's potential for transforming the world, as well as moments of humor and playfulness. The idea of a film based on the work of the French painter and conceptual artist Yves Klein had been in Jarman's head for some time, at least as early as 1987.[62] One of his journals for that year contains a series of poems based on the work of Klein, each accompanied by a photocopied illustration from a monograph about Klein's work. The initial idea for a monochrome film with sound track subsequently changed to a work punctuated by judo throws (Klein was skilled in the art, and had made training films while studying in Japan) and then to a more standard artist biopic. The diary entry in *Modern Nature* for May 24, 1989, discusses Jarman's participation in a "loathsome inept youth-oriented arts programme" devoted to the work of Klein. He suggests to the producers that they have an interview "followed by as many minutes or seconds of blank blue soundless TV," although they failed to take

his advice.[63] He concludes the entry by saying, "IKB spirit in matter."
IKB is "International Klein Blue," the deep, ultramarine blue that Klein
used for his most famous monochrome paintings and installations.

Jarman had long been an admirer of Klein and his work, and there
are certainly enough similarities in their aesthetic interests to account
for this. Klein was much given to mystical pronouncements about art,
and his work often involved alchemical thinking. Like Jarman, he was
very much interested in the four elements and particularly fire, creating sculptures out of jets of flame, and paintings by scorching canvases with blowtorches. He experimented with what he called the
architecture of air, and with the mystical properties of gold. One of
Klein's ongoing preoccupations concerned the transformative potential of aesthetic space, evidenced most famously in a work called *The
Void.* This was an empty room, painted white, in which was manifested
a "sensuous pictorial state," a spatialization of his monochrome paintings, which would "act upon the sensuous vehicles or bodies of the
gallery visitors."[64] Entering the space, writes Klein, "one is literally im-
pregnated by the pictorial sensibility, refined and stabilized beforehand
by the painter in the given space."[65] This challenge to the boundaries of
the artwork and to the relation between artwork and viewer is a precursor to the radical reimagining of cinema that takes place with *Blue.*

Jarman's ideas for a Klein film continued to evolve for a number of
years, often under the names of "Bliss" or "Blueprint." O'Pray notes
that at a benefit screening of *The Garden* at the London Lumiere, on
January 6, 1991, "Jarman and Tilda Swinton put on a pre-screening event
titled 'Symphonie Monotone,'" clearly in homage to Yves Klein's work
of the same name:

> They sat at a table on stage creating sounds by running their
> moistened fingers around the rim of wine glasses, as in the
> Last Supper Sequence of *The Garden,* and recited passages
> from various writers on the theme of 'blue'. On the cinema
> screen was projected a 35mm film of a detail from an Yves
> Klein blue painting shot at the Tate Gallery. At various points
> slide images were projected on to the blue field. Sitting on the
> floor before the stage was a group of musicians led by Simon
> Turner playing gentle, almost hippie-style music. Now and

then the young boy actor Jody Graber from *The Garden* would run out into the audience with small blue and gold painted stones which he gave to individuals.[66]

The event was very much in the spirit of Klein's installations and performances, and it evolved into a series of concerts; the next was held at the Electric Cinema on Portobello Road on February 3, followed by others in Bari, Ghent, Rome, Berlin, and Tokyo.[67]

Another important precursor to *Blue* is the book *Chroma*. Produced after the Blue concerts, but before the film *Blue*, *Chroma* is very much a link between these works and *Wittgenstein*. Much of the script for the film *Blue* is in fact contained in the chapter "Into the Blue." Like most of Jarman's books, *Chroma* can be seen as an autobiographical experiment for a subject-in-process. Instead of using calendrical time as an organizing principle, *Chroma* is organized around the consideration of various colors. Most of the chapter titles are phrases that emphasize the metaphoric uses of color: "On Seeing Red"; "White Lies"; "Green Fingers." The chapters offer a collage of memories prompted by colors; theories about color from writers and philosophers such as Pliny, Cornelius Agrippa, Leonardo da Vinci, Isaac Newton, Goethe, and Wittgenstein; and lines of poetry involving color from Sappho, Dante, Wilfred Owen, T. S. Eliot, and others.

One of the more interesting projects the book takes on is to historicize color, often by offering a history of the development of a particular pigment or its uses. Of the red dyes, for example, he writes:

It is in these colours that the modern pharmaceutical industry was born. The great dye factories experimenting in scientific and artificial colour in the nineteenth century. The invention of malveine, aniline, fuchsin, the red dyes, were the foundations of Bayer and Ciba, and many other multinationals. Colour was turned into explosives. The fiery orange of nitre. Not only were they making explosives but they were also making drugs. The pills you swallow came from the dyers' works. In antiquity, colour (chroma) was considered a drug (pharmakon). Colour therapy.[68]

The method is similar here to that of *Modern Nature,* only now with colors rather than plants supplying the initial occasion for reflection.

Indeed, with its project of historicizing something that we consider to be ahistorical, the book could easily have been called "Modern Color." Historicizing inevitably means politicizing, or, at the very least, making visible connections that generally go unnoticed.

Jarman is careful to emphasize, following Wittgenstein, the contextual nature of color perception: "I know my colours are not yours. Two colours are never the same, even if they're from the same tube. Context changes the way we perceive them" (ibid., 42). This observation itself comes in the context of a letter that Jarman writes to the reader and posts in a red envelope, given its urgent nature: "I wrote this book in an absence of time. If I have overlooked something you hold precious—write it in the margin. . . . I had to write quickly as my right eye was put out in August by the 'sight oh! megalo virus' . . . and then it was a run-in with the dark" (ibid.). The reference here is to the cytomegalovirus, an opportunistic infection that was destroying Jarman's sight, and the treatment for which is one of the dominant subjects of *Blue*. The concern with color in both the book and the film is ultimately a concern with the politics of vision, both in the starkly literal sense of an AIDS-related blindness and in the metaphoric sense about diverse experiences of the world.

Thus we see that consideration of color is persistently linked to a history of sexuality, both implicitly and explicitly. In the chapter titled "Marsilio Ficino," Jarman considers the effect of the Neoplatonist philosopher on changing ideas about same-sex love in the Renaissance. He interrupts himself to object: "I know this is a long way from light and colour . . . but is it? For Leonardo took the first step into light, and Newton, a notorious bachelor, followed him with Optics. In this century Ludwig Wittgenstein wrote his *Remarks on Colour*. Colour seems to have a queer bent!" (58). One reason why color has a queer bent, the book suggests, is that if color perception is contextual, then lives lived outside the mainstream can lead to fresh perceptions, not just of color but of the world in general. This becomes, to some degree, the project of the film *Blue*: challenging the viewer to see with new eyes.

Blue consists of an unvarying field of IKB projected by film onto the screen, accompanied by a sound track. The sound track incorporates a number of different elements: four voices (those of Nigel Terry, John Quentin, Tilda Swinton, and Jarman) read a script that is a mix of autobiographical accounts, largely of Jarman's treatment for blindness, reflections on the color blue, and a fantastical account of a young man named Blue. This is accompanied by a minimalist score by Simon Fisher Turner, and occasional sound effects. In an opening sequence, for example, Nigel Terry says, "I am sitting with some friends in this café drinking coffee served by young refugees from Bosnia. The war rages across the newspapers and through the ruined streets of Sarajevo." We hear, behind this, first the ambient noises of a café, then the sound of bombs exploding, and then the café noises again. Although the majority of the narration is in the first person, present tense, the film opens by addressing a "you":

> You say to the boy open your eyes
> When he opens his eyes and sees the light
> You make him cry out. Saying
> O Blue come forth
> O Blue arise
> O Blue ascend
> O Blue come in

The film closes with a similarly enigmatic, sensual address:

> The smell of him
> Dead good looking
> In beauty's summer
> His blue jeans
> Around his ankles
> Bliss in my ghostly eye
> Kiss me
> On the lips
> On the eyes
> Our name will be forgotten
> In time
> No one will remember our work
> Our life will pass like the traces of a cloud
> And be scattered like
> Mist that is chased by the

Rays of the sun
For our time is the passing of a shadow
And our lives will run like
Sparks though the stubble

I place a delphinium, Blue, upon your grave

In these lyrical lines, it is difficult to tell what the pronouns are doing, or to stabilize the action. Is the boy dead good-looking, or is the good-looking boy dead? Who is encompassed by the "our" in "our name will be forgotten / In time / No one will remember our work"? The final line suggests that the addressee of the film is the boy named Blue, and that he now exists only in the mind's eye of memory. Shakespearean themes (mortality and fame) and echoes ("beauty's summer") in the narration recall the dreamy landscape and images of *The Angelic Conversation,* although the tone is now more elegiac.

Before addressing further the details of the sound track, I want to discuss the most commented upon aspect of the film, the unwavering field of blue. Following some of the more Kleinian pronouncements on the sound track ("From the bottom of your heart, pray to be released from the image. . . . The image is the prison of the soul"), some critics have argued that the blue screen is essentially an act of negation, denial, or rejection. O'Pray, for example, writes that "The blue colour field in *Blue* is offered as a denial, perhaps a transcending of his enthrallment with the real. It is such an extreme negation of his imagistic sensibility that it is perhaps an instance of Freud's notion that a feeling can be so intense that its only outlet is through its opposite."[69] Tim Lawrence writes, "Inspired by Klein, *Blue* is a refusal of representation. Unwilling to reduce people with AIDS to a fixed category, the monochrome screen dramatically reveals the artificiality of art. Jarman's move is powerful precisely because it is staged in a cinema rather than an art gallery."[70] While Klein did emphatically reject the line and the image in painting, his monochromes are not necessarily a refusal of representation, as is indicated by calling them "monochrome propositions." As this would suggest, for both Klein and Jarman the blue field is not an absence but a throbbing site of possibility. Nor is the monochrome in any way a rejection of art, or of the revolutionary potential of art, in which both Jarman and Klein strongly believed. On the contrary, in

Klein's more mystical pronouncements, the blue field is meant to offer the most potent point of access to the universe.

In Jarman's script, "the image" is very closely connected to the "facts of the world," and thus to what Jarman elsewhere calls "received information": "All received information should makes us inverts sad."[71] Hence the appeal on the sound track to Klein's favorite saint, Saint Rita, "the Saint of the Lost Cause. The saint of all who are at their wit's end, who are hedged in and trapped by the facts of the world." The rejection of the image should therefore be understood as a rejection of the conventional apprehension of reality, which is inevitably imprisoning for those who do not belong to heterosoc: "The image is a prison of the soul, your heredity, your education, your vices and aspirations, your qualities, your psychological world." There are also, as Lawrence argues, more particular and political reasons to refuse conventional representation in relation to AIDS, the limitations of which Jarman had previously remarked upon, and which will be discussed in some detail later in this chapter. But art here is figured as the potential solution to the limitations of convention, not the problem.

In her comprehensive study of Klein's career, Sidra Stich begins by observing that "his art is often misunderstood as an extreme form of pure abstraction based on reductivist and formalist tenets."[72] Klein's friend and colleague, the art critic Pierre Restany, similarly takes pains to differentiate Klein's monochromes from famous precedents like those of Kasimir Malevich, or the color field painters of the 1940s and 1950s. Klein is not interested in abstraction or in pure form, or in confining his art to the surface of the painting: "The great lesson that Klein derived from blue was its extradimensional character. Through blue and beyond blue, he felt himself grazed by the quivering of the absolute, a tangible representation of infinite space."[73] To emphasize the spatial qualities of the blue, the paintings were not hung on the walls but rather extended out from them by means of metal rods. As Stich further explains:

> A critical aspect of Klein's approach to monochrome painting was thus his desire to deobjectivify the work of art. He conceived of his paintings as living presences, not as material

things with restrictive boundaries. In addition, he treated
colour as an illuminating surface, never as a planar form. For
him, colour was the real and abstract medium of space, the
sensibility that inhabits extradimensional space and impreg-
nates both people and environments.[74]

Klein's monochromes thus challenge the relation between spectator
and painter by moving in a number of different directions: they push
out (literally and metaphorically) into the space of the gallery, and
they simultaneously offer access to the void. The paintings are not of
space, but rather are an attempt to become space itself.

The void that Klein gestures toward or opens up in his blue paintings is not a sphere of absence or negativity, but rather a productive
zone of infinite space and possibility. The rejection of lines is bound
up with a rejection of the creation of the illusion of perspective, which
Klein saw as a limitation of color's potential and not an opening up of
aesthetic space at all. Jarman reflects this understanding of the void
when he counsels, "To be an astronaut of the void, leave the comfortable house that imprisons you with reassurance." The entire film invites
us to be an astronaut of the void, by contemplating the "living presence" of the screen, and leaving behind the comfortable house of conventional apprehension.

Paul Julian Smith writes that, "Like Klein's paintings, *Blue* reveals
that monochrome is never simple or single: the colour seems to pulse
before our eyes and is constantly inflected by the tiny imperfections of
the medium."[75] (This becomes more and more obvious as the prints
age and deteriorate.) Moreover, as Peter Schwenger explains, there are
various mental processes that will cause us to see images where none
exist.[76] It is important to reiterate that while there are no visual images,
neither are we confronted with stasis: the screen glows with the projection of frame after frame of blue. The film is still a motion picture.
In that regard, the film resembles the kinetic sculptures that Klein made
in collaboration with Jean Tinguely, which featured rapidly rotating
disks of blue: "The rotation speed of the blue disk created an impression of stability; the rotating movement was not perceived as such, but
as a vibration of the surrounding space. Speed, like the pressure of air,

became a quality of the Void, a manifestation of energy."[77] Similarly, the glow of blue invades the space of the cinema, enveloping the spectator.

Blue thus further develops a number of investigations that pre-occupied Jarman throughout his artistic career. The first is the relation between the spectatorial space, the screen and the space of the film, an investigation undertaken in order to remake that relation. Here, the productive void of blue becomes the logical extension of the notion of the cinema as heterotopia, as the screen disappears as boundary in favor of pure color-space. Related to this is the investigation within his films of painting, and the studio as ontological laboratory, a place to experiment with being-in-space. Both *Imagining October* and *Caravaggio* explore the work performed by painting in remaking the social field. Whereas his own paintings of the 1980s and 1990s abandoned even the abstract or formal investigations that marked his earlier landscape paintings, the films became increasingly interested in exploring the possibilities of aesthetic space, whether this is a painting or a film. Thus the films after *Caravaggio* take up this particular project in their increasingly nonrealistic construction of space. *War Requiem,* for example, complements the aims of Britten's oratorio by its particular invocation of memorial architecture. Just as Britten's score juxtaposes the requiem mass and Owen's poetry, set to more modern music, Jarman's film juxtaposes intimate, "human" spaces with the cold formality of the public monument. *Edward II* takes this in a more formal direction yet, banishing all private space in favor of shifting, antihuman underground zones, a materialization of the oppressive Thatcherite moral climate in which privacy has essentially disappeared for certain groups. And, as we have noted, *Wittgenstein* banishes sets altogether, playing out its scenes in pools of light against black backgrounds. *Blue* is thus neither a bizarre and anomalous exercise nor a rejection of art or cinema. It is, as Peter Wollen argues, an attempt to inculcate in the viewer a new way of seeing, "an evocation of pure vision."[78]

As Schwenger observes, this new vision is linked to the mind's eye, and to the images that are created in the mind by the sound track. This, of course, is where the film departs from Klein. One of the most startling, unrealizable images conjured by the narration involves Blue's travels:

Blue walks into the labyrinth. Absolute silence is demanded of all its visitors, so their presence does not disturb the poets who are directing the excavations. Digging can only proceed on the calmest of days as rain and wind destroy the finds.

The archaeology of sound has only just been perfected and the systematic cataloguing of words has until recently been undertaken in a haphazard way. Blue watched as a word or phrase materialized in scintillating sparks, a poetry of fire which cast everything into darkness with the brightness of its reflections.[79]

The image of words emerging, materializing, and exploding into light mirrors the action of the sound track in the listener's mind. Here is the realization of Jarman's dream of bridging the barrier between audience and spectacle, as the film's image track is constructed in the viewer's head. This intimacy of film and audience is furthered by the physical properties of the medium: the blue screen lulls us into receptivity, while we are surrounded and penetrated by the soundtrack. Sound is a more intimate medium than vision. It is vision that allows for the separation between ourselves and the object or the image, and we can shut our eyes to close off the experience. There is less voluntary control of the sense of sound, and it serves to connect us rather than separate us from the world, helping us to orient ourselves in space. Moreover, we often can feel its physical effects on and in our body; at times in the film the sound becomes almost unbearable in its force, particularly in conjunction with the absence of a stabilizing image sequence, inducing in us the distress of the narrator. Analogously to the mutual impregnation of Klein's paintings and the viewer, here there is a mutual incorporation of audience and film. The film attempts to imagine a seeing that is more like a hearing: a vision that connects us to the world, rather than separating us from it.

There is a final formal aspect of the film to note, one that further structures the relation to the content of the narration. Although the words in the script are clearly Jarman's, many of them describing his own experience with HIV, they are not spoken by him. The bulk of the script is read by John Quentin and Nigel Terry, whose voices, while similar to each other, are nonetheless easily distinguishable. Jarman has a rather distinctive voice, with which the British audience at the time of the film's release was likely familiar, and so it would likely have recognized that these very personal observations are disconnected from the person who experienced them. Even if the audience was not familiar enough with Jarman's voice to recognize it, the film does not allow for the fiction of Nigel Terry representing Jarman, because of the alternation between his and Quentin's voice. If the audience does accept that the two voices "represent" Jarman, this is disrupted mid-way through the film, when we briefly hear the real Jarman's voice, before the narration is resumed by Terry and Quentin. Whether or not one recognizes any of the voices, what is certain is that no stable image of the speaker can be built up, even in the mind's eye. It is not any particular person that one identifies or empathizes with, but rather an experience or a feeling.[80] If one is identifying with Jarman, it is nonetheless through a depersonalizing relay structure.

There are strong reasons for Jarman to refuse to allow the specta-tor to form a stable image of the narrating persona, most immedi-ately because of the politics of representation around PWAs and AIDS in general. Although a number of his films directly or indirectly con-cerned themselves with AIDS, he never directly represented an HIV-positive person as such. Douglas Crimp observed that early on in the epidemic, "the portrait of the person with AIDS had become some-thing of a genre," with a fairly narrow range of visual signifiers.[81] He quotes a curator describing a representative show: "The majority of the sitters are shown alone; many are in the hospital; or at home, sick, in bed. Over 90 percent are men. Some are photographed with their parents, or at least their mothers. Only four are shown with lovers or friends. . . . The majority of sitters are clearly ravaged by the disease. . . . Not one is shown in a work environment; only a fraction are pictured outside."[82] Crimp concludes: "Certainly we can say that these represen-tations do not help us, and that they probably hinder us, in our strug-gle, because the best they can do is elicit pity, and pity is not solidarity. We must continue to demand and create our own counterimages, images of PWA self-empowerment, of the organized PWA movement and of the larger AIDS activist movement."[83] For Jarman, however, the second of these schools of representation is no less dangerous: "I shall not win the battle against the virus—in spite of the slogans like 'Living th AIDS'. The virus was appropriated by the well—so we have to live with AIDS while they spread the quilt for the moths of Ithaca across the wine dark sea. Awareness is heightened by this, but something else is lost. A sense of reality drowned in theatre." The quilt he refers to is, of course, the AIDS quilt, about which he famously expressed reservations, particularly regarding the surrounding ceremonies: "when the panels were unveiled a truly awful ceremony took place, in which a group of what looked like refrigerated karate experts, all dressed in white, turned and chanted some mumbo jumbo—horrible, quasi-religious, false."[84]

The quilt in its memorializing function participates in what John Paul Ricco calls a "retro-teleo-logic" that reads backwards from AIDS to equate gay men with the disease itself. He argues instead for what he calls a "disappeared aesthetics" that resists this logic by taking up loss fully, and which he says is exemplified by *Blue:* "this aesthetics, as a tactic of becoming-disappeared, eludes logics of positivity and negativity, by doubly refusing visibility and invisibility. A disappeared aesthetics visualizes nothing but a potentiality or a preference to not-visualize, and thereby points to the ethical-political dimensions of visuality itself."[85] This is a highly productive reading of the film, within the context of a very stimulating meditation on art and AIDS. His point about the film's interest in the ethics and politics of seeing is very much to point. Less certain is whether the blue screen shows a preference to not-visualize or is an example of pure visuality.

Jarman shares Ricco's concerns about the "ethical-political dimensions of visuality": "AIDS was too vast a subject to 'film'. All the art failed. It was well-intentioned but decorative—the graffiti artist Keith Haring raised consciousness but failed to turn the tragedy beyond the domestic."[86] Jarman here identifies two key problems with AIDS and art, one philosophical and one practical. The larger problem is addressed by Lee Edelman, who notes that "AIDS lacks a coherent medical referent." The most that can be agreed upon is that it involves a devastation of the immune system and is identified by any of a wide range of symptoms: "the signifier ['AIDS'] both connotes and denominates a dense and contradictory array of medical diagnoses, social experiences, projective fantasies, and 'political' agendas."[87] The more particular problem with AIDS and representation is the movement beyond the domestic, or (to misquote the script) the "comfortable house that [perhaps inadvertently] imprisons [us] with reassurance," which returns us to the problem of representing PWAs, and the necessity of moving from the domestic to the political while still moving the audience.

This is the function of the particular relation that the film structures with its audience, which we might see as a version of empathy. In a discussion of the ethics of representing trauma, LaCapra suggests that "Being responsive to the traumatic experience of others, notably of victims, implies not the appropriation of their experience but what I would call empathic unsettlement."[88] "Empathic unsettlement" is a good term for the response that the film attempts to evoke. Whereas sympathy involves a community of feeling with the suffering other, empathy involves a projection out of the self, to the site of the other. "Empathy" first appears, in the early twentieth century, as a term in aesthetics, and is commonly defined as "the power of entering into the experience of or understanding objects or emotions outside ourselves" (OED). This is similar to the process Kaja Silverman, following Max Scheler, describes as heteropathic identification, whereby we identify fully with the other, at the site of the other.[89] Scheler writes that

> identification can come about in *one* way through the total
> eclipse and absorption of another self by one's own, it being
> thus, as it were, completely dispossessed and deprived of all
> rights in its conscious existence and character. It can also come
> about the other way, where 'I' (the formal subject) am so over-
> whelmed and hypnotically bound and fettered by the other 'I'
> (the concrete individual), that my formal status as a subject is
> usurped by the other's personality, with all *its* characteristic
> aspects; in such a case, I live, not in 'myself,' but entirely in
> 'him', the other person.[90]

Scheler's distinction is useful because it identifies the implications of the spatial dynamics of the identification process. An ex-corporative or heteropathic form of identification, like empathy, is a more potentially transformative relation than sympathy, which leaves the self changed;

in LaCapra's account, empathy aims to leave the self unsettled, displaced, undone.

In the case of *Blue*, the intimacy of the voices in our ears encourages an identification with the experience described, at the site of that experience. With no images on the screen, we are given no way to distance or hold ourselves away from the narrative. Much of this intimate dialogue has to do with severely restricted vision, the experience of which is mimicked by the screen and further enhanced by the sound track. Early in the film, for example, a narrator tells us, in the present tense, "I step off the kerb and a cyclist nearly knocks me down. Flying in from the dark he nearly parted my hair. I step into a blue funk." After the first sentence, we hear a bell ring, the sounds of a bicycle speeding past, and, in a receding voice, "Look where the fuck you're going," allowing us to experience the disorientation and surprise that the narration is recounting. After the last sentence—"I step into a blue funk"—we hear the clanging of an iron door shutting on us, a metaphoric sound that doubles the mood of the narration and encloses us within it. We experience the film at the site of the narrator.

Because there is no way in which the voices of the actors are inflected or infected with HIV, it is far easier for the non-PWA to identify with this site than if confronted with the usual images of PWAs, which bring with them all of their accumulated cultural meanings. Gabriele Griffin further notes that "The absence of a literal, visual representation of the body in *Blue* means that Jarman refuses to situate or contain the look directed at the screen, thereby activating the viewer into an interrogation of her or his visual expectations and, simultaneously, denying an easy categorization of what is seen into same and/or other."[91] Because we are not able to assemble the voices and stabilize them into a recognizable image of a PWA, we cannot establish a comfortable distance from the narration. The gently ironic voices do not encourage the usual pity or sympathy for the sufferer, but rather encourage us to feel the horror of being in the situation, a "normal" person caught in a nightmare scenario. For example, the extended reading, more than two minutes long, of the innumerable and devastating possible side effects of an experimental drug invokes what might be called the sublime of disaster, and one begins to feel giddy with the recitation. The statement finishes with the improbable officialese: "If you are concerned with any of the above side effects or if you would like any further information, please ask your doctor." As intended, the mind reels with the question as to who would not be concerned with such horrors, and wondering what kind of "further information" could possibly assuage one's fears in the face of such a list. The black humor is quickly replaced by a more somber mood as the narrator says: "In order to be put on the drug you have to sign a piece of paper stating you understand that all these illnesses are a possibility. I really can't see what I am to do. I am going to sign it." The excruciating length of the recitation evokes what Jarman identifies as the vastness of the subject of AIDS, and the horror of possibility that accompanies it.

The rejection of the familiar images of the PWA goes hand in hand with the film's purposeful failure to differentiate between varieties of suffering. Over the course of the narration we are placed in a number of different wards, waiting rooms, and examination rooms, but it is not always clear whether these are specifically for AIDS patients or eye patients or for a more general hospital population. There are further confusions, as one cranky patient in the hospice observes to the narrator, "You can't be too careful who you mix with there, there's no way of telling the visitors, patients, or staff apart. The staff have nothing to identify them except they are all into leather." It is not clear whether the other patients we hear described are PWAs or whether they are gay, although in the popular imagination the former inevitably implies the latter. The sound track introduces a more fundamental and parodic confusing of sexual identities themselves, in a song that begins, "I am a mannish / Muff diving / Size queen" and concludes with the repeated claim, "I am a Not Gay." The refusal of the category "gay" is in the first instance bound up with the queer politics of the period, but it goes further in the context of the film's rejection of "the facts of the world," and in the particular version of empathetic identification it is fostering.

To say one is a "Not Gay" is to refuse to allow the audience a recognizable category through which to see and understand the narrator: it is to frustrate, in other words, an incorporative sympathy that would leave the audience secure in its knowing. Rather than identifying what the narrator is, the audience must instead identify with the particularities of his situation. This includes a full range of human emotions, as opposed to just the suffering acceptance or heroic optimism of the PWA, as well the particularities of his existence: his grief at the loss of friends, his love for H.B., his fantasies about a blue-eyed boy.

Jarman's film is to some degree a formal experiment that takes up Klein's explorations of the color-space, and in particular his project of reeducating vision by avoiding the known, and instead offering up the infinities of the void. Jarman, however, has a more political project than Klein: the reeducation of the audience regarding the AIDS epidemic. Part of this involves getting beyond the horrifying and yet familiar, and therefore inadvertently comforting image of the tragic HIV sufferer. Through its particular visual and aural address, the film fosters a relation of empathy in the audience; a particular kind of transport that encourages us to identify not with Jarman, which might lead to a benign but useless sympathy, but with the experience of being HIV positive.

Like Jarman's garden at Dungeness, *Blue* is a work of art that the audience fully inhabits. To sit in the theater is to become a part of the spectacle itself, as the blue light from the screen illuminates and makes present the community of the audience. But it also makes the spectator's mind the apparatus of projection, as the sound track constructs the image track in our heads, making us project ourselves outward to the site of the narration. We are offered a boundless void of possibility and potentiality, although the proffered transformation is not without its pain. But here, as elsewhere with Jarman's work, privation can potentially lead to a fuller apprehension of being. The restriction of sight in *Blue* opens up a boundlessness of vision.

The Raft of the Medusa

DEATH IS UNDOUBTEDLY A CONVENIENCE FOR CRITICS. There is an almost irresistible logic to seeing *Blue* as Jarman's final statement on filmmaking instead of simply as his last completed film. *Blue* does seem to offer an emphatic and deeply fitting conclusion to Jarman's career, the end point of an aesthetic, intellectual, and political journey that ends on this strangely exhilarating note. The press certainly saw the film that way, but then it had been in the habit of seeing each of his films as his final film for some time, something at which Jarman alternately bristled and laughed. In a late interview he noted: "I've written my epitaph about six times now, apparently. Every single film is scotched up as my last. Surely they'll stop on that business. Especially if I get another run together."[1] Seeing *Blue* as the culmination of a career rather than the last work in an interrupted life offers the critic an unwarranted narrative consolation that should be resisted.

Jarman did in fact have a number of projects in various stages of development at the time of his death. There was, for example, a long-considered adaptation of James Purdy's novel *Narrow Rooms,* the funding of which apparently fell apart over casting choices. In *Modern Nature* he mentions putting together a feature-length compilation of some of his super-8 films, which appeared after his death as *Glitterbug.* And he had been discussing with Tariq Ali of the BBC a treatment for a feature film, cowritten with David Lewis, about AIDS and activism, using the story of the Théodore Géricault painting *The Raft of the Medusa* (1819) as a starting point.

Coincidentally, a play by Joe Pintauro of the same name, and also dealing with AIDS, had premiered a couple of years earlier in New York. Pintauro's play is a standard character drama about a disparate and representative group of HIV-positive characters and their therapist.

The title is the only allusion the play makes to the Géricault's dramatic painting of the survivors of the wreck of the *Medusa* off the coast of Senegal in 1816. After it ran aground, the ship's officers and their families took to the longboats, while the remaining 150 men were consigned to a hastily constructed raft. The raft, however, proved too difficult for the boats to tow and so it was quickly cut loose. The castaways endured unimaginable horrors, including madness, murder, and cannibalism, before the surviving fifteen men were rescued by a passing ship. Of these, five more died before the ship reached the shore.[2]

Jarman's film would have made greater use of the wreck than Pintauro's play, placing it in a wider political context, and as with much of his work, history would be used as a site of reflection and resistance. As with *Caravaggio,* the film would have been to some degree an investigation of the painter's style, in particular Géricault's use of color, chiaroscuro, and his anatomy studies. Although, like Pintauro, Jarman uses the raft of survivors as a metaphor for those living with AIDS, the film also would have included scenes of Géricault painting the picture and subsequently exhibiting it, as well as the story of two of the survivors, Henri Savigny and Alexandre Corréard. After the rescue, these two tried tirelessly to get compensation for the survivors, but to no avail, as the French government simply wished to ignore the whole disaster. In response to the survivors' demands, wrote Corréard, the government "sought to besmirch our character, reduce us to odious beings."[3] The result was a public scandal. Later, Corréard set up a bookshop and publishing house called At the Wreck of the Medusa, which became a meeting place for malcontents and radicals. If the raft provides a potent metaphor for the perilous state of those living with HIV, cut loose by their governments and smeared by the media, for Jarman the subsequent activities of the survivors provide at least one way of addressing the situation, an example that he tirelessly followed.

There is a final intriguing detail that the proposal for the film notes: after Géricault painted *The Raft of the Medusa,* a second competing version was produced for the newly emergent technology of the diorama, and this version toured England, as did the painting itself.[4] To the accompaniment of an orchestral score and dramatic lighting, a huge scroll of canvas unwound to portray the events leading to the terrifying spectacle of the wreck. In mentioning this, Jarman argues that the diorama is the forerunner of IMAX. The inclusion of the diorama opens up the question of the ethics of representation, the role of the political artist, the efficacy of spectacle in motivating empathy, and the efficacy of empathy in motivating political change. Which is to say: how does one most ethically and effectively represent disaster, in order to move or unsettle the viewer? The proposed film, much like *Blue*, would have offered a rather different answer than more mainstream AIDS films like *Philadelphia* (1993), whose principal strategy was the evocation of sympathy or pity.

Jarman's work and the example of his life moved (and continue to move) many people. In an article in the *Guardian* published on the tenth anniversary of Jarman's death, the filmmaker Alex Cox testified to Jarman's influence on his career and, in particular, his opposition to "the well-made film, which looks nice and doesn't confuse people and makes a clear distinction between 'historical' and 'contemporary' subjects" (although he also pointed despairingly to the ongoing success of the well-made historical film).[5] More recently, Seamus McGarvey, who worked on *The Garden*, has argued that Jarman's "influence is absolutely incalculable. You can see it in lots of filmmakers' work, from advertising, to pop culture, to music. I mean, he kind of kick-started a real disturbance in art and filmmaking. Where would British filmmakers be without his influence? Derek's spectral influence still reigns over British film."[6]

Jarman's influence is not confined to the world of film, which makes sense given the diverse fields he worked in and the wide range of artists to whom he offered encouragement and mentoring. For example, since his death a geographically and stylistically diverse group of musicians have offered tributes to him: the American composer Robert Moran wrote "32 Cryptograms for Derek Jarman,"[7] inspired by a screening of *Blue* at the New York International Film Festival that Jarman attended; Italian techno artist Ghittoni recorded "Derek Jarman Blues" using a sample of dialogue from *Blue* ("Kiss me. Kiss me again."); Donna McKeavitt wrote *Translucence: A Song Cycle* using words by Jarman; Prospect Cottage provided the inspiration for Robin Rimbaud's *The Garden Is Full of Metal*; and in Japan, very early after Jarman's death, *Eternal Blue Extreme: An Asian Tribute to Derek Jarman* appeared.

Books and articles on his work now appear with some regularity (although there has as yet been no extended treatment of his paintings and installations),[8] the garden is frequently visited by journalists, documentaries have been produced,[9] the films continue to be reissued on DVD around the world, and curators include his work in major exhibitions. The garden at Dungeness was prominently featured in the Tate Britain's exhibition *The Art of the Garden* in 2005 and a screening of *Blue* accompanied *Colour after Klein* at the Barbican the same year; in the spring and summer of 2007, Jarman's work figured in *Panic Attack! Art in the Punk Years* at the Barbican, and in *The Last Days of the British Underground 1978–1988* at the ICA, which was accompanied by a retrospective of his films. The same summer a glossy hipster magazine, *Dazed & Confused,* devoted a ten-page spread to the man they called "The Last Bohemian." In 2008, a new documentary by Isaac Julien appeared, *Derek,* featuring footage of a late interview conducted by Colin MacCabe and narration by Tilda Swinton. The documentary was the center of an installation by Julien at the Serpentine Gallery *(Derek Jarman: Brutal Beauty)* and appeared in conjunction with a series of lectures and screenings, including screenings of *Imagining October* at the Tate Britain. Around the same time, the Canadian poet and film scholar Keith Garebian produced a book of poetry, *Blue: The Derek Jarman Poems.*

For an artist whose work often seemed so determinedly topical, so directly involved in the political struggles of his time, the continuing interest might be a little surprising, especially given the changes that have occurred in the intervening years: the advances in treatment for HIV, for example, the repeal of Section 28 in 2000, the long reign of New Labour, the rise of the Saatchi Gallery and the YBAs (Young British Artists) on the British art scene in the 1990s, and so on. But it may be that the topicality of the work sometimes obscured the very serious commitment in the work to a truly radical rethinking of the nature of the work of art and its place in the world, a rethinking that has an obvious ongoing relevance for artists and writers. Jarman's first film, after all, documented his own studio; his final film was a tribute to an artist he greatly admired; in between were countless representations of painters, musicians, writers, thinkers, and a whole series of reflections on how art represents and transforms the world. Art's role in presenting or stimulating new perspectives is obviously important here, but more profound is the questioning in Jarman's work of what precisely the work of art was. Where does the film actually take place?

In the studio, in the auditorium, or in the audience's head? When does a film start, and when does it end? What are the boundaries of a painting and what dimensions does it occupy? How does a spectator experience or inhabit a film or a painting or a garden, and what is the nature of that relation? And, most important, can it be transformative? What can art accomplish?

These aesthetic investigations were combined with Jarman's activist engagement with history. His long-standing interest in Jung gave him an understanding of how powerful the affective pull of myth could be, but his concern with politics meant that the myths he engaged with were some of the founding myths of the present moment, and particularly of the English nation. Jarman's engagement with the art of the past was profound, complex, and productive: alternately rewriting some histories, claiming ownership of others, and writing new histories for new communities and new nations. The historical double vision invoked by Caravaggio's paintings of biblical figures became a model for the complex and palimpsestic temporalities created in Jarman's written and filmic works. Like Caravaggio, Jarman continually insisted on the presence of the past; his work compels us to see how the past haunts the present. Any attempt to shape the future requires an engagement with the past.

Jarman's aesthetic and historical investigations were thus a crucial part of his engagement with the very pressing political issues of his day. For him, and for the worlds that he lived in, the question of the work that art could accomplish was more than just theoretical, and it became increasingly more urgent as his career advanced. His political interventions on behalf of gay, queer, and AIDS activist organizations ranged from participating in protests, writing letters, and holding fundraisers to more profound attempts to shift dominant understandings of the outlines of the nation through his artistic practice. The result was an incredibly diverse body of work through which can be charted, among other things, the history and fortunes of sexual minorities in Britain in the latter half of the twentieth century. The scope of Jarman's learning and interest, and the generosity of his vision, made this the fullest and richest engagement possible. This more than anything will ensure that the work his art performs will continue on for some time to come.

Acknowledgments

OVER THE COURSE OF WORKING ON THIS BOOK and on earlier essays about Jarman, I have been helped by a number of people who read chapters or grant applications, edited articles for collections, or offered advice at crucial points. I am glad to be able to acknowledge here Ellis Hanson, Daniel O'Quinn, Richard Dellamora, Eric Savoy, Susan Bennett, Stephen Bruhm, Peter Schwenger, Amy Sargeant, Peter Sinnema, Richard Morrison, and the anonymous readers for the University of Minnesota Press. Friends and colleagues at the University of Calgary, including Mary Polito, Jackie Jenkins, and Stephen Guy-Bray, helped to make a happy and productive working environment.

Friends in London and Rome have been generous with their time and hospitality, and I thank Caroline Duncan, Malcolm Tute, Gabriella Zolese, and Dinesh Sethi. I benefited greatly over the years from visits and talks with Graeme Marsden, who has been an unfailing source of information, conversation, encouragement, and productive disagreement.

Staff at various libraries and archives provided invaluable assistance, particularly Janet Moat, head of Special Collections at the British Film Institute; the amazingly friendly staff of the Pacific Film Archives at Berkeley; the staff of the Hall-Carpenter Archives at the London School of Economics; and the interlibrary loan staff at the University of Calgary.

Early in the project I made a decision not to interview Jarman's friends and collaborators and to restrict my focus to the "publicly available" Jarman. I'm not sure whether this was a wise decision; certainly those whom I have had contact with—Tony Peake, James Mackay, and Keith Collins—have been very helpful.

Financial support for this research was provided by the Social Sciences and Humanities Research Council of Canada and the University

Research Grants Committee of the University of Calgary. These grants allowed me to hire at various points some very able research assistants: Aaron Giovannone, Karen Walker, Michael Brisbois, and Andrew Bretz. I am grateful for fellowships from the Killam Trust and the Calgary Institute for the Humanities, which allowed me valuable time for writing.

Finally, I am grateful to my partner, Glenn Mielke, who has taught me much about film, among many other things.

Notes

Introduction

1. Jarman, *Modern Nature*, 49, 87.

2. One might further observe, however, that in the narrative of the film, two airmen (with parachutes) do bail out of a plane that is returning from a bombing run over Europe, and it is at least conceivable that this would have occurred near Dungeness, located as it is on the east coast of England, south of Dover. Bartlett has invented the scene out of material provided by the film, with such vividness that he can picture it in his head. Who knows what Mrs. Oiller saw? For an account of the location shooting, see Michael Powell's *A Life in Movies*, 541–44.

3. Quoted in Hobsbawm, *Nations and Nationalism since 1780*, 12.

4. Critics have tended to agree with Jarman's assessment. See, for example, the chapter on British Expressionism in Jim Leach's *British Cinema*, 66–85. Sarah Street places Pressburger and Powell and Jarman in a tradition of British modernism (*British National Cinema*, 161–65, 181–84). In *The Last of England*, Jarman writes that "There is only one English feature director whose work is in the first rank [Powell]" (216).

5. Pressburger and Powell were heavily criticized during World War II for their insufficiently nationalistic *The Life and Death of Colonel Blimp*; Powell's career as a filmmaker in Britain more or less came to an end with the extremely hostile response to *Peeping Tom*.

6. Street, *British National Cinema*, 183.

7. Jarman, *The Last of England*, 88.

8. Morrison, "Derek Jarman," 20.

9. Houlbrook, *Queer London*, 110; Houlbrook is quoting the Law Society in the second quotation.

10. McDonough, "Situationist Space," 252.

11. Ibid., 178.

12. Benjamin, "The Work of Art in the Age of Its Technological Reproducibility: Second Version," 117.

13. Ibid., 104.

14. Ibid., 108.

15. Hansen, "Room-for-Play," 17.

16. O'Pray, "'New Romanticism' and the British Avant-Garde Film in the Early 80s," 256–62.

17. See most recently, Wymer, *Derek Jarman;* or O'Pray, *Derek Jarman: Dreams of England.*

1. Artistic and Sexual Revolutions

1. *The Last of England* shows Jarman standing in front of an early self-portrait, 45. For the details of this solo show of twenty-five works, see Peake, *Derek Jarman,* 72.

2. Jarman, *Dancing Ledge,* 69.

3. Ibid., 97.

4. Ibid., 105.

5. Debord and Sanguinetti, *The Veritable Split in the International,* 19–20.

6. Marcus, *Lipstick Traces.* Writers aligned with Situationist ideals are fairly scathing on Marcus's work, which places Situationism within a mostly aesthetic tradition. Jappe, for example, writes that "some of the connections he makes between very different phenomena—between the SI and the Sex Pistols, for example—are fanciful, and betray a lack of historical understanding" (Jappe, *Guy Debord,* 177). Other writers on the punk movement in art, however, point to some very clear continuities between major punk figures and the SI. See, for example, Wilson, "Modernity Killed Every Night," 144–51.

7. There is a growing body of work on the Situationist International. Many important documents are gathered in Ken Knabb's *Situationist International Anthology.* See also Tom McDonough's *Guy Debord and the Situationist International.* Virtually all of the Situationist texts are available at the Situationist International Online, an excellent resource.

8. *Internationale Situationniste* 1 (June 1958). Reprinted in Knabb, *Situationist International Anthology,* 45.

9. For Lefebvre's account of this, see Ross, "Lefebvre on the Situationists," 267–84.

10. Jappe, *Guy Debord,* 59.

11. Sadler, *The Situationist City,* 78–79 and 181nn31, 32. The psychogeography is reproduced in Blazwick, *An Endless Adventure . . . An Endless Passion . . . An Endless Banquet,* 45–49. Although an update on it was published in the *Internationale Situationniste* ("Venice Has Conquered Ralph Rumney"), by the time Rumney had finished it he had been expelled (a common fate for the group).

12. Jappe, *Guy Debord,* 50.

13. McDonough, "Situationist Space," 250.

14. Knabb, *Situationist International Anthology,* 45.

15. Jappe, *Guy Debord*, 59.

16. For the films of Debord, see Knabb, *Guy Debord*.

17. Sadler, *The Situationist City*, 43.

18. Vidler, "*Terres Inconnues*," 16.

19. Sadler, *The Situationist City*, 9.

20. See, for example, the chapter "Human Associations" in Smithson and Smithson, *Ordinariness and Light*, 39–60.

21. Alloway, "The Development of British Pop," 27–67.

22. Mellor, *The Sixties Art Scene in London*, 59–67; Crow, *The Rise of the Sixties*, 57–58.

23. See Sadler, *The Situationist City*, and the IS journal. The SI did have a sporadic presence in London through the 1960s, including among its adherents T. J. Clark and Donald Nicholson-Smith, who, along with the other British SI members, were expelled in 1967 and went on to form King Mob. For more on the Situationist presence in England, see Blazwick, *An Endless Adventure*, which includes documents from the 1960s to the 1980s.

24. The issues were "The Changing Guard," *Times Literary Supplement*, August 6, 1964, and "Any Advance? The Changing Guard—2," September 3, 1964.

25. Alloway, "The Independent Group," 50. This exhibition precedes slightly the New Realism show at the Sidney Janis gallery in New York, in the fall of 1962, that brought together all of the major American pop artists.

26. Curtis, "'A Highly Mobile and Plastic Environ,'" 51.

27. Jarman, *Dancing Ledge*, 123.

28. Ibid., 73.

29. In an overview of 1960s architecture, Simon Sadler notes that "Bohemians like to refashion the material culture of the past rather than see it swept up by philistine renewal. London's artfully déclassé sixties intelligentsia gentrified a decayed Islington, no-go riverside warehouses and forgotten corners of Kensington and Chelsea. Whenever stationed in London, the most radical avant-garde of the day, the Situationist International, used its wanderings to satisfy a taste for the Dickensian" (Sadler, "British Architecture in the Sixties," 133).

30. Skurka and Gil, *Underground Interiors*, 47.

31. These dates come from Tony Peake's filmography, and as he indicates, the dating of most of these films is uncertain at best.

32. Jarman, *The Last of England*, 197.

33. Houlbrook, *Queer London*, 91.

34. For an insider's account of the GLF and a reprinting of key documents, see Walter, *Come Together*. For an oral history of the GLF, see Power, *No Bath but Plenty of Bubbles*. Jeffrey Weeks gives a brief history of the movement in the context of the history of gay politics in the twentieth century in *Coming Out*, 185–206.

35. Birch, "A Community of Interests," 51.

36. Ibid., 54.

37. For a firsthand account of the communes, see ibid., 51–59.

38. MacCabe, "A Post-National European Cinema," 15.

39. Jarman, "Dancer from the Dance," 20.

40. "Among the more regular attenders or supporters were Derek Jarman, Jim Anderson of *Oz* magazine and Graham Chapman" (Power, *No Bath but Plenty of Bubbles*, 68–69).

41. Ibid., 41.

42. Peake, *Derek Jarman*, 159–60.

43. Jarman, *Dancing Ledge*, 70–72.

2. Liberation, Space, and the Early Films

1. Wymer, *Derek Jarman*, 27.

2. Jarman, *Kicking the Pricks*, 54.

3. For a Foucauldian discussion of the home movie and its relation to the modern family, see Zimmermann, *Reel Families*.

4. Watney, "Home Movie Man," 40–41.

5. Field and O'Pray, "On Imaging October, Dr. Dee and Other Matters," 49.

6. Jarman, *Kicking the Pricks*, 134.

7. For these films, see Peake, *Derek Jarman*, 112–13.

8. Mekas, "On the Baudelairean Cinema," 85–86. According to David Curtis, Smith's *Flaming Creatures* first played in London in the spring of 1967 at the UFO Club; P. Adams Sitney showed a program of the New American Cinema, including films by Smith, at the National Film Theatre in 1968, which subsequently toured a number of English universities (Curtis, "English Avant-Garde Film," 176–82).

9. Dwoskin, *Film Is . . . : The International Free Cinema*, 62–65. For an even more contemporary account, see Johnston and Dawson, "Declarations of Independence," 28–32; Jarman, "More British Sounds," 144–47.

10. Curtis, "English Avant-Garde Film," 180.

11. Street, *British National Cinema*, 170.

12. O'Pray, *Derek Jarman*, 70. In an early interview in the tabloid *Ritz*, Jarman mentions specifically Larcher's "Monkeys Birthday" and "Mare's Tale," when talking about influences. First and foremost, however, is Kenneth Anger. See Lyme, "Derek Jarman Talks to Francis Lyme," 23.

13. From an interview with Clive Hodgson to accompany "Derek Jarman: Programme 2, Apprentice Work," a program of super-8s at the National Film Theatre on December 18, 1979. BFI Special Collections: Derek Jarman.

14. The names of these films, and what is included in them, seem to have changed quite regularly. See Peake's Filmography in *Derek Jarman* for full details, 573–87.

15. Peake, *Derek Jarman*, 195.

16. Field and O'Pray, "On Imaging October, Dr. Dee and Other Matters," 47.

17. Jarman, *Dancing Ledge*, 130.

18. Ibid., 129.

19. Hamlin, *Film Art Phenomena*, 44–45.

20. *The Devils* opens at the court of Louis XIII with a masque involving the king acting out the Birth of Venus. *Fellini Satyricon* (1969) also has an opening theater sequence.

21. Jarman, *Dancing Ledge*, 155.

22. Jarman, Preface to *Lindsay Kemp and Company*, 7.

23. Jarman, *Dancing Ledge*, 155.

24. Ibid., 6.

25. Jameson, *The Geopolitical Aesthetic*, 12.

26. Hoberman, *On Jack Smith's Flaming Creatures, and Other Secret-Flix of Cinemaroc*, 130–31.

27. Jarman, *The Last of England*, 81.

28. Giuseppi Pelosi was convicted of the crime and served nine years, but in 2005 he retracted his confession and suggested it was a politically motivated killing.

29. See, for example, Pencak, *The Films of Derek Jarman*, 171–84; Dillon, *Derek Jarman and Lyric Film;* Gardner, "Perverse Law," 31–64.

30. Jarman, "P.P.P. in the Garden of Earthly Delights," 22–29. The script appears in the same notebook as that of *Imagining October.* BFI Special Collections: Derek Jarman.

31. Nowell-Smith, "Pasolini's Originality," 14.

32. For Pasolini's views on this, see "Observations on the Sequence Shot," in Pasolini, *Heretical Empiricism*, 233–37.

33. Pasolini, *Pasolini on Pasolini*, 83.

34. Jarman, *Dancing Ledge*, 196.

35. BFI Special Collections: Derek Jarman.

36. Rayns, "Unblocked Talents," 12–13.

37. Babusco, "Piercing Pleasures," 21–22.

38. Dillon discusses the "scenes of narcissistic reflection and homoerotic doubling" at some length in his discussion of the film (*Derek Jarman and Lyric Film*, 69).

39. Dyer, *Now You See It*, 169.

40. *Financial Times*, October 29, 1976; cited in Wyke, "Playing Roman Soldiers," 260.

41. Included in Isaac Julien's documentary *Derek* (2008).

42. Andrew Moor takes the opposite view, arguing that "Sebastian's unendorsed self-sacrifice is motivated by his pious separation of divine and earthly pleasures;

while conversely Adrian and Anthony's loving relationship seems to fuse these polarities ideally" ("Spirit and Matter," 52).

43. Kaye, "Losing His Religion," 88.

44. Pasolini, "Pasolini on Film," 76.

45. Kracauer, *Theory of Film*, 79.

46. See, for example, Cook, *Fashioning the Nation*, 6.

47. Silverman, *Threshold of the Visible World*, 12–14.

48. Comolli, "Historical Fiction," 41–53.

49. For a discussion of the history of the visual representation of the saint in relation to the film, see Wyke, "Shared Sexualities," 234–40. For a discussion of the representation of Saint Sebastian in relation to gay culture, see Kaye, "Losing His Religion," 86–105.

50. Jarman, *Dancing Ledge*, 144.

51. Jackson, *Strategies of Deviance*, 176.

52. Wyke, "Playing Roman Soldiers," 263.

53. Deleuze, *Sacher-Masoch*, 107.

54. Ibid., 58.

55. Ibid., 112.

56. Iles, "Derek Jarman," 65.

57. Deleuze, *Sacher-Masoch*, 30.

58. Ricco, *The Logic of the Lure*, 12, 75.

59. This was particularly the case with the Gay Liberation Front. For the GLF, writes Keith Birch, coming out "meant a rejection of self-oppression and of the internalization of heterosexual values" ("A Community of Interests," 54). In the American context, David M. Halperin points to the prescriptive liberationist politics of *The Joy of Gay Sex*, noting that "The notion that gay liberation had put an end to earlier (and now disavowed) forms of homosexual existence rooted in past experiences of oppression and homophobia was typical of the period" (*How to Do the History of Homosexuality*, 18).

60. Dyer, "Pasolini and Homosexuality," 62. Michael John Pinfold makes a similar argument about *Sebastiane*, arguing that it "perpetrat[es] a view of male sexuality which is about domination and control" ("The Performance of Queer Masculinity in Derek Jarman's *Sebastiane*," 77). This is the conclusion of a larger reading that suggests that the film "represents all expressions of male sexuality as unproblematic" (ibid.), which strikes me as unlikely.

61. Waugh, "Derek Jarman's *Sebastiane*," 69–71. The review was originally published in the Toronto publication *The Body Politic* 41 (March 1978), 19. This echoes the indignant review in the newspaper *Gay Left* ("A socialist journal for gay men"), which labeled it "gay exploitation," seeing the film's success "as a measure of our continued exploitation and oppression" (Derbyshire, "At Last a Film We Can Call Our Own?" 19).

62. Jarman, *Dancing Ledge*, 150.

63. Jarman, "The Making of *Sebastiane*."

64. Jarman, *At Your Own Risk*, 83.

65. Ibid., 84.

66. For a stimulating discussion of queer art and processes of becoming, see Ricco, *The Logic of the Lure*.

67. Jarman, *Dancing Ledge*, 22.

68. In an interview with Keith Hawes in *Gay News* for the release of *Jubilee*, Jarman says that *Sebastiane* "was always for me a destroyed film; it had a vibrancy that was destroyed by its academic seriousness" (*Gay News* 137 [February 23, 1978], 23). In *At Your Own Risk*, he distances himself entirely from the Sebastian story: "Can one feel sorry for this Latin closet case?" (83).

3. The Elizabethan Future

1. The rock critics were hilariously sanctimonious in their rejection of the film. One reviewer declared it "an irresponsible movie. Don't remember punk this way" ("A Jubilee for Punks," *Melody Maker* 53.8 [February 25, 1978]: 3); Nick Kent similarly called it "a disturbingly irresponsible film" ("On the Town: The Unpleasant Vision of 'Punk 1984,'" *NME* [February 28, 1978]: 41, 43).

2. Jarman, *Dancing Ledge*, 172.

3. For a discussion of the connection of Blake with the film, see Dillon, *Derek Jarman and Lyric Film*, 74–84.

4. Interview with Keith Howes in *Gay News* 137 (February 23, 1978), 23.

5. See, for example, Vermorel, *Fashion and Perversity*; Savage, *England's Dreaming*.

6. O'Pray, *Derek Jarman*, 94.

7. Upton, "Anarchy in the UK."

8. Frith and Horne, *Art into Pop*, 124.

9. O'Brien, "The Woman Punk Made Me," 194. On women and the punk movement, see also O'Brien's *She Bop II*, 132–78; Whitely, *Women and Popular Music*, 107–14.

10. Savage, *England's Dreaming*, 278. The "Grundy interview" was the appearance of the Sex Pistols and a few female fans (including Siouxsie Sue), on Bill Grundy's show *Today*.

11. Howes and Wall, "Punk: Wot's in It for Us?" 21–25.

12. Medhurst, "What Did I Get?" 220.

13. Savage, *England's Dreaming*, 147–50. On the filming, see also Jarman, *Dancing Ledge*, 26–27; Peake, *Derek Jarman*, 242–43.

14. Coincidentally, Julien Temple uses a similar temporal structure in both of his punk films, *The Great Rock 'N' Roll Swindle* (1980) and *The Filth and the Fury* (2000).

15. Jarman, *The Last of England*, 188.

16. Isaac Julien's *Young Soul Rebels* (1991) addresses some of the cultural issues around the Jubilee year, showing some of the connections and the tensions between the various subcultures (gay, black, punk) that characterized both the production of Jarman's film and the reception.

17. BFI Special Collections: Derek Jarman.

18. Sladen, "Introduction," 9.

19. Warr, "Feral City," 120.

20. Savage, *England's Dreaming*, 230.

21. Ibid., 260. For a less sympathetic reading of the use of Nazi iconography, see Sabin, "'I Won't Let That Dago By,'" 208.

22. McCole, *Walter Benjamin and the Antinomies of Tradition*, 7.

23. Vermorel, *Fashion and Perversity*, 184.

24. Jarman, *Dancing Ledge*, 164.

25. Ibid., 173.

26. Interview in *Gay News* 137 (February 23, 1978), 23.

27. Jarman, *The Last of England*, 60.

28. Field and O'Pray, "On Imaging October, Dr. Dee and Other Matters," 58.

29. For example, Jon Savage mentions a punk concert at which Kenneth Anger films were screened: *Scorpio Rising* and *Kustom Kar Kommandos* (*England's Dreaming*, 207).

30. BFI Special Collections: Derek Jarman.

31. Westwood denounced the film in a critique written on one of her famous T-shirts. In "An Open T-shirt to Derek Jarman from Vivienne Westwood" she declared: "And Aerial *[sic]* who flashed the sun in a mirror, and considered a diamond and had great contact lenses: 'Consider the world's diversity and worship it. By denying its multiplicity, you deny your own true nature. Equality prevails not for God but for man's sake'—consider that! What an insult to my VIRILITY! I'm a punk, man (and you use the values you give to punks as a warning). I am supposed to see old Elizabeth's England as some state of grace? Well, I rather consider that all this grand stuff and looking at diamonds is something to do with a gay (which you are) boy's love of dressing up and playing at charades" (quoted in Jarman, *At Your Own Risk*, 87).

32. Jarman, *Dancing Ledge*, 196.

33. Savage, *England's Dreaming*, 230.

34. Jarman, *Dancing Ledge*, 188.

35. Ibid., 21.

36. Ibid., 188. For a more extended discussion of Jarman's interest in and use of alchemy, see Ellis, "Queer Period."

37. Rayns, "Submitting to Sodomy," 63–64.

38. Collick, *Shakespeare, Cinema and Society*, 102.

39. MacCabe, "A Post-National European Cinema," 13.

40. Jarman, *Dancing Ledge*, 203.

41. Bevington and Holbrook, "Introduction," 4.

42. See, for example, Vincent Canby's contemptuous dismissal of the film (*New York Times*, September 22, 1980, C20).

43. For a discussion of these masques, see Barthelemy, *Black Face Maligned Race*, 8–41. Stephen Orgel notes in *The Jonsonian Masque* that even by 1605, when *The Masque of Blacknesse* was performed, the idea of using blackface in a masque was not new (*The Jonsonian Masque*, 34).

44. Orgel, "Marginal Jonson," 158.

45. Orgel, *The Jonsonian Masque*, 6–7.

46. Bennett, *Performing Nostalgia*, 119, 129.

47. See, for example, Paul Brown, "'This thing of darkness I acknowledge mine,'" 48–71; Barker and Hulme, "Nymphs and Reapers Heavily Vanish," 191–205; Halpern, "'The Picture of Nobody,'" 262–92. For an account of postcolonialist productions of the play, see Bennett, *Performing Nostalgia*, 119–50.

48. MacCabe, "A Post-National European Cinema," 11–12.

49. Zabus and Dwyer, "'I'll be wise hereafter,'" 365–66.

50. Chedgzoy, *Shakespeare's Queer Children*, 202.

51. Ibid.

52. Loomba, *Gender, Race, Renaissance Drama*, 43.

53. Boose, "'The Getting of a Lawful Race,'" 37.

54. Gillies, *Shakespeare and the Geography of Difference*, 32.

55. In the film, Ariel is dressed in a white boiler suit, which perhaps places him in the same camp.

56. All quotations from the text are from Shakespeare, *The Tempest*, ed. Stephen Orgel.

57. Holderness, "Shakespeare Rewound," 72.

58. Hall, *Things of Darkness*, 22.

59. Ibid., 25.

60. Goldberg, *Sodometries*, 181.

61. As Alan Stewart has argued, following Jonathan Goldberg, "sodomy is by definition a disturbance of alliance/marriage arrangements" (*Close Readers*, xxviii). Alan Bray argues that accusations of sodomy were generally made in association with other crimes, such as atheism or sedition, which suggests that the crime always had a social dimension. Bray particularly isolates the issue of class: friendships that cut across class lines were likely to be identified as sodomitical (Bray, *Homosexuality in Renaissance England*).

62. Chedgzoy, *Shakespeare's Queer Children*, 204.

63. MacCabe, "A Post-National European Cinema," 12.

64. Loomba, *Gender, Race, Renaissance Drama*, 45.

65. Singh, "Caliban versus Miranda," 198.

66. Bennett, *Performing Nostalgia*, 132.

67. MacCabe, "A Post-National European Cinema," 16–17.

68. Jarman, *Dancing Ledge*, 202.

69. Ross, *No Respect*, 151.

70. Harris and Jackson, "Stormy Weather," 96.

71. Jablonski, *Harold Arlen*, 51–53.

72. Mast, *Can't Help Singin'*, 231–32.

73. For an account of the witch hunts of the 1950s, see Jeffrey-Poulter, *Peers, Queers and Commons*; Sinfield, *Literature, Politics and Culture in Postwar Britain*, 60–85. On race in postwar Britain, see especially Gilroy, *'There Ain't No Black in the Union Jack.'*

74. Sabin, "'I Won't Let That Dago By,'" 199–218. On antifascist organizations of the 1970s, including ANL and RAR, see Copsey, *Anti-Fascism in Britain*, 115–52. On the National Front, see Thurlow, *Fascism in Britain*, 230–44.

75. Marcus, *Lipstick Traces*, 117.

76. Smith, *New Right Discourse on Race and Sexuality*, 26.

77. Ibid., 210.

78. Tobin, "Lesbianism and the Labour Party," 56–66.

79. On the parallels between Sycorax and Prospero in the text, and their common origin in the character of Medea from Ovid's *Metamorphoses*, see Stephen Orgel's introduction to his edition of the play, 19–20.

80. Warr, "Feral City," 120.

81. Rosenfeld, "The End of Everything Was 20 Years Ago Today," 26–29.

4. The Caravaggio Years

1. On the videos, see Peake, *Derek Jarman*, 288–89, 312. The poet Jeremy Reed offers an evocative account of Jarman and Marc Almond in Soho at this time in "Coda: What Colour Is Time? Derek Jarman's Soho," 203–6.

2. Jarman, *The Last of England*, 36.

3. Sidney, "The Defense of Poesy," 121.

4. O'Pray, *Dreams of England*, 138.

5. Jarman, *The Last of England*, 90.

6. Peake, *Derek Jarman*, 341.

7. Jarman, *The Last of England*, 99.

8. Peake, *Derek Jarman*, 345.

9. The lines rewrite a couple of lines from Blake's "Auguries of Innocence": "The Harlots cry from Street to Street / Shall weave old Englands winding Sheet" (115–16) (in Erdman, *The Poetry and Prose of William Blake*).

10. Jarman, *The Last of England*, 112.

11. Jarman, *Dancing Ledge*, 197.

12. This is reminiscent as well of Eisenstein, who frequently inserts fantasy images to clarify the meaning at particular moments: the stone lions that come to life in *Battleship Potemkin*, for example, or a series of harps seen in *October* when peace is being discussed.

13. Both O'Pray and Peake, for example, mention this.

14. I am thinking in particular of Michel Foucault's "Friendship as a Way of Life," 135–40.

15. Peake, *Derek Jarman*, 341; Jarman discusses it in *Derek Jarman's Garden*, 43.

16. Jarman, *The Last of England*, 145.

17. Commentary accompanying a program of super-8 shorts shown at Berkeley.

18. Holmes, "New Romantic Shakespeare," 61.

19. Vendler, *The Art of Shakespeare's Sonnets*, 638.

20. Ibid., 639.

21. Fineman, *Shakespeare's Perjured Eye*, 17.

22. Jarman, *Dancing Ledge*, 133.

23. Herbert, *Fortune and Men's Eyes*.

24. Dillon, *Derek Jarman and Lyric Film*.

25. "Cocteau was one of the early key practitioners of film poetry and Jean Cau was certain that *Un Chant d'Amour* was heavily influenced by—if not derivative of—Cocteau's *Blood of a Poet*. Genet certainly viewed Kenneth Anger's short film *Fireworks* (1947) in 1949 and the two bear comparison in their visions of homoerotic desire" (Giles, *Criminal Desires*, 81).

26. Ibid., 135.

27. Jarman himself draws attention to the shared "obsession with the language of closed structures, the ritual of the closet and the sanctuary . . . the prison cells of Genet's *Un Chant d'Amour*, the desert encampment of *Sebastiane*" (*The Last of England*, 60).

28. Ibid., 133.

29. Ibid., 54.

30. Field and O'Pray, "On Imaging October, Dr. Dee and Other Matters," 55.

31. Jarman, *The Last of England*, 54.

32. Jarman, *Modern Nature*, 23.

33. O'Quinn, "Gardening, History, and the Escape from Time," 118.

34. Field and O'Pray, "On Imaging October, Dr. Dee and Other Matters," 49.

35. Ibid., 56.

36. Jarman, *Queer Edward II*, 86.

37. Hibbard, *Caravaggio*, 30.

38. Harvey, "See Rome and Die," 56, 60.

39. For an extended discussion of this in the poetic realm, see Guy-Bray, *Loving In Verse*.

40. Jarman, *Dancing Ledge*, 9, 14, 22. Both Bersani and Dutoit (in *Caravaggio*) and Dillon comment on the Pasolini/Caravaggio remarks. In what follows, I will be depending more on Bersani and Dutoit's discussion of the painter *(Caravaggio's Secrets)* than their monograph on Jarman's film. Their evident distaste for what they see as Jarman's politics makes for an ungenerous if often insightful reading, where, for the most part, any positive features of Jarman's films seem to occur in spite of his intentions. By contrast, their highly productive reading of Caravaggio's work offers many very useful avenues into what Jarman might have learned from Caravaggio.

41. Warwick, "Introduction," 19.

42. Gardner, "Perverse Law," 42.

43. Posner, "Caravaggio's Homo-Erotic Early Works," 301–19.

44. For a critical discussion of biographies of Caravaggio and the known facts of his life, see Puglisi, "Caravaggio's Life and *Lives* over Four Centuries," 23–35.

45. Jarman, *The Last of England*, 90.

46. Bersani and Dutoit, *Caravaggio's Secrets*, 10.

47. Cardinal del Monte's relationship with Caravaggio is addressed in Francis Haskell's *Patrons and Painters*, which cites a contemporary account from 1617 describing him as "a living corpse . . . given entirely to spiritual matters, perhaps so as to make up for the license of his younger days" (28–29).

48. Quoted in Friedlaender, *Caravaggio Studies*, 14.

49. Ibid., 15.

50. Jarman, *War Requiem*, 15.

51. Lynne Tillman offers a number of examples in other reviews of *Caravaggio* ("Love Story," 23).

52. Jarman, *Derek Jarman's Caravaggio*, 45.

53. Hibbard, *Caravaggio*, 4, 12.

54. Warwick, "Introduction," 16.

55. Friedlaender, *Caravaggio Studies*, 17.

56. Hibbard, *Caravaggio*, 77.

57. Bersani and Dutoit, *Caravaggio's Secrets*, 46. Subsequent references are given in the text.

58. Tweedie, "The Suspended Spectacle of History," 386.

59. Foucault, "Friendship as a Way of Life," 135.

60. Murray, *Like a Film*, 132.

61. Dillon, *Derek Jarman and Lyric Film*, 139.

62. Posner argues, apropos of the wreath, that the painting of the sick Bacchus "may be meant to symbolize 'Lewdness' or 'Lust,' which are represented in Cesare

Ripa's iconological handbook by a faun with a bunch of grapes and crown of rocket *(eruca)*. . . . Since ivy is mentioned by Ripa only a few pages earlier specifically as a symbol of lewdness, the artist could easily have felt justified in using the more familiar plant as a substitute for rocket" (314).

5. Thatcherism, AIDS, and War

1. Jarman, *The Last of England,* 173. "Kicking the Pricks" was Jarman's preferred title, which I will be using to differentiate the book from the film; it was later republished under that name.

2. O'Pray, *Derek Jarman,* 156.

3. Maslin, "Glimpses of a Depressing Future."

4. Jarman, *The Last of England,* 12.

5. Bordwell, *The Cinema of Eisenstein,* 43.

6. Eisenstein, *Selected Works,* vol. 1, 40–41.

7. Nesbit, *Savage Junctures,* 11.

8. Jarman, *The Last of England,* 13–14.

9. Nesbit, *Savage Junctures,* 21.

10. Eisenstein, *Selected Works,* 64. Subsequent references are given in the text.

11. Bersani and Dutoit, *Caravaggio,* 56.

12. Hill, *British Cinema of the 1980s,* 161.

13. Jarman, *The Last of England,* 193.

14. Anderson, "Only Connect," 53.

15. Jarman, *The Last of England,* 136.

16. Jackson, *The Humphrey Jennings Film Reader,* xv.

17. Kuhn, *Family Secrets,* 134.

18. Ibid., 137.

19. Anderson, "Only Connect," 57.

20. Dillon, *Derek Jarman and Lyric Film,* 163–67.

21. Vendler, *The Art of Shakespeare's Sonnets,* 16.

22. On the films of this era, see Friedman, *Fires Were Started.*

23. Among the other responses was Julian Petley, "The British Cinema under Fire: The Price of Portraying a Less Than Perfect Britain," *The Listener,* January 21, 1988.

24. Bersani and Dutoit, *Caravaggio,* 17, 61.

25. Kuhn, *Family Secrets,* 145; Humphrey, "Authorship, History and the Dialectic of Trauma," 209.

26. Jarman, *Modern Nature,* 297.

27. Peake, *Derek Jarman,* 378.

28. Jarman, *The Last of England,* 188.

29. Ibid., 170.

30. On a further poignant note, the archaeologist is played by one of the lovers from *The Angelic Conversation.*

31. Jarman, *The Last of England,* 167.

32. "Spring" is the credited name for Rupert Adley (Peake, *Derek Jarman,* 368).

33. Pope and Leonard, "Divas and Disease, Mourning and Militancy," 319; they are quoting Galás's description of her own work.

34. Hill, *British Cinema of the 1980s,* 158–59.

35. Jarman, *The Last of England,* 16.

36. Quoted in Peake, *Derek Jarman,* 377.

37. Jarman, *The Last of England,* 17.

38. Ibid.

39. Watney, *Policing Desire,* 137.

40. Bergonzi, *Heroes' Twilight,* 131.

41. Quoted in Jarman, *War Requiem,* 30.

42. Ibid., xii.

43. Matt Houlbrook has questioned the existence of any officially organized witch hunt, although he does acknowledge the increase in prosecutions in the 1950s (34–35), as well as increasingly hostile press attention, when "the queer became a more visible and dangerous part of everyday discourse . . . defined as a potent threat to Britain's very existence" (*Queer London,* 192).

44. Jeffrey-Poulter, *Peers, Queers and Commons,* 265.

45. Ibid., 257.

46. Brett, "Musicality, Essentialism, and the Closet," 21.

47. Carpenter, *Benjamin Britten,* 194.

48. Jarman, *War Requiem,* 29.

49. Ibid.

50. Kennedy, *Britten,* 118.

51. Tambling, *Opera, Ideology and Film,* 119.

52. Quoted in Carpenter, *Benjamin Britten,* 404–5.

53. Kennedy, *Britten,* 209.

54. Breen, *Wilfred Owen,* 171.

55. Kerr, *Wilfred Owen's Voices,* 271.

56. Fussell, *The Great War and Modern Memory,* 294.

57. Jeffrey-Poulter, *Peers, Queers and Commons,* 265.

58. Dyer, "Homosexuality and Heritage," 204–28; Neale, "'Chariots of Fire,' Images of Men," 47–53; Finch and Kwietniowski, "Melodrama and *Maurice,*" 72–80.

59. See, for example, Monk, "The British Heritage-Film Debate Revisited," 176–98.

60. Higson, "Re-presenting the National Past," 113.

61. On the relation between stage and film version, as well as the relations between Branagh, Olivier, and Henry, see Collier, "Post-Falklands, Post-Colonial," 143–54.

62. Branagh, *Beginnings*, 236.

63. Manheim, "The Function of Battle Imagery in Kurosawa's Histories and the *Henry V* Films," 133.

64. Lippard and Johnson, "Private Practice, Public Health," 288.

65. Jarman, *War Requiem*, 29.

66. Das, "'Kiss Me, Hardy,'" 69.

67. Day Lewis, "Introduction," in *The Collected Poems of Wilfred Owen*, 18–19.

68. Jarman, *War Requiem*, 16.

69. Foucault, "Friendship as a Way of Life," 135.

70. Foucault, "Sexual Choice, Sexual Act," 153.

71. Jarman, *At Your Own Risk*, 27.

6. Time and the Garden

1. Jarman, *Derek Jarman's Garden*, 14.

2. Riley and Ferry, "Fighting for the Beaches of Dungeness," 46, 47.

3. Published posthumously, *Derek Jarman's Garden* is a more straightforward description of the garden, the house, and the landscape around it. Jarman's words are accompanied by the photographs of Howard Sooley, who collaborated on the making of the garden.

4. Jarman, *Modern Nature*, 30.

5. Postle, "Country Gardens," 20. See also Daniels, "Suburban Prospects," in the same volume. On the emergence of the cottage garden as an icon of Englishness, see chapter 3 of Helmreich, *The English Garden and National Identity*, 66–90.

6. On the history of the cottage garden, see Scott-James, *The Cottage Garden*.

7. Hunt, *The Afterlife of Gardens*, 42. See also Beck, "Gardens as a 'Third Nature,'" 327–34.

8. John Parkinson's *Paradisi in Sole Paradisus Terrestris* (1629), for example, gives instructions on how to create patterns using plants and "dead materials" such as bones, tiles, or stones.

9. Wollen, "Facets of Derek Jarman," 19.

10. The classic work on English Renaissance gardens is Roy Strong's *The Renaissance Garden in England*. Also highly informative is John Dixon Hunt's *Garden and Grove*.

11. The text is reproduced in Jarman, *Derek Jarman's Garden*, 117.

12. Hunt, *The Afterlife of Gardens*, 112.

13. Jarman, *Modern Nature*, 30.

14. Jarman, *Derek Jarman's Garden*, 12.

15. Ibid., 5.

16. Ibid., 43.

17. Some of these designs are reproduced in Wollen, *Derek Jarman: A Portrait*, 60.

18. In *Chroma* Jarman says of his paintings at eighteen: "My paintings are in the browns and greens of landscape. Dark and sombre, stone circles and mysterious woods. They are the ancestors of my garden in Dungeness" (82).

19. Hill, *The Gardener's Labyrinth*, 114.

20. Jarman, *Modern Nature*, 41.

21. Woodward, *Gerard's Herball*, 5.

22. Prest, *The Garden of Eden*.

23. Debus, *The English Paracelsians*.

24. Jarman, *Modern Nature*, 23.

25. Ibid., 179.

26. Jarman, *Queer Edward II*, 2.

27. Morrison, "Derek Jarman: The Final Interview," 17–22.

28. Jarman, *Modern Nature*, 75. Deborah Esch offers a lengthy discussion of this aspect of *Modern Nature* in *In the Event*, 116–34.

29. Jarman, *Modern Nature*, 161–68. For a discussion and photographs of the exhibition, see Iles, "Derek Jarman," 64–77.

30. Jarman, *Modern Nature*, 152.

31. Ibid., 314.

32. Ibid., 56.

33. Jarman, *Queer Edward II*, 30.

34. Jarman, *Modern Nature*, 297. This is echoed by a comment in Tom Joslin's *Silverlake Chronicles: The View from Here*: "certainly having AIDS and being a walking dead, if you will, separates one from the everyday world."

35. Jarman, *Modern Nature*, 53–54.

36. See Daniel O'Quinn's discussion of these "sacred sodomitical spaces" in "Gardening, History, and the Escape from Time," 113–26.

37. Ross Chambers offers a discussion of the AIDS diary as prophylaxis in *Facing It*, 5–6.

38. Rayns, "The 'I-Movie.'"

39. "The film is structured like a dream allegory, in a poetic tradition, rather like Chaucer's Canterbury Tales. The film is a dream allegory of the author, in this case, myself. I could have put somebody else into it but really dreams are always in the first person, though some people often invent proxies. I go to sleep and go on a mental journey" ("Gardener's Question Time: An Interview with Derek Jarman," *The Garden* Press Kit).

40. *Derek Jarman's Garden*, 91. For a discussion of American films dealing with AIDS, see Hart, *The AIDS Movie*.

41. Chambers, *Facing It*, 17.

42. Jarman, *Modern Nature*, 211.

43. Ibid., 56.

44. Ibid., 149.

45. Loughlin, *Alien Sex*, 274.

46. Perriam, "Queer Borders," 117.

47. Jarman, *Modern Nature*, 22.

48. Loughlin, *Alien Sex*, 271.

49. Jarman, *Modern Nature*, 14.

50. Hunt, *Greater Perfections*, 37–38.

51. Bersani and Dutoit, *Caravaggio's Secrets*, 42.

52. Sontag, *AIDS and Its Metaphors*, 46.

7. Blindness and Insight

1. Rich, "New Queer Cinema," 16.

2. For histories of the movement, see Lucas, *OutRage! An Oral History* and *Impertinent Decorum*, 158–69.

3. Lucas, *OutRage!* 58.

4. Rich, "New Queer Cinema," 16.

5. Ibid., 21.

6. Arroyo, "Death Desire and Identity," 80.

7. Jarman, "Queer Questions," 35.

8. Jarman, *Queer Edward II*, 20.

9. Photo caption accompanying Michael O'Pray's "Damning Desire," 9.

10. See, for example, MacCabe, who states that the film is "much more unambiguous in its misogyny than any of his other work" (15). MacCabe's description of the "gay dialectic where identification with the position of the woman is set against rejection of the woman's body" (ibid.) is as odd as his consequent reading of the film. Kate Chedgzoy discusses the charges of misogyny in some detail, noting that "The spectacle of heterosexual men rushing to vindicate their own sexual politics by criticizing Jarman's misogyny is not an edifying one" (*Shakespeare's Queer Children*, 209). See also Bette Talvacchia, who discusses all of the female figures in the film ("Historical Phallicy," 118–26). For an extended reading of Isabella from a queer perspective, see Niall Richardson, "The Queer Performance of Tilda Swinton in Derek Jarman's *Edward II*," 427–44.

11. Rich, "New Queer Cinema," 18.

12. Talvacchia discusses the implications of vampiric Isabella from a feminist perspective in some detail ("Historical Phallicy," 125–26).

13. Jarman, quoted in O'Pray, "Damning Desire," 11.

14. On the history of Hammer and Bray, see Kinsey, *Hammer Films;* Hunter,

House of Horror. Hammer sold Bray in 1970, but it remained a studio, where films such as Ken Russell's *The Music Lovers* and *The Rocky Horror Picture Show* were subsequently made (Kinsey, *Hammer Films*, 355).

15. Benshoff, *Monsters in the Closet*, 231.

16. Hanson, "Undead," 325.

17. Jarman, *Queer Edward II*, 4.

18. Talvacchia, "Historical Phallicy," 119, 120.

19. Bruzzi, *Undressing Cinema*, 36.

20. Founded in 1986 by Lloyd Newson, one of the dancers in the scene, DV8 is a British collective that frequently addresses issues of sexuality in its works. Just prior to their appearance in *Edward II* they had performed (and filmed) *Dead Dreams of Monochrome Men,* a piece about loneliness, desire, and the effects of homophobia.

21. Arroyo, "Death Desire and Identity," 85.

22. Normand, "'Edward II', Derek Jarman, and the State of England," 184–85. For another discussion of the relation between the play and the film, see Cartelli, "Queer Edward II," 213–23.

23. Jarman, quoted in O'Pray, "Damning Desire," 11.

24. Normand, "'Edward II', Derek Jarman, and the State of England," 181.

25. Romney, "Edward II," 42.

26. On the latter, see Arroyo, "Death Desire and Identity," 80. On the former, see Romney, "Edward II," 41–42. Chedgzoy discusses the "heterophobia" charges (*Shakespeare's Queer Children*, 208–9).

27. The slogans for the text were provided by Greg Taylor. Thomas Cartelli notes the interesting parallels between these and Marlowe's own famous and provocative pronouncements about boys, religion, and the sexuality of Christ ("Queer Edward II," 218).

28. Jarman, *Queer Edward II*, 22.

29. LaCapra, *Writing History, Writing Trauma*, 42.

30. Cartelli, "Queer Edward II," 220.

31. On this, see in particular Christian Braad Thomson, *Fassbinder:* "Fassbinder never has 'pure' heroes. Rather, he demonstrates one of the most melancholy consequences of oppression, that the damage to the souls of the victims makes them unable to find alternative norms, so that the only possibility left to them is to recapitulate the norms that have led to their oppression" (205).

32. Jarman, *Queer Edward II*, 116.

33. Ibid., 84.

34. This ending apparently has some historical justification. Jarman writes in the script that "We've adopted the conspiracy theory for the end of the film. Manuel Fieschi, writing to Edward III, told him that his father had escaped from

Berkeley Castle, to Corfe, and from there to Avignon" (ibid., 158). For a discussion of the letter and the conspiracy, see Cuttino and Lyman, "Where Is Edward II?" 522–44; Haines, *King Edward II*, 219–38. Ian Mortimer has taken up the claim that Edward was not murdered in *The Greatest Traitor* (2003), *The Perfect King* (2006), and "The Death of Edward II in Berkeley Castle," 1175–1214.

35. Jarman, *Queer Edward II*, 154.

36. Dillon, *Derek Jarman and Lyric Film*, 213.

37. Jarman, *Queer Edward II*, 146.

38. The poker (originally a "plumber's iron") is almost certainly an invention by a chronicler writing thirty years after Edward's death (Cuttino and Lyman, "Where Is Edward II?" 524).

39. Jarman, quoted in O'Pray, "Damning Desire," 14.

40. 5.1.26–27; 5.1.152–53; 5.1.110–11 (Christopher Marlowe, *Edward II*).

41. De Jongh, "The Last Picture Show."

42. Eagleton, "A Suitable Case for Treatment." An expanded version of this was published as "My Wittgenstein."

43. Monk, "Between Earth and Ice," 16. The *Evening Standard* was less circumspect: "According to Monk, Eagleton's scathing dismissal of the Martian in Jarman's film as mere 'camp' and 'embarrassing whimsy' turns out to be a sign of professional ignorance. The Martian is Wittgenstein's own" (de Jongh, "The Last Picture Show").

44. Jarman and Butler, "Wittgenstein," 76.

45. Eagleton, "Introduction to Wittgenstein," 12.

46. Ibid., 9.

47. Glock, *A Wittgenstein Dictionary*, 31.

48. Eagleton, "Introduction to Wittgenstein," 10.

49. Jarman, *At Your Own Risk*, 134.

50. Jarman and Butler, "Wittgenstein," 70.

51. Wittgenstein, *Remarks on Colour*, 27e.

52. O'Pray, *Derek Jarman*, 198.

53. Jarman and Butler, "Wittgenstein," 132. Subsequent references are given in the text.

54. Brenner, *Wittgenstein's Philosophical Investigations*, 120.

55. Jarman, "This Is Not a Film of Ludwig Wittgenstein," 64.

56. Wittgenstein, *Remarks on Colour*, 9e.

57. Jarman, "This Is Not a Film of Ludwig Wittgenstein," 63.

58. Jarman and Butler, "Wittgenstein," 108.

59. Ibid.

60. Ibid., 67.

61. Ibid., 74.

62. Wollen, *"Blue,"* 120–21; Peake, *Derek Jarman,* 398–99.

63. Jarman, *Modern Nature,* 82.

64. Klein, "Overcoming the Problematics of Art," 48.

65. Ibid.

66. O'Pray, *Dreams of England,* 201.

67. Peake, *Derek Jarman,* 474. A CD exists of the Rome concert: *Live Blue Roma (The Archaeology of Sound)* (London: Mute Records, 1995). The script for this performance is considerably less autobiographical than that of the film.

68. Jarman, *Chroma,* 38. Subsequent references are given in the text.

69. O'Pray, *Derek Jarman,* 203.

70. Lawrence, "AIDS, the Problem of Representation, and Plurality in Derek Jarman's *Blue,"* 252.

71. Jarman, *Modern Nature,* 23.

72. Stich, *Yves Klein,* 9.

73. Restany, *Yves Klein,* 44.

74. Stich, *Yves Klein,* 66.

75. Smith, *"Blue* and the Outer Limits," 19.

76. Schwenger, "Derek Jarman and the Colour of the Mind's Eye," 420.

77. Restany, *Yves Klein,* 50.

78. Peter Wollen, *"Blue,"* 130.

79. This quotation supplies the subtitle, *The Archaeology of Sound,* for *Live Blue Roma,* a CD recording of the last of the concerts that preceded the film.

80. Perhaps coincidentally, this translates to some degree Yves Klein's unrealized ideas about novel writing. He "proposed the creation of novels that would have neither characters nor plot but intense abstract power. Rather than conveying a message or being rooted in subject matter, such works of literature would present an atmosphere or ambience and feelings. Like single-color paintings, they would offer purity, and contrary to what one might think, they would have great variety and be of differing levels of quality" (Stich, *Yves Klein,* 53).

81. Douglas Crimp, *Melancholia and Moralism,* 88.

82. Crimp quoting William Olander, in ibid., 93.

83. Ibid., 100.

84. Jarman, *Derek Jarman's Garden,* 91.

85. Ricco, *The Logic of the Lure,* 35, 42.

86. Jarman, *Derek Jarman's Garden,* 91.

87. Edelman, "The Mirror and the Tank," 9, 10.

88. LaCapra, *Writing History, Writing Trauma,* 41.

89. Silverman, *Male Subjectivity at the Margins,* 264–65.

90. Scheler, *The Nature of Sympathy,* 18–19.

91. Griffin, *Representations of HIV and AIDS,* 19.

Coda

1. Morrison, "Derek Jarman," 22.

2. Eitner, Géricault, 158–63.

3. Quoted in Alhadeff, The Raft of the Medusa, 18.

4. The details of the panorama can be found in Eitner, Géricault. It was billed as a "Marine Peristrephic Panorama of the Medusa"; the sixth scene largely copied Géricault's painting (212). Interestingly enough, the diorama killed the audience for the painting itself in some cities.

5. Cox, "This Is Indecent," 14–15.

6. McGarvey, "The Last Bohemian," 82.

7. Moran, "32 Cryptograms for Derek Jarman," 540–42.

8. A couple of valuable overviews and many good reproductions can be found in Wollen, Derek Jarman and "Facets of Derek Jarman," 15–31, and O'Pray, "Derek Jarman," 65–75. See also Iles, "Derek Jarman," 64–77.

9. Kimpton-Nye, Derek Jarman.

Works Cited

Albanese, Denise. "Making It New: Humanism, Colonialism, and the Gendered Body in Early Modern Culture." In *Feminist Readings of Early Modern Culture: Emerging Subjects*, ed. Valerie Traub, M. Lindsay Kaplan, and Dympna Callaghan, 16–43. Cambridge: Cambridge University Press, 1996.

Alhadeff, Albert. *The Raft of the Medusa: Géricault, Art, and Race.* Munich: Prestel, 2002.

Alloway, Lawrence. "The Development of British Pop." In Lippard 27–67.

———. "The Independent Group: Postwar Britain and the Aesthetics of Plenty." In *The Independent Group: Postwar Britain and the Aesthetics of Plenty*, ed. David Robbins, 49–50. Cambridge: MIT Press, 1990.

Anderson, Benedict. *Imagined Communities: Reflections on the Origin and Spread of Nationalism.* London: Verso, 1991.

Anderson, Lindsay. "Only Connect: Some Aspects of the Work of Humphrey Jennings." *Sight and Sound* (April–June 1954). Reprinted in *Humphrey Jennings: Film-Maker, Painter, Poet*, ed. Mary-Lou Jennings, 53–59. London: BFI, 1982.

Arroyo, José. "Death Desire and Identity: The Political Unconscious of 'New Queer Cinema.'" In *Activating Theory: Lesbian, Gay, Bisexual Politics*, ed. Joseph Bristow and Angelia R. Wilson, 70–96. London: Lawrence & Wishart, 1993.

Babusco, Jack. "Piercing Pleasures: Derek Jarman's *Sebastiane*." *Gay News* 105 (October 21, 1976), 21–22.

Barker, Francis, and Peter Hulme. "Nymphs and Reapers Heavily Vanish: The Discursive Con-texts of *The Tempest*." In *Alternative Shakespeares*, ed. John Drakakis, 191–205. London: Routledge, 1985.

Barthelemy, Gerald. *Black Face Maligned Race: The Representation of Blacks in English Drama from Shakespeare to Southerne.* Baton Rouge and London: Louisiana State University Press, 1987.

Beck, Thomas A. "Gardens as a 'Third Nature': The Ancient Roots of a Renaissance Idea." *Studies in the History of Gardens and Designed Landscapes* 22 (2002): 327–34.

Belsey, Catherine. *The Subject of Tragedy: Identity and Difference in Early Modern Drama.* London and New York: Methuen, 1985.

Benjamin, Walter. "The Work of Art in the Age of Its Technological Reproducibility: Second Version." In *Walter Benjamin: Selected Writings*, vol. 3, ed. Howard Eiland and Michael W. Jennings. Trans. Edmund Jephcott, Howard Eiland, et al., 101–33. Cambridge, Mass.: Belknap Press, 2002.

Bennett, Susan. *Performing Nostalgia: Shifting Shakespeare and the Contemporary Past*. London and New York: Routledge, 1996.

Benshoff, Harry M. *Monsters in the Closet: Homosexuality and the Horror Film*. Manchester: Manchester University Press, 1997.

Bergonzi, Bernard. *Heroes' Twilight: A Study of the Literature of the Great War*. London: Constable, 1965.

Bersani, Leo, and Ulysses Dutoit. *Caravaggio*. BFI Modern Classics. London: BFI, 1999.

———. *Caravaggio's Secrets*. Cambridge: MIT Press, 1998.

Bevington, David. "*The Tempest* and the Jacobean Court Masque." In Bevington and Holbrook 218–43.

Bevington, David, and Peter Holbrook. "Introduction." In Bevington and Holbrook 1–19.

———, eds. *The Politics of the Stuart Court Masque*. Cambridge: Cambridge University Press, 1998.

Birch, Keith. "A Community of Interests." In *Radical Records: Thirty Years of Gay and Lesbian History*, ed. Bob Cant and Susan Hemmings, 51–59. London: Routledge, 1988.

Blazwick, Iwona, ed. *An Endless Adventure . . . An Endless Passion . . . An Endless Banquet: A Situationist Scrapbook*. London: Verson/ICA, 1989.

Boose, Lynda E. "'The Getting of a Lawful Race': Racial Discourse in Early Modern England and the Unpresentable Black Woman." In *Women, "Race," and Writing in Early Modern England*, ed. Margo Hendricks and Patricia Parker, 35–54. London and New York: Routledge, 1994.

Bordwell, David. *The Cinema of Eisenstein*. Cambridge: Harvard University Press, 1993.

Brakhage, Stan. *Telling Time: Essays of a Visionary Filmmaker*. Kingston, N.Y.: Documentext, 2003.

Branagh, Kenneth. *Beginnings*. London: Chatto & Windus, 1989.

Bray, Alan. *Homosexuality in Renaissance England*. New York: Columbia University Press, 1995.

Breen, Jennifer, ed. *Wilfred Owen: Selected Poetry and Prose*. New York: Routledge, 1988.

Brenner, William H. *Wittgenstein's Philosophical Investigations*. Albany: State University of New York Press, 1999.

Brett, Philip. "Musicality, Essentialism, and the Closet." In *Queering the Pitch: The New Gay and Lesbian Musicology*, ed. Philip Brett, Elizabeth Wood, and Gary C. Thomas, 9–26. New York: Routledge, 1986.

Brown, Paul. "'This thing of darkness I acknowledge mine': *The Tempest* and the Discourse of Colonialism." In *Political Shakespeare: New Essays in Cultural Materialism*, ed. Jonathan Dollimore and Alan Sinfield, 48–71. Ithaca, N.Y., and London: Cornell University Press, 1985.

Bruno, Giuliana. *Atlas of Emotions: Journeys in Art, Architecture, and Film*. London: Verso, 2002.

———. *Streetwalking on a Ruined Map*. Princeton, N.J.: Princeton University Press, 1993.

Bruzzi, Stella. *Undressing Cinema: Clothing and Identity in the Movies*. London: Routledge, 1996.

Carpenter, Humphrey. *Benjamin Britten: A Biography*. London: Faber and Faber, 1992.

Cartelli, Thomas. "*Queer Edward II*: Postmodern Sexualities and the Early Modern Subject." In *Marlowe, History, and Sexuality: New Essays on Christopher Marlowe*, ed. Paul Whitfield White, 213–23. New York: AMS Press, 1998.

Chambers, Ross. *Facing It: AIDS Diaries and the Death of the Author*. Ann Arbor: University of Michigan Press, 1998.

Chedgzoy, Kate. *Shakespeare's Queer Children: Sexual Politics and Contemporary Culture*. Manchester: Manchester University Press, 1995.

Collick, John. *Shakespeare, Cinema and Society*. Manchester: Manchester University Press, 1989.

Collier, Suzannne. "Post-Falklands, Post-Colonial: Contextualizing Branagh as Henry V on Stage and on Film." *Essays in Theatre / Études Théâtrales* 10 (1990): 143–54.

Comolli, Jean-Louis. "Historical Fiction: A Body Too Much." *Screen* 19 (1978): 41–53.

Cook, Pam. *Fashioning the Nation: Costume and Identity in British Cinema*. London: BFI, 1996.

Copsey, Nigel. *Anti-Fascism in Britain*. Manchester: Manchester University Press, 2000.

Cox, Alex. "This Is Indecent." *Guardian*, February 19, 2004, Supp. 14–15.

Craig, Hugh. "Jonson, the Antimasque and the 'Rules of Flattery.'" In Bevington and Holbrook 176–96.

Crimp, Douglas. *Melancholia and Moralism: Essays on AIDS and Queer Politics*. Cambridge: MIT Press, 2002.

Crow, Thomas. *The Rise of the Sixties*. New York: Harry N. Abrams, 1996.

Curtis, Barry. "'A Highly Mobile and Plastic Environ.'" In *Art and the 60s: This Was Tomorrow*, ed. Chris Stephens and Katharine Stout, 46–63. London: Tate, 2004.

Curtis, David. "English Avant-Garde Film: An Early Chronology." *Studio International* 190.978 (November / December 1975): 176–82.

Cuttino, G. P., and Thomas W. Lyman. "Where Is Edward II?" *Speculum* 53.3 (1978): 522–44.

Daniels, Stephen. "Suburban Prospects." In *Art of the Garden*, 22–30. London: Tate, 2004.

Das, Santanu. "'Kiss Me, Hardy': Intimacy, Gender, and Gesture in World War I Trench Literature." *Modernism/Modernity* 9.1 (2002): 51–74.

Day Lewis, C., ed. *The Collected Poems of Wilfred Owen*. London: Chatto & Windus, 1964.

Debord, Guy, and Gianfranco Sanguinetti. *The Veritable Split in the International*. London: Chronos Publications, 1990.

Debus, Allen G. *The English Paracelsians*. New York: Science History Publishers, 1965.

de Jongh, Nicholas. "The Last Picture Show." *Evening Standard*, March 25, 1993.

Deleuze, Gilles. *Sacher-Masoch: An Interpretation*. Trans. Jean McNeil. London: Faber and Faber, 1971.

Derbyshire, Phil. "At Last a Film We Can Call Our Own?" *Gay Left* 4 (summer 1977): 19.

Dillon, Steven. *Derek Jarman and Lyric Film*. Austin: University of Texas Press, 2004.

Dwoskin, Steve. *Film Is . . . : The International Free Cinema*. London: Peter Owen, 1975.

Dyer, Richard. "Homosexuality and Heritage." In *The Culture of Queers*, 204–28. London: Routledge, 2002.

———. *Now You See It: Studies on Lesbian and Gay Film*. London: Routledge, 1990.

———. "Pasolini and Homosexuality." In *Pier Paolo Pasolini*, ed. Paul Willemen, 53–63. London: BFI, 1977.

Eagleton, Terry. "A Suitable Case for Treatment." *Guardian*, March 18, 1993.

———. "Introduction to Wittgenstein." In *Wittgenstein: The Terry Eagleton Script/ The Derek Jarman Film*, 5–13. London: BFI, 1991.

———. "My Wittgenstein." *Common Knowledge* 3.1 (1994): 152–57.

Edelman, Lee. "The Mirror and the Tank: 'AIDS,' Subjectivity, and the Rhetoric of Activism." In *Writing AIDS: Gay Literature, Language, and Analysis*, ed. Timothy F. Murphy and Suzanne Poirier, 9–38. New York: Columbia University Press, 1993.

Eisenstein, S. M. *Selected Works*, vol. 1: *Writings, 1922–34*. Ed. and trans. Richard Taylor. London: BFI, 1987.

Eitner, Lorenz E. A. *Géricault: His Life and Work*. London: Orbis Publishing, 1983.

Ellis, Jim. "Queer Period: Derek Jarman's Renaissance." In *Out Takes: Queer Theory and Film*, ed. Ellis Hanson, 288–315. Durham, N.C.: Duke University Press, 1999.

Erdman, David V., ed. *The Poetry and Prose of William Blake*. New York: Doubleday, 1965.

Esch, Deborah. *In the Event: Reading Journalism, Reading Theory*. Stanford, Calif.: Stanford University Press, 1999.

Field, Simon, and Michael O'Pray. "On Imaging October, Dr. Dee and Other Matters: An Interview with Derek Jarman." *Afterimage* 12 (autumn 1985): 40–59.

Finch, Mark, and Richard Kwietniowski. "Melodrama and *Maurice:* Homo Is Where the Het Is." *Screen* 29.3 (1988): 72–80.

Fineman, Joel. *Shakespeare's Perjured Eye: The Invention of Poetic Subjectivity in the Sonnets.* Berkeley: University of California Press, 1986.

Foucault, Michel. "Different Spaces." In *Aesthetics, Method and Epistemology,* ed. James D. Faubion, 175–86. Essential Works of Foucault 2. New York: New Press, 1998.

———. "Friendship as a Way of Life." In Rabinow 135–40.

———. "Sexual Choice, Sexual Act." In Rabinow 141–56.

Friedlaender, Walter. *Caravaggio Studies.* New York: Schocken, 1969.

Friedman, Lester, ed. *Fires Were Started: British Cinema and Thatcherism.* Minneapolis: University of Minnesota Press, 1993.

Frith, Simon, and Howard Horne. *Art into Pop.* London: Metheun, 1987.

Fussell, Paul. *The Great War and Modern Memory.* New York: Oxford University Press, 1975.

Gardner, David. "Perverse Law: Jarman as Gay Criminal Hero." In Lippard 31–64.

Giles, Jane. *Criminal Desires: Jean Genet and Cinema.* Vol. 2, *Persistence of Vision.* London: Creation Books, 2002.

Gillies, John. *Shakespeare and the Geography of Difference.* Cambridge: Cambridge University Press, 1994.

Gilroy, Paul. *'There Ain't No Black in the Union Jack': The Cultural Politics of Race and Nation.* London: Hutchinson, 1987.

Glock, Hans-Johann. *A Wittgenstein Dictionary.* Oxford: Blackwell, 1996.

Goldberg, Jonathan. *Sodometries: Renaissance Texts/Modern Sexualities.* Stanford, Calif.: Stanford University Press, 1992.

Gordon, D. J. "Roles and Mysteries." In *The Renaissance Imagination,* ed. Stephen Orgel, 3–23. Berkeley: University of California Press, 1975.

Griffin, Gabriele. *Representations of HIV and AIDS: Visibility Blue/s.* Manchester: Manchester University Press, 2000.

Guy-Bray, Stephen. *Loving in Verse: Poetic Influence as Erotic.* Toronto: University of Toronto Press, 2000.

Haines, Roy Martin. *King Edward II.* Montreal: McGill-Queens University Press, 2003.

Hall, Kim F. *Things of Darkness: Economies of Race and Gender in Early Modern England.* Ithaca, N.Y., and London: Cornell University Press, 1995.

Halperin, David M. *How to Do the History of Homosexuality.* Chicago and London: University of Chicago Press, 2002.

Halpern, Richard. "'The Picture of Nobody': White Cannibalism in *The Tempest.*" In *The Production of English Renaissance Culture,* ed. David Lee Miller, Haron O'Dair, and Harold Weber, 262–92. Ithaca, N.Y.: Cornell University Press, 1994.

Hamlin, Nicky. *Film Art Phenomena.* London: BFI, 2003.

Hansen, Miriam Bratu. "Room-for-Play: Benjamin's Gamble with Cinema." *October* 109 (2004): 3–45.

Hanson, Ellis. "Undead." In *Inside/Out: Lesbian Theories, Gay Theories,* ed. Diana Fuss, 324–40. London: Routledge, 1991.

Harris, Diana, and MacDonald Jackson. "Stormy Weather: Derek Jarman's *The Tempest.*" *Literature/Film Quarterly* 25 (1997): 90–98.

Hart, Kylo-Patrick R. *The AIDS Movie: Representing a Pandemic in Film and Television.* Binghamton, N.Y.: Haworth Press, 2000.

Harvey, Stephen. "See Rome and Die." *Village Voice* 31 (1986), 56, 60.

Haskell, Francis. *Patrons and Painters.* Rev. ed. New Haven: Yale University Press, 1980.

Helmreich, Anne. *The English Garden and National Identity.* Cambridge: Cambridge University Press, 2002.

Herbert, John. *Fortune and Men's Eyes.* New York: Grove Press, 1967.

Hibbard, Howard. *Caravaggio.* New York: Harper and Row, 1983.

Higson, Andrew. "Re-presenting the National Past: Nostalgia and Pastiche in the Heritage Film." In Friedman 109–29.

———. *Waving the Flag: Constructing a National Cinema in Britain.* Oxford: Clarendon Press, 1995.

Hill, John. *British Cinema of the 1980s.* Oxford: Oxford University Press, 1999.

Hill, Thomas. *The Gardener's Labyrinth.* London, 1577.

Hoberman, J. *On Jack Smith's Flaming Creatures, and Other Secret-Flix of Cinemaroc.* New York: Granary Books, 2001.

Hobsbawm, Eric. *Nations and Nationalism since 1780: Programme, Myth, Reality.* Cambridge: Cambridge University Press, 1990.

Holderness, Graham. "Shakespeare Rewound." *Shakespeare Survey* 45 (1993): 63–74.

Holmes, Michael Morgan. "New Romantic Shakespeare: AIDS, Poetry, and Community Survival in Derek Jarman's *The Angelic Conversation.*" *Post Script* 17.2 (1998): 56–72.

Houlbrook, Matt. *Queer London: Pleasures and Perils in the Sexual Metropolis, 1918–1957.* Chicago and London: University of Chicago Press, 2005.

Howes, Keith. "*Jubilee.*" *Gay News* 137 (February 23, 1978), 22.

Howes, Keith, and Alan Wall, "Punk: Wot's in It for Us?" *Gay News* 136 (February 9, 1978), 21–25.

Humphrey, Daniel. "Authorship, History and the Dialectic of Trauma: Derek Jarman's *The Last of England.*" *Screen* 44.2 (2003): 208–15.

Hunt, John Dixon. *The Afterlife of Gardens.* Philadelphia: University of Pennsylvania Press, 2004.

———. *Garden and Grove: The Italian Renaissance Garden in the English Imagination, 1600–1750.* Rev. ed. Philadelphia: University of Pennsylvania Press, 1996.

———. *Greater Perfections: The Practice of Garden Theory*. Philadelphia: University of Pennsylvania Press, 1999.

Iles, Chrissie. "Derek Jarman." In *Derek Jarman: Brutal Beauty,* ed. Melissa Larner, 64–77. London: Koenig Books, 2008.

Jablonski, Edward. *Harold Arlen: Rhythm, Rainbows, and Blues*. Boston: Northeastern University Press, 1996.

Jackson, Earl, Jr. *Strategies of Deviance: Studies in Gay Male Representation*. Bloomington: Indiana University Press, 1995.

Jackson, Kevin, ed. *The Humphrey Jennings Film Reader*. London: Carcanet, 1993.

Jameson, Fredric. *The Geopolitical Aesthetic: Cinema and Space in the World System*. Bloomington: Indiana University Press, 1992.

Jappe, Anselm. *Guy Debord*. Trans. Donald Nicholson-Smith. Berkeley: University of California Press, 1999.

Jarman, Derek. *At Your Own Risk: A Saint's Testament*. Woodstock, N.Y.: Overlook Press, 1993.

———. *Blue*. Woodstock, N.Y.: Overlook Press, 1994.

———. *Chroma: A Book of Colour—June '93*. London: Century, 1994.

———. "Dancer from the Dance: An Interview with Derek Jarman." *Square Peg* 10 (1985): 20–22.

———. *Dancing Ledge*. Ed. Shaun Allen. London: Quartet Books, 1984.

———. *Derek Jarman's Caravaggio*. London: Thames and Hudson, 1986.

———. *Derek Jarman's Garden: With Photographs by Howard Sooley*. London: Thames and Hudson, 1995.

———. *The Last of England*. Ed. David L. Hirst. London: Constable, 1987.

———. "The Making of *Sebastiane*." *Gay News* 104 (October 7–20, 1976).

———. *Modern Nature*. London: Vintage, 1992.

———. "P. P. P. in the Garden of Earthly Delights/Nijinksy's Last Dance." *Afterimage* 12 (autumn 1985): 22–29.

———. Preface to *Lindsay Kemp and Company: Photographs by Anno Wilms*. London: Gay Men's Press, 1987.

———. *Queer Edward II*. London: BFI, 1991.

———. "Queer Questions." *Sight and Sound* 2.5 (September 1992): 35.

———. *Up in the Air: Collected Film Scripts*. London: Vintage, 1996.

———. *War Requiem: The Film*. London: Faber and Faber, 1989.

———. "This Is Not a Film of Ludwig Wittgenstein." In *Wittgenstein*, 63–66. London: BFI, 1991.

Jarman, Derek, and Ken Butler. "Wittgenstein: The Derek Jarman Film." In Jarman, *Wittgenstein*, 69–151. London: BFI, 1991.

Jeffrey-Poulter, Stephen. *Peers, Queers and Commons: The Struggle for Gay Law Reform from 1950 to the Present*. New York: Routledge, 1991.

Johnston, Claire, and Jan Dawson. "Declarations of Independence." *Sight and Sound* 39.1 (winter 1969/1970): 28–32.

———. "More British Sounds." *Sight and Sound* 39.3 (summer 1970): 144–47.

Kaye, Richard A. "Losing His Religion: Saint Sebastian as Contemporary Gay Martyr." In *Outlooks: Lesbian and Gay Sexualities and Visual Cultures,* ed. Peter Horne and Reina Lewis, 86–105. London: Routledge, 1996.

Keith, Michael, and Steve Pile. "Introduction Part I: The Politics of Place." In *Place and the Politics of Identity,* ed. Michael Keith and Steve Pile, 1–21. London: Routledge, 1993.

Kennedy, Michael. *Britten.* Rev. ed. London: J. M. Dent, 1993.

Kerr, Douglas. *Wilfred Owen's Voices: Language and Community.* Oxford: Clarendon Press, 1993.

Kimpton-Nye, Andy. *Derek Jarman: Life as Art.* 2004.

Kinsey, Wayne. *Hammer Films: The Bray Studios Years.* London: Reynolds & Hearn, 2002.

Klein, Yves. *Overcoming the Problematics of Art: The Writings of Yves Klein.* Trans. Klaus Ottoman. Puttnam, Conn.: Spring Publications, 2007.

Knabb, Ken, ed. *Guy Debord: Complete Cinematic Works.* Oakland, Calif.: AK Press, 2003.

———, ed. and trans. *Situationist International Anthology.* Berkeley: Bureau of Public Secrets, 1981.

Kracauer, Siegfried. *Theory of Film: The Redemption of Physical Reality.* New York: Oxford University Press, 1960.

Kuhn, Annette. *Family Secrets: Acts of Memory and Imagination.* London: Verso, 2002.

LaCapra, Dominick. *Writing History, Writing Trauma.* Baltimore: Johns Hopkins University Press, 2001.

Lawrence, Tim. "AIDS, the Problem of Representation, and Plurality in Derek Jarman's *Blue.*" *Social Text* 52/53 (1997): 241–64.

Leach, Jim. *British Cinema.* Cambridge: Cambridge University Press, 2004.

Lippard, Chris, ed. *By Angels Driven: The Films of Derek Jarman.* Townbridge, Wiltshire: Flicks Books, 1996.

Lippard, Chris, and Guy Johnson. "Private Practice, Public Health: The Politics of Sickness and the Films of Derek Jarman." In Friedman 278–93.

Lippard, Lucy, ed. *Pop Art.* New York: Frederick A. Praeger, 1966.

Loomba, Ania. *Gender, Race, Renaissance Drama.* Manchester and New York: Manchester University Press, 1989.

Loughlin, Gerald. *Alien Sex: The Body and Desire in Cinema and Theology.* Oxford: Blackwell, 2004.

Lucas, Ian. *Impertinent Decorum: Gay Theatrical Maneouvres.* London and New York: Cassell, 1994.

———. *OutRage! An Oral History.* London and New York: Cassell, 1998.

Lyme, Francis. "Derek Jarman Talks to Francis Lyme." *Ritz* 15 (1978): 23.

MacCabe, Colin. "A Post-National European Cinema: A Consideration of Derek Jarman's *The Tempest* and *Edward II*." In *Screening Europe: Image and Identity in Contemporary European Cinema,* ed. Duncan Petrie, 9–18. London: BFI, 1992.

Manheim, Michael. "The Function of Battle Imagery in Kurosawa's Histories and the *Henry V* Films." *Literature/Film Quarterly* 22 (1994): 129–35.

Marcus, Greil. *Lipstick Traces: A Secret History of the Twentieth Century.* Cambridge: Harvard University Press, 1989.

Marlowe, Christopher. *Edward II.* Ed. W. Moelwyn Merchant. New Mermaids. London: Ernest Bean, 1967.

Maslin, Janel. "Glimpses of a Depressing Future." *New York Times,* September 28, 1988.

Mast, Gerald. *Can't Help Singin': The American Musical on Stage and Screen.* Woodstock, N.Y.: Overlook Press, 1987.

McCole, John. *Walter Benjamin and the Antinomies of Tradition.* Ithaca, N.Y.: Cornell University Press, 1993.

McDonough, Tom, ed. *Guy Debord and the Situationist International: Texts and Documents.* Cambridge: MIT Press, 2002.

———. "Situationist Space." In McDonough 241–66.

McGarvey, Seamus. "The Last Bohemian." *Dazed & Confused* 2.49 (May 2007): 82.

Medhurst, Andy. "What Did I Get? Punk, Memory and Autobiography." In Sabin 219–31.

Mekas, Jonas. "On the Baudelairean Cinema." In *Movie Journal: The Rise of the New American Cinema, 1959–1971,* 85–86. New York: Macmillan, 1972.

Mellor, David. *The Sixties Art Scene in London.* London: Phaedon Press, 1993.

Michaels, Eric. *Unbecoming.* Ed. Paul Foss. Rev. ed. Durham, N.C.: Duke University Press, 1997.

Monk, Claire. "The British Heritage-Film Debate Revisited." In *British Historical Cinema,* ed. Claire Monk and Amy Sargeant, 176–98. London: Routledge, 2002.

Monk, Ray. "Between Earth and Ice." *Times Literary Supplement,* March 19, 1993, 16.

Moor, Andrew. *Powell and Pressburger: A Cinema of Magic Spaces.* London: I. B. Taurus, 2005.

———. "Spirit and Matter: Romantic Mythologies in the Films of Derek Jarman." In *Territories of Desire in Queer Culture,* ed. David Alderson and Linda Anderson, 49–67. Manchester: Manchester University Press, 2000.

Moran, Robert. "32 Cryptograms for Derek Jarman." *Rocky Road to Kansas.* Argo 444, 540–42.

Morrison, Richard. "Derek Jarman: The Final Interview, Thursday, November 18, 1993." *Art & Understanding* 3.1 (1994): 17–22.

Mortimer, Ian. "The Death of Edward II in Berkeley Castle." *English Historical Review* 120 (2005): 1175–1214.

————. *The Greatest Traitor.* New York: Thomas Dunne, 2003.

————. *The Perfect King.* London: Jonathan Cape, 2006.

Murray, Timothy. *Like a Film.* London: Routledge, 1993.

Neale, Steve. "'Chariots of Fire,' Images of Men." *Screen* 23.2 (1982): 47–53.

Nesbit, Anne. *Savage Junctures: Sergei Eisenstein and the Shape of Thinking.* London: I. B. Tauris, 2003.

Normand, Lawrence. "'Edward II', Derek Jarman, and the State of England." In *Constructing Christopher Marlowe,* ed. J. A. Downie and J. T. Parnell, 177–93. Cambridge: Cambridge University Press, 2000.

Nowell-Smith, Geoffrey. "Pasolini's Originality." In *Pier Paolo Pasolini,* ed. Paul Willemen, 4–20. London: BFI, 1977.

O'Brien, Lucy. *She Bop II: The Definitive History of Women in Rock, Pop and Soul.* London: Continuum, 2002.

————. "The Woman Punk Made Me." In Sabin 186–98.

O'Pray, Michael. "Damning Desire." *Sight and Sound* 1.6 (October 1991): 8–14.

————. "Derek Jarman: The Art of Films/Films of Art." In Wollen 65–75.

————. *Derek Jarman: Dreams of England.* London: BFI, 1996.

————. "'New Romanticism' and the British Avant-Garde Film in the Early 80s." In *The British Cinema Book,* ed. Robert Murphy, 256–62. 2d ed. London: BFI, 2001.

O'Quinn, Daniel. "Gardening, History, and the Escape from Time: Derek Jarman's *Modern Nature.*" *October* 89 (1999): 113–26.

Orgel, Stephen. *The Jonsonian Masque.* Cambridge: Harvard University Press, 1965.

————. "Marginal Jonson." In Bevington and Holbrook 144–75.

Owen, Wilfred. *Poems.* London: Chatto & Windus, 1922.

————. *Wilfred Owen: Selected Poetry and Prose.* Ed. Jennifer Breen. New York: Routledge, 1988.

Park, James. *Learning to Dream: The New British Cinema.* London: Faber and Faber, 1984.

Pasolini, Pier Paolo. *Heretical Empiricism.* Ed. Louise K. Barnett. Trans. Ben Lawton and Louise K. Barnett. Bloomington: Indiana University Press, 1988.

————. "Pasolini on Film." In *Pier Paolo Pasolini,* ed. Paul Willemen, 67–77. London: BFI, 1977.

————. *Pasolini on Pasolini: Interviews with Oswald Stack.* London: BFI, 1969.

Peake, Tony. *Derek Jarman.* London: Little, Brown, 1999.

Pencak, William. *The Films of Derek Jarman.* Jefferson, N.C.: McFarland, 2002.

Perriam, Chris. "Queer Borders: Derek Jarman, *The Garden.*" In *New Exoticisms: Changing Patterns in the Construction of Otherness,* ed. Isabel Santaolalla. Postmodern Studies 29, 115–25. Amsterdam: Rodopi, 2000.

Pinfold, Michael John. "The Performance of Queer Masculinity in Derek Jarman's *Sebastiane.*" *Film Comment* 23.1 (1998): 74–83.

Pope, Rebecca A., and Susan J. Leonard. "Divas and Disease, Mourning and Militancy: Diamanda Galás's Operatic *Plague Mass*." In *The Work of Opera*, ed. Richard Dellamora and Daniel Fischlin, 315–33. New York: Columbia University Press, 1997.

Posner, Donald. "Caravaggio's Homo-Erotic Early Works." *Art Quarterly* 34 (1971): 301–19.

Postle, Martin. "Country Gardens." In *Art of the Garden*, 12–21. London: Tate, 2004.

Powell, Michael. *A Life in Movies*. London: Faber and Faber, 1986.

Power, Lisa. *No Bath but Plenty of Bubbles: An Oral History of the Gay Liberation Front, 1970–1973*. London: Cassell, 1996.

Prest, John. *The Garden of Eden: The Botanic Garden and the Re-Creation of Paradise*. New Haven: Yale University Press, 1981.

Pugilisi, Catherine. "Caravaggio's Life and *Lives* over Four Centuries." In Warwick 23–35.

Rabinow, Paul, ed. *Ethics: Subjectivity and Truth*. Essential Works of Foucault 1. New York: New Press, 1997.

Rayns, Tony. "The 'I-Movie.'" *The Garden* Press Kit. London: The Sales Co.

———. "Submitting to Sodomy." *Afterimage* 12 (1985): 60–65.

———. "Unblocked Talents." *Time Out*, no. 346 (November 5–11, 1976): 12–13.

Reed, Jeremy. "Coda: What Colour Is Time? Derek Jarman's Soho." In *London Eyes: Reflections in Text and Image*, ed. Gail Cunningham and Stephen Barber, 203–6. Oxford: Berghahn Books, 2007.

Rees, A. L. *A History of Experimental Film and Video*. London: BFI, 1999.

Restany, Pierre. *Yves Klein*. Trans. John Shepley. New York: Harry N. Abrams, 1982.

Ricco, John Paul. *The Logic of the Lure*. Chicago: University of Chicago Press, 2002.

Rich, B. Ruby. "New Queer Cinema." *Sight and Sound* 2.5 (September 1993). Reprinted in *New Queer Cinema: A Critical Reader*, ed. Michele Aaron, 15–22. Edinburgh: Edinburgh University Press, 2004.

Richardson, Niall. "The Queer Performance of Tilda Swinton in Derek Jarman's *Edward II*: Gay Male Misogyny Reconsidered." *Sexualities* 6 (2003): 427–44.

Riley, Helen, and Brian Ferry. "Fighting for the Beaches of Dungeness." *New Scientist* (June 5, 1986): 46–52.

Romney, Jonathan. "*Edward II*." *Sight and Sound* (November 1991): 41–42.

Rosenfeld, Kathryn. "The End of Everything Was 20 Years Ago Today: Punk Nostalgia." *New Art Examiner* 27.4 (1999–2000): 26–29.

Ross, Andrew. *No Respect: Intellectuals and Popular Culture*. London and New York: Routledge, 1989.

Ross, Kristin. "Lefebvre on the Situationists." In McDonough 267–84.

Sabin, Roger. "'I Won't Let That Dago By': Rethinking Punk and Racism." In Sabin 199–218.

————, ed. *Punk Rock So What? The Cultural Legacy of Punk.* London: Routledge, 1999.

Sadler, Simon. "British Architecture in the Sixties." In *Art and the 60s: This Was Tomorrow,* ed. Chris Stephens and Katharine Stout, 116–33. London: Tate, 2004.

————. *The Situationist City.* Cambridge: MIT Press, 1998.

Savage, Jon. *England's Dreaming.* New York: St. Martin's Griffin, 2001.

Scheler, Max. *The Nature of Sympathy.* Trans. Peter Heath. New Haven: Yale University Press, 1954.

Schwenger, Peter. "Derek Jarman and the Colour of the Mind's Eye." *University of Toronto Quarterly* 65.2 (1996): 419–26.

Scott-James, Anne. *The Cottage Garden.* London: Allen Lane, 1981.

Shakespeare, William. *The Tempest.* Ed. Stephen Orgel. Oxford and New York: Oxford University Press, 1987.

Sidney, Sir Philip. "The Defense of Poesy." In *Selected Prose and Poetry,* ed. Robert Kimbrough, 99–160. Madison: University of Wisconsin Press, 1983.

Silverman, Kaja. *Male Subjectivity at the Margins.* London: Routledge, 1991.

————. *The Threshold of the Visible World.* London: Routledge, 1996.

Sinfield, Alan. *Literature, Politics and Culture in Postwar Britain.* Oxford: Basil Blackwell, 1989.

Singh, Jyotsna G. "Caliban versus Miranda: Race and Gender Conflicts in Postcolonial Rewritings of *The Tempest.*" In *Feminist Readings of Early Modern Culture: Emerging Subjects,* ed. Valerie Traub et al., 191–209. Cambridge: Cambridge University Press, 1996.

Skurka, Norma, and Oberto Gil. *Underground Interiors: Decorating for Alternative Lifestyles.* New York: Galahad Books, 1972.

Sladen, Mark. "Introduction." In Sladen and Yedgar 9–17.

Sladen, Mark, and Ariella Yedgar, eds. *Panic Attack! Art in the Punk Years.* London: Merrel, n.d.

Smith, Anna Marie. *New Right Discourse on Race and Sexuality: Britain, 1968–1990.* Cambridge: Cambridge University Press, 1994.

Smith, Paul Julian. "*Blue* and the Outer Limits." *Sight and Sound* (October 1993): 18–19.

Smithson, Alison, and Peter Smithson. *Ordinariness and Light.* Cambridge: MIT Press, 1970.

Sonnabend, Yolanda. "The 'Fabric of This Vision': Designing *The Tempest* with Derek Jarman." In Wollen 77–80.

Sontag, Susan. *AIDS and Its Metaphors.* London: Penguin, 1989.

Stewart, Alan. *Close Readers: Humanism and Sodomy in Early Modern England.* Princeton, N.J.: Princeton University Press, 1997.

Stich, Sidra. *Yves Klein.* Stuttgart: Cantz Verlag, 1994.

Street, Sarah. *British National Cinema.* London: Routledge, 1997.

Strong, Roy. *The Renaissance Garden in England*. London: Thames and Hudson, 1979, 1998.

Talvacchia, Bette. "Historical Phallicy: Derek Jarman's *Edward II*." *Oxford Art Journal* 16.1 (1993): 112–28.

Tambling, Jeremy. *Opera, Ideology and Film*. Manchester: Manchester University Press, 1987.

Thomsen, Christian Braad. *Fassbinder: The Life and Work of a Provocative Genius*. Trans. Martin Chalmers. London: Faber and Faber, 1991; reprint, Minneapolis: University of Minnesota Press, 2004.

Thurlow, Richard. *Fascism in Britain*. Rev. ed. London: I. B. Tauris, 1998.

Tillman, Lynne. "Love Story." *Art in America* 75.1 (January 1987): 21–23.

Tobin, Ann. "Lesbianism and the Labour Party: The GLC Experience." *Feminist Review* 34 (1990): 56–66.

Tweedie, James. "The Suspended Spectacle of History: The Tableau Vivant in Derek Jarman's *Caravaggio*." *Screen* 44.4 (2003): 379–403.

Upton, Julian. "Anarchy in the UK: Derek Jarman's *Jubilee* Revisited." *Bright Lights Film Journal* 30 (October 2000): n.p.

Vendler, Helen. *The Art of Shakespeare's Sonnets*. Cambridge, Mass.: Belknap Press, 1997.

Vermorel, Fred. *Fashion and Perversity: A Life of Vivienne Westwood and the Sixties Laid Bare*. London: Bloomsbury, 1997.

Viano, Maurizio. *A Certain Realism: Making Use of Pasolini's Film Theory and Practice*. Berkeley: University of California Press, 1993.

Vidler, Anthony. "*Terres Inconnues*: Cartographies of a Landscape to Be Invented." *October* 115 (2006): 13–30.

Walter, Aubrey, ed. *Come Together: The Years of Gay Liberation 1970–73*. London: Gay Men's Press, 1980.

Warr, Tracey. "Feral City." In Sladen and Yedgar 116–21.

Warwick, Genevieve, ed. *Caravaggio: Realism, Rebellion, Reception*. Newark: University of Delaware Press, 2006.

———. "Introduction: Caravaggio in History." In Warwick 13–22.

Watney, Simon. "Home Movie Man." *Marxism Today* (October 1987): 40–41.

———. *Policing Desire: Pornography, AIDS, and the Media*. Minneapolis: University of Minnesota Press, 1987.

Waugh, Thomas. *The Fruit Machine: Twenty Years of Writing on Queer Cinema*. Durham, N.C.: Duke University Press, 2000.

Weeks, Jeffrey. *Coming Out: Homosexual Politics in Britain from the Nineteenth Century to the Present*. Rev. ed. London: Quartet Books, 1990.

Wees, William. *Light Moving in Time*. Berkeley: University of California Press, 1992.

Whitely, Sheila. *Women and Popular Music: Sexuality, Identity and Subjectivity*. London: Routledge, 2000.

Wilson, Andrew. "Modernity Killed Every Night." In Sladen and Yedgar 144–51.

Wittgenstein, Ludwig. *Remarks on Colour*. Ed. G. E. M. Anscombe. Trans. Linda L. McAlister and Margarete Schättle. Berkeley: University of California Press, 1977.

Wollen, Peter. *"Blue." New Left Review* 6 (November/December 2000): 120–33.

Wollen, Roger, ed. *Derek Jarman: A Portrait*. London: Thames and Hudson, 1996.

———. "Facets of Derek Jarman." In Wollen 15–31.

Woodward, Marcus, ed. *Gerard's Herball*. 1636. London: Spring Books, 1964.

Wyke, Maria. "Playing Roman Soldiers: The Martyred Body, Derek Jarman's *Sebastiane*, and the Representation of Male Homosexuality." In *Parchments of Gender: Deciphering the Bodies of Antiquity*, ed. Maria Wyke, 243–66. Oxford: Clarendon Press, 1998.

———. "Shared Sexualities: Roman Soldiers, Derek Jarman's *Sebastiane*, and British Homosexuality." In *Imperial Projections: Ancient Rome in Modern Popular Culture*, ed. Sandra Joshel, Margareet Malamud, and Donald T. McGuire Jr., 229–48. Baltimore: Johns Hopkins University Press, 2001.

Wymer, Rowland. *Derek Jarman*. Manchester: Manchester University Press, 2005.

Zabus, Chantal, and Kevin A. Dwyer. "'I'll Be Wise Hereafter': Caliban in Postmodern British Cinema." In *The Contact and the Culmination*, ed. Marc Delrez and Benedicte Ledent, 271–89. Liège, Belgium: Liège Language and Literature, 1997.

Zimmermann, Patricia R. *Reel Families: A Social History of Amateur Film*. Bloomington: Indiana University Press, 1996.

Select Filmography of Derek Jarman

Features

Sebastiane. Directed by Paul Humfress and Derek Jarman. Produced by James Whaley and Howard Malin. With Leonardo Treviglio, Barney James, Neil Kennedy. Distac, 1976.

Jubilee. Directed by Derek Jarman. Produced by Howard Malin and James Whaley. With Jenny Runacre, Toyah Willcox, Little Nell, Jordan. Megalovision, 1978.

The Tempest. Directed by Derek Jarman. Produced by Guy Ford and Mordecai Schreiber. With Heathcote Williams, Karl Johnson, Toyah Willcox, Elisabeth Welch, Jack Birkett. Kendon Films, 1979.

The Angelic Conversation. Directed by Derek Jarman. Produced by James Mackay. With Paul Reynolds, Philip Williamson. Derek Jarman, 1985.

Caravaggio. Directed by Derek Jarman. Produced by Sarah Radclyffe. With Nigel Terry, Sean Bean, Tilda Swinton. British Film Institute, 1986.

The Last of England. Directed by Derek Jarman. Produced by James Mackay and Don Boyd. Anglo-International Films, 1987.

War Requiem. Directed by Derek Jarman. Produced by Don Boyd. With Nathaniel Parker, Tilda Swinton, Lawrence Olivier. Anglo International Films, 1989.

The Garden. Directed by Derek Jarman. Produced by James Mackay. With Tilda Swinton, Johnny Mills, Kevin Collins. Basilisk, 1990.

Edward II. Directed by Derek Jarman. Produced by Steve Clark-Hall and Antony Root. With Steven Waddington, Tilda Swinton, Nigel Terry, Andrew Tiernan. Working Title, 1991.

Wittgenstein. Directed by Derek Jarman. Produced by Tariq Ali. With Karl Johnson, Tilda Swinton, Michael Gough. Channel Four, 1993.

Blue. Directed by Derek Jarman. Produced by James Mackay and Takashi Asai. With John Quentin, Nigel Terry, Tilda Swinton, and Derek Jarman. Basilisk, 1993.

Glitterbug. Produced by James Mackay. Basilisk Communications, 1994.

Short Films

Studio Bankside (1972)
A Journey to Avebury (1973)
Garden of Luxor (1973)
The Art of Mirrors (1973)
Fire Island (1974)
Duggie Fields (1974)
Picnic at Rae's (1974)
Gerald's Film (1975)
Ula's Fete (1976)
Jordan's Dance (1977)
Sloane Square (1974–76)
In the Shadow of the Sun (1974–80)
Imagining October (1984)

Music Videos

The Smiths, *The Queen Is Dead* (1986)
Marianne Faithfull, *Broken English* (1979)

As Designer

The Devils (Ken Russell, UK 1971)
Savage Messiah (Ken Russell, UK 1972)

Index

Jim Ellis is associate professor of English at the University of Calgary, where he teaches sixteenth- and seventeenth-century literature and contemporary British film.